BOOK 5 – DERIVATIVES AND PORTFOLIO MANAGEMENT

LEVEL 2 BOOK 5: DERIVATIVES AND PORTFOLIO MANAGEMENT

©2009 Kaplan, Inc. All rights reserved.

Published in September 2009 by Kaplan Schweser.

Printed in the United States of America.

ISBN: 1-4277-9476-6

PPN: 4550-0116

READINGS AND LEARNING OUTCOME STATEMENTS

READINGS

The following material is a review of the Derivatives and Portfolio Management principles designed to address the learning outcome statements set forth by CFA Institute.

STUDY SESSION 16

Reading Assignments

Derivatives and Portfolio Management, CFA Program Curriculum, Volume 6, Level 2 (CFA Institute, 2010)

STUDY SESSION 17

Reading Assignments

Derivatives and Portfolio Management, CFA Program Curriculum, Volume 6, Level 2 (CFA Institute, 2010)

STUDY SESSION 18

Reading Assignments

Derivatives and Portfolio Management, CFA Program Curriculum, Volume 6, Level 2 (CFA Institute, 2010)

LEARNING OUTCOME STATEMENTS (LOS)

The CFA Institute Learning Outcome Statements are listed below. These are repeated in each topic review; however, the order may have been changed in order to get a better fit with the flow of the review.

STUDY SESSION 16

The topical coverage corresponds with the following CFA Institute assigned reading:
58. Forward Markets and Contracts
The candidate should be able to:
  a. explain how the value of a forward contract is determined at initiation, during the life of the contract, and at expiration. (page 14)
  b. calculate and interpret the price and the value of an equity forward contract, assuming dividends are paid either discretely or continuously. (page 16)
  c. calculate and interpret the price and the value of 1) a forward contract on a fixed-income security, 2) a forward rate agreement (FRA), and 3) a forward contract on a currency. (page 20)
  d. evaluate credit risk in a forward contract and explain how market value is a measure of the credit risk to a party in a forward contract. (page 28)

The topical coverage corresponds with the following CFA Institute assigned reading:
59. Futures Markets and Contracts
The candidate should be able to:
  a. explain why the futures price must converge to the spot price at expiration. (page 36)
  b. determine the value of a futures contract. (page 37)
  c. explain how forward and futures prices differ. (page 38)
  d. describe the monetary and nonmonetary benefits and costs associated with holding the underlying asset, and explain how they affect the futures price. (page 42)
  e. describe backwardation and contango. (page 43)
  f. discuss whether futures prices equal expected spot prices. (page 43)
  g. describe the difficulties in pricing Eurodollar futures and creating a pure arbitrage opportunity. (page 46)
  h. calculate and interpret the price of Treasury bond futures, stock index futures, and currency futures. (page 46)

STUDY SESSION 17

The topical coverage corresponds with the following CFA Institute assigned reading:
60. Option Markets and Contracts
The candidate should be able to:
  a. calculate and interpret the prices of a synthetic call option, synthetic put option, synthetic bond, and synthetic underlying stock, and infer why an investor would want to create such instruments. (page 58)
  b. calculate and interpret prices of interest rate options and options on assets using one- and two-period binomial models. (page 61)

c. explain the assumptions underlying the Black-Scholes-Merton model and their limitations. (page 74)

d. explain how an option price, as represented by the Black-Scholes-Merton model, is affected by each of the input values (the option Greeks). (page 76)

e. explain the delta of an option and demonstrate how it is used in dynamic hedging. (page 79)

f. explain the gamma effect on an option's price and delta and how gamma can affect a delta hedge. (page 83)

g. discuss the effect of the underlying asset's cash flows on the price of an option. (page 84)

h. demonstrate the methods for estimating the future volatility of the underlying asset (i.e., the historical volatility and the implied volatility methods). (page 85)

i. illustrate how put-call parity for options on forwards (or futures) is established. (page 85)

j. compare and contrast American options on forwards and futures with European options on forwards and futures, and identify the appropriate pricing model for European options. (page 87)

The topical coverage corresponds with the following CFA Institute assigned reading:

61. Swap Markets and Contracts
The candidate should be able to:

a. distinguish between the pricing and valuation of swaps. (page 98)

b. explain the equivalence of the following swaps to combinations of other instruments: interest rate swaps to a series of off-market forward rate agreements (FRAs) and a plain vanilla swap to a combination of an interest rate call and interest rate put. (page 99)

c. calculate and interpret the fixed rate on a plain vanilla interest rate swap and the market value of the swap during its life. (page 100)

d. calculate and interpret the fixed rate, if applicable, and the foreign notional principal for a given domestic notional principal on a currency swap, and determine the market values of each of the different types of currency swaps during their lives. (page 107)

e. calculate and interpret the fixed rate, if applicable, on an equity swap and the market values of the different types of equity swaps during their lives. (page 111)

f. explain and interpret the characteristics and uses of swaptions, including the difference between payer and receiver swaptions. (page 113)

g. identify and calculate the possible payoffs and cash flows of an interest rate swaption. (page 113)

h. calculate and interpret the value of an interest rate swaption on the expiration day. (page 114)

i. evaluate swap credit risk for each party and during the life of the swap, distinguish between current credit risk and potential credit risk, and illustrate how swap credit risk is reduced by both netting and marking to market. (page 115)

j. define swap spread and relate it to credit risk. (page 116)

The topical coverage corresponds with the following CFA Institute assigned reading:

62. Interest Rate Derivative Instruments
The candidate should be able to:

a. demonstrate how both a cap and a floor are packages of options on interest rates and options on fixed-income instruments. (page 126)

b. compute the payoff for a cap and a floor and explain how a collar is created. (page 128)

The topical coverage corresponds with the following CFA Institute assigned reading:
63. Using Credit Derivatives to Enhance Return and Manage Risk
The candidate should be able to:
a. describe the characteristics of a credit default swap, and compare and contrast a credit default swap with a corporate bond. (page 134)
b. explain the advantages of using credit derivatives over other credit instruments. (page 136)
c. explain the use of credit derivatives by the various market participants. (page 136)
d. discuss credit derivatives trading strategies and how they are used by hedge funds and other managers. (page 137)

STUDY SESSION 18

The topical coverage corresponds with the following CFA Institute assigned reading:
64. Portfolio Concepts
The candidate should be able to:
a. discuss mean-variance analysis and its assumptions, and calculate the expected return and the standard deviation of return for a portfolio of two or three assets. (page 147)
b. explain the minimum-variance and efficient frontiers, and discuss the steps to solve for the minimum-variance frontier. (page 152)
c. discuss diversification benefits, and explain how the correlation in a two-asset portfolio and the number of assets in a multi-asset portfolio affect the diversification benefits. (page 156)
d. calculate the variance of an equally weighted portfolio of n stocks, explain the capital allocation and the capital market lines (CAL and CML) and the relation between them, and calculate the values of one of the variables given the values of the remaining variables. (page 159)
e. explain the capital asset pricing model (CAPM), including its underlying assumptions and the resulting conclusions. (page 169)
f. discuss the security market line (SML), the beta coefficient, the market risk premium, and the Sharpe ratio, and calculate the value of one of these variables given the values of the remaining variables. (page 170)
g. explain the market model, and state and interpret the market model's predictions with respect to asset returns, variances, and covariances. (page 177)
h. calculate an adjusted beta, and discuss the use of adjusted and historical betas as predictors of future betas. (page 179)
i. discuss reasons for and problems related to instability in the minimum-variance frontier. (page 181)
j. discuss and compare macroeconomic factor models, fundamental factor models, and statistical factor models. (page 182)
k. calculate the expected return on a portfolio of two stocks, given the estimated macroeconomic factor model for each stock. (page 186)

l. discuss the arbitrage pricing theory (APT), including its underlying assumptions and its relation to the multifactor models, calculate the expected return on an asset given an asset's factor sensitivities and the factor risk premiums, and determine whether an arbitrage opportunity exists, including how to exploit the opportunity. (page 187)

m. explain the sources of active risk, define and interpret tracking error, tracking risk, and the information ratio, and explain factor portfolio and tracking portfolio. (page 190)

n. compare and contrast the conclusions and the underlying assumptions of the CAPM and the APT models, and explain why an investor can possibly earn a substantial premium for exposure to dimensions of risk unrelated to market movements. (page 194)

The topical coverage corresponds with the following CFA Institute assigned reading:

65. A Note on Harry M. Markowitz's "Market Efficiency: A Theoretical Distinction and So What?"

The candidate should be able to:

a. discuss the efficiency of the market portfolio in the CAPM and the relation between the expected return and beta of an asset when restrictions on borrowing at the risk-free rate and on short selling exist. (page 212)

b. discuss the practical consequences that follow when restrictions on borrowing at the risk-free rate and on short selling exist. (page 213)

The topical coverage corresponds with the following CFA Institute assigned reading:

66. International Asset Pricing

The candidate should be able to:

a. explain international market integration and segmentation and the impediments to international capital mobility. (page 217)

b. discuss the factors that favor international market integration. (page 218)

c. state the assumptions of the domestic capital asset pricing model (CAPM). (page 219)

d. justify the extension of the domestic CAPM to an international context (the extended CAPM) and describe the assumptions needed to make the extension. (page 219)

e. determine whether the real exchange rate has changed in a period, given the beginning-of-period (nominal) exchange rate, the inflation rates in the period, and the end-of-period (nominal) exchange rate. (page 220)

f. calculate the expected 1) exchange rate and 2) domestic-currency holding period return on a foreign bond (security), given expected, predictable inflation rates, the beginning-of-period nominal exchange rate, and the constant real exchange rate. (page 222)

g. calculate the end-of-period real exchange rate and the domestic-currency *ex-post* return on a foreign bond (security), given the end-of-period exchange rate, the beginning-of-period real exchange rate, and the inflation rates during the period. (page 222)

h. calculate a foreign currency risk premium and explain a foreign currency risk premium in terms of interest rate differentials and forward rates. (page 223)

i. state the risk pricing relation and the formula for the international capital asset pricing model (ICAPM). (page 225)

j. calculate the expected return on a stock, given its world market beta and currency exposure as well as the appropriate risk-free rates and risk premiums. (page 228)

k. explain the effect of market segmentation on the ICAPM. (page 229)

l. define currency exposure and explain exposures in terms of correlations. (page 229)

m. discuss the likely exchange rate exposure of a company based on a description of the company's activities, and explain the impact of both real and nominal exchange rate changes on the valuation of the company. (page 232)

n. discuss the currency exposures of national economies, equity markets, and bond markets. (page 233)

o. contrast the traditional trade approach (j-curve) and the money demand approach to modeling the relation between real exchange rate changes and domestic economic activity. (page 233)

The topical coverage corresponds with the following CFA Institute assigned reading:

67. **The Theory of Active Portfolio Management**
The candidate should be able to:

a. justify active portfolio management when security markets are nearly efficient. (page 248)

b. discuss the steps and the approach of the Treynor-Black model for security selection. (page 249)

c. describe how an analyst's accuracy in forecasting alphas can be measured and how estimates of forecasting can be incorporated into the Treynor-Black approach. (page 255)

The topical coverage corresponds with the following CFA Institute assigned reading:

68. **The Portfolio Management Process and the Investment Policy Statement**
The candidate should be able to:

a. explain the importance of the portfolio perspective. (page 263)

b. describe the steps of the portfolio management process and the components of those steps. (page 263)

c. define investment objectives and constraints and explain and distinguish among the types of investment objectives and constraints. (page 264)

d. discuss the role of the investment policy statement in the portfolio management process and explain the elements of an investment policy statement. (page 267)

e. explain how capital market expectations and the investment policy statement help influence the strategic asset allocation decision, and discuss how investors' investment time horizon may influence their strategic asset allocation. (page 268)

f. contrast the types of investment time horizons, determine the time horizon for a particular investor, and evaluate the effects of this time horizon on portfolio choice. (page 268)

g. justify ethical conduct as a requirement for managing investment portfolios. (page 269)

FORWARD MARKETS AND CONTRACTS

Study Session 16

EXAM FOCUS

This topic review covers the calculation of price and value for forward contracts, specifically equity forward contracts, T-bond forward contracts, currency forwards, and forward (interest) rate agreements. You need to have a good understanding of the no-arbitrage principle that underlies these calculations because it is used in the topic reviews of futures and swaps pricing as well. There are several important price and value formulas in this review. A clear understanding of the sources and timing of forward contract settlement payments will enable you to be successful on this portion of the exam without depending on pure memorization of these complex formulas. In the past, candidates have been tested on their understanding of the relationship of the payments at settlement to interest rate changes, asset price changes, and index level changes. The pricing conventions for the underlying assets have been tested separately. The basic contract mechanics are certainly "fair game," so don't overlook the easy stuff by spending too much time trying to memorize the formulas.

WARM-UP: FORWARD CONTRACTS

The party to the forward contract that agrees to buy the financial or physical asset has a **long forward position** and is called the *long*. The party to the forward contract that agrees to sell/deliver the asset has a **short forward position** and is called the *short*.

We will illustrate the basic forward contract mechanics through an example based on the purchase and sale of a Treasury bill. Note that while forward contracts on T-bills are usually quoted in terms of a discount percentage from face value, we use dollar prices here to make the example easy to follow.

Consider a contract under which Party A agrees to buy a $1,000 face value 90-day Treasury bill from Party B 30 days from now at a price of $990. Party A is the long and Party B is the short. Both parties have removed uncertainty about the price they will pay or receive for the T-bill at the future date. If 30 days from now T-bills are trading at $992, the short must deliver the T-bill to the long in exchange for a $990 payment. If T-bills are trading at $988 on the future date, the long must purchase the T-bill from the short for $990, the contract price.

Each party to a forward contract is exposed to **default risk**, the probability that the other party (the counterparty) will not perform as promised. Typically, no money changes hands at the inception of the contract, unlike futures contracts in which each party posts an initial deposit called the **margin** as a guarantee of performance.

At any point in time, including the settlement date, the party to the forward contract with the negative value will owe money to the other side. The other side of the contract will have a positive value of equal amount. Following this example, if the T-bill price is $992 at the (future) settlement date and the short does not deliver the T-bill for $990 as promised, the short has defaulted.

 Professor's Note: For the basics of forward contracts, please see the online Schweser Library.

WARM-UP: FORWARD CONTRACT PRICE DETERMINATION

The No-Arbitrage Principle

The price of a forward contract is *not* the price to purchase the contract because the parties to a forward contract typically pay nothing to enter into the contract at its inception. Here, *price refers to the contract price of the underlying asset under the terms of the forward contract.* This price may be a U.S. dollar or euro price but it is often expressed as an interest rate or currency exchange rate. For T-bills, the price will be expressed as an annualized percentage discount from face value; for coupon bonds, it will usually be expressed as a yield to maturity; for the implicit loan in a forward rate agreement (FRA), it will be expressed as annualized London Interbank Offered Rate (LIBOR); and for a currency forward, it is expressed as an exchange rate between the two currencies involved. However it is expressed, this rate, yield, discount, or dollar amount is the forward price in the contract.

The price that we wish to determine is the forward price that makes the *values* of both the long and the short positions zero at contract initiation. We will use the *no-arbitrage principle*: there should not be a riskless profit to be gained by a combination of a forward contract position with positions in other assets. This principle assumes that (1) transactions costs are zero, (2) there are no restrictions on short sales or on the use of short sale proceeds, and (3) both borrowing and lending can be done in unlimited amounts at the risk-free rate of interest. This concept is so important, we'll express it in a formula:

forward price = price that would not permit profitable riskless arbitrage in frictionless markets

A Simple Version of the Cost-of-Carry Model

In order to explain the no-arbitrage condition as it applies to the determination of forward prices, we will first consider a forward contract on an asset that costs nothing to store and makes no payments to its owner over the life of the forward contract. A zero-coupon (pure discount) bond meets these criteria. Unlike gold or wheat, it has no storage costs; unlike stocks, there are no dividend payments to consider; and unlike coupon bonds, it makes no periodic interest payments.

The general form for the calculation of the forward contract price can be stated as follows:

$$FP = S_0 \times \left(1 + R_f\right)^T$$

or

$$S_0 = \frac{FP}{\left(1 + R_f\right)^T}$$

where:
FP $=$ forward price
S_0 $=$ spot price at inception of the contract $(t = 0)$
R_f $=$ annual risk-free rate
T $=$ forward contract term in years

Example: Calculating the no-arbitrage forward price

Consider a 3-month forward contract on a zero-coupon bond with a face value of $1,000 that is currently quoted at $500, and assume a risk-free annual interest rate of 6%. Determine the price of the forward contract under the no-arbitrage principle.

Answer:

$$T = \frac{3}{12} = 0.25$$

$$FP = S_0 \times \left(1 + R_f\right)^T = \$500 \times 1.06^{0.25} = \$507.34$$

Now, let's explore in more detail why $507.34 is the no-arbitrage price of the forward contract.

Cash and Carry Arbitrage When the Forward Contract is Overpriced

Suppose the forward contract is actually trading at $510 rather than the no-arbitrage price of $507.34. A short position in the forward contract requires the delivery of this bond three months from now. The arbitrage that we examine in this case amounts to borrowing $500 at the risk-free rate of 6%, buying the bond for $500, and simultaneously taking the short position in the forward contract on the zero-coupon bond so that we are obligated to deliver the bond at the expiration of the contract for the forward price and receive $510.

At the settlement date, we can satisfy our obligation under the terms of the forward contract by delivering the zero-coupon bond for a payment of $510, regardless of its market value at that time. We will use the $510 payment we receive at settlement from the forward contract (the forward contract price) to repay the $500 loan. The total amount to repay the loan, since the term of the loan is three months, is:

$$\text{loan repayment} = \$500 \times (1.06)^{0.25} = \$507.34$$

The payment of $510 we receive when we deliver the bond at the forward price is greater than our loan payoff of $507.34, and we will have earned an arbitrage profit of $510 – $507.34 = $2.66. Notice that this is equal to the difference between the actual forward price and the no-arbitrage forward price. The transactions are illustrated in Figure 1.

Figure 1: Cash and Carry Arbitrage When Forward is Overpriced

Today		*Three Months From Today*	
Spot price of bond	$500		
Forward price	$510		
Transaction	*Cash flow*	*Transaction*	*Cash flow*
Short forward	$0	Settle short position by delivering bond	$510.00
Buy bond	–$500		
Borrow at 6%	+$500	Repay loan	– $507.34
Total cash flow	$0	Total cash flow = arbitrage profit	+$2.66

Professor's Note: Here's a hint to help you remember which transactions to undertake for cash and carry arbitrage. You always want to buy underpriced assets and sell overpriced assets, so if the futures contract is overpriced, you want to take a short position that gives you the obligation to sell at a fixed price. Because you go short in the forward market, you take the opposite position in the spot market and buy the asset. You need money to buy the asset, so you have to borrow. Therefore, the first step in cash and carry arbitrage at its most basic is:

forward overpriced ⇒ short (sell) forward ⇒ long (buy) spot asset ⇒ borrow money

Reverse Cash and Carry Arbitrage When the Forward Contract is Underpriced

Suppose the forward contract is actually trading at $502 instead of the no-arbitrage price of $507.34. We reverse the arbitrage trades from the previous case and generate an arbitrage profit as follows. We sell the bond short today for $500 and simultaneously take the long position in the forward contract, which obligates us to purchase the bond in 90 days at the forward price of $502. We invest the $500 proceeds from the short sale at the 6% annual rate for three months.

In this case, at the settlement date, we receive the investment proceeds of $507.34, accept delivery of the bond in return for a payment of $502, and close out our short position by delivering the bond we just purchased at the forward price.

The payment of $502 we make as the long position in the contract is less than investment proceeds of $507.34, and we have earned an arbitrage profit of $507.34 – $502 = $5.34. The transactions are illustrated in Figure 2.

Figure 2: Reverse Cash and Carry Arbitrage When Forward is Underpriced

Today		Three Months From Today	
Spot price of bond	$500		
Forward price	$502		
Transaction	*Cash flow*	*Transaction*	*Cash flow*
Long forward	$0	Settle long position by buying bond	–$502.00
Short sell bond	+$500	Deliver bond to close short position	$0.00
Invest short-sale proceeds at 6%	–$500	Receive investment proceeds	+ $507.34
Total cash flow	$0	Total cash flow = arbitrage profit	+$5.34

Professor's Note: In this case, because the forward contract is underpriced, the trades are reversed from cash and carry arbitrage:

forward underpriced $\Rightarrow$ long (buy) forward $\Rightarrow$ short sell spot asset $\Rightarrow$ invest money

We can now determine that the no-arbitrage forward price that yields a zero *value* for both the long and short positions in the forward contract at inception is the no-arbitrage price of $507.34.

Professor's Note: This long explanation has answered the question, "What is the forward price that allows no arbitrage?" You'll have to trust me, but a very clear understanding here will make what follows easier and will serve you well as we progress to futures, options, and swaps.

LOS 58.a: Explain how the value of a forward contract is determined at initiation, during the life of the contract, and at expiration.

If we denote the value of the long position in a forward contract at time t as V_t, the value of the long position at contract initiation, $t = 0$, is:

$$V_0 \left(\text{of long position at initiation} \right) = S_0 - \left[\frac{FP}{\left(1 + R_f \right)^T} \right]$$

Note that the no-arbitrage relation we derived in the prior section ensures that the value of the long position (and of the short position) at contract initiation is zero.

If $S_0 = \dfrac{FP}{\left(1 + R_f \right)^T}$, then $V_0 = 0$.

The value of the long position in the forward contract during the life of the contract after t years ($t < T$) have passed (since the initiation of the contract) is:

$$V_t \left(\text{of long position during life of contract} \right) = S_t - \left[\frac{FP}{\left(1 + R_f \right)^{T-t}} \right]$$

This is the same equation as above, but the spot price, S_t, will have changed, and the period for discounting is now the number of years remaining until contract expiration ($T - t$). This is a zero-sum game, so the value of the contract to the short position is the negative of the long position value:

$$V_t \left(\text{of short position during life of contract} \right) = \left[\frac{FP}{\left(1 + R_f \right)^{T-t}} \right] - S_t$$
$$= -V_t \left(\text{of long position during life of contract} \right)$$

Notice that the forward price, *FP*, is the forward price agreed to at the initiation of the contract, not the current market forward price. In other words, as the spot and forward market prices change over the life of the contract, one side (i.e., short or long position) wins and the other side loses. For example, if the market spot and forward prices increase after the contract is initiated, the long position makes money, the value of the long position is positive, and the value of the short position is negative. If the spot and forward prices decrease, the short position makes money.

Professor's Note: Unfortunately, you must be able to use the forward valuation formulas on the exam. If you're good at memorizing formulas, that prospect shouldn't scare you too much. However, if you don't like memorizing formulas, here's another way to remember how to value a forward contract. The long position will pay the forward price (FP) at maturity (time T) and receive the spot price (S_T). The value of the contract to the long position at maturity is what he will receive less what he will pay: $S_T - FP$. Prior to maturity (at time T), the value to the long is the present value of S_T (which is the spot price at time t of S_t) less the present value of the forward price: $S_t - \left[\dfrac{FP}{(1+R_f)^{T-t}}\right]$.

So, on the exam, think "long position is spot price minus present value of forward price."

Example: Determining value of a forward contract prior to expiration

In our 3-month zero-coupon bond contract example, we determined that the no-arbitrage forward price was $507.34. Suppose that after two months the spot price on the zero-coupon bond is $515, and the risk-free rate is still 6%. Calculate the value of the long and short positions in the forward contract.

Answer:

$$V_2 \left(\text{of long position after two months}\right) = \$515 - \frac{\$507.34}{1.06^{1/12}} = \$515 - \$504.88 = \$10.12$$

$$V_2 \left(\text{of short position after two months}\right) = -\$10.12$$

Another way to see this is to note that because the spot price has increased to $515, the current no-arbitrage forward price is:

$$FP = \$515 \times 1.06^{1/12} = \$517.51$$

The long position has made money (and the short position has lost money) because the forward price has *increased* by $10.17 from $507.34 to $517.51 since the contract was initiated. The value of the long position today is the present value of $10.17 for one month at 6%:

$$V_2 \left(\text{long position after two months}\right) = \frac{\$10.17}{1.06^{1/12}} = \$10.12$$

At contract expiration, we do not need to discount the forward price because the time left on the contract is zero. Since the long can buy the asset for FP and sell it for the market price S_T, the value of the long position is the amount the long position will receive if the contract is settled in cash:

$$V_T \left(\text{of long position at maturity} \right) = S_T - FP$$

$$V_T \left(\text{of short position at maturity} \right) = FP - S_T = -V_T \left(\text{of long position at maturity} \right)$$

Figure 3 summarizes the key concepts you need to remember for this LOS.

Figure 3: Forward Value of Long Position at Initiation, During the Contract Life, and at Expiration

Time	Forward Contract Valuation
At initiation	Zero, because the contract is priced to prevent arbitrage
During the life of the contract	$S_t - \left[\dfrac{FP}{(1 + R_f)^{T-t}} \right]$
At expiration	$S_T - FP$

How Might Forward Contract Valuation Be Tested?

Look for these ways in which the valuation of a forward contract might appear as part of an exam question:

- To mark-to-market for financial statement reporting purposes.
- To mark-to-market because it is required as part of the original agreement. For example, the two parties might have agreed to mark-to-market a 180-day forward contract after 90 days to reduce credit risk.
- To measure credit exposure.
- To calculate how much it would cost to terminate the contract.

LOS 58.b: Calculate and interpret the price and the value of an equity forward contract, assuming dividends are paid either discretely or continuously.

Equity Forward Contracts With Discrete Dividends

Recall that the no-arbitrage forward price in our earlier example was calculated for an asset with no periodic payments. A stock, a stock portfolio, or an equity index may have expected dividend payments over the life of the contract. In order to price such a contract, we must either adjust the spot price for the present value of the expected dividends (PVD) over the life of the contract or adjust the forward price for the future value of the dividends (FVD) over the life of the contract. The **no-arbitrage price of an equity forward contract** in either case is:

$$FP\left(\text{on an equity security}\right) = \left(S_0 - PVD\right) \times \left(1 + R_f\right)^T$$

$$FP\left(\text{on an equity security}\right) = \left[S_0 \times \left(1 + R_f\right)^T\right] - FVD$$

 Professor's Note: In practice, we would calculate the present value from the ex-dividend date, not the payment date. On the exam, use payment dates unless the ex-dividend dates are given.

For equity contracts, use a 365-day basis for calculating T if the maturity of the contract is given in days. For example, if it is a 60-day contract, T = 60 / 365. If the maturity is given in months (e.g., two months) calculate T using maturity divided by number of months (e.g., T = 2 / 12).

Example: Calculating the price of a forward contract on a stock

Calculate the no-arbitrage forward price for a 100-day forward on a stock that is currently priced at $30.00 and is expected to pay a dividend of $0.40 in 15 days, $0.40 in 85 days, and $0.50 in 175 days. The annual risk-free rate is 5% and the yield curve is flat.

Answer:

Ignore the dividend in 175 days because it occurs after the maturity of the forward contract.

$$PVD = \frac{\$0.40}{1.05^{15/365}} + \frac{\$0.40}{1.05^{85/365}} = \$0.7946$$

$$FP = \left(\$30.00 - \$0.7946\right) \times 1.05^{100/365} = \$29.60$$

The time line of cash flows is shown in the following figure.

Pricing a 100-Day Forward Contract on Dividend-Paying Stock

To calculate the **value of the long position in a forward contract on a dividend-paying stock**, we make the adjustment for the present value of the remaining expected discrete dividends at time t (PVD_t) to get:

$$V_t \left(\text{long position} \right) = \left[S_t - PVD_t \right] - \left[\frac{FP}{\left(1 + R_f \right)^{\left(T - t \right)}} \right]$$

Professor's Note: This formula still looks like the standard "spot price minus present value of forward price." However, now the "spot price" has been adjusted by subtracting out the present value of the dividends because the long position in the forward contract does not receive the dividends paid on the underlying stock. So, now think "adjusted spot price less present value of forward price."

Example: Calculating the value of an equity forward contract on a stock

After 60 days, the value of the stock in the previous example is $36.00. Calculate the value of the equity forward contract on the stock to the long position, assuming the risk-free rate is still 5% and the yield curve is flat.

Answer:

There's only one dividend remaining (in 25 days) before the contract matures (in 40 days) as shown below, so:

$$PVD_{60} = \frac{\$0.40}{1.05^{25/365}} = \$0.3987$$

$$V_{60} \left(\text{long position} \right) = \$36.00 - \$0.3987 - \left[\frac{\$29.60}{1.05^{40/365}} \right] = \$6.16$$

Valuing a 100-Day Forward Contract After 60 Days

Equity Forward Contracts With Continuous Dividends

To calculate the **price of an equity index forward contract**, rather than take the present value of each dividend on (possibly) hundreds of stocks, we can make the calculation as if the dividends are paid continuously (rather than at discrete times) at the dividend yield rate on the index. Using continuous time discounting, we can calculate the no-arbitrage forward price as:

$$FP\left(\text{on an equity index}\right) = S_0 \times e^{\left(R_f^c - \delta^c\right) \times T} = \left(S_0 \times e^{-\delta^c \times T}\right) \times e^{R_f^c \times T}$$

where:
R_f^c = continuously compounded risk-free rate
δ^c = continuously compounded dividend yield

> *Professor's Note: The relationship between the discrete risk-free rate R_f and the continuously compounded rate R_f^c is $R_f^c = ln\left(1 + R_f\right)$. For example, 5% compounded annually is equal to ln(1.05) = 0.04879 = 4.879% compounded continuously. The 2-year 5% future value factor can then be calculated as either $1.05^2 = 1.1025$ or $e^{0.04879 \times 2} = 1.1025$.*

0.0096

Example: Calculating the price of a forward contract on an equity index

The value of the S&P 500 index is 1,140. The continuously compounded risk-free rate is 4.6% and the continuous dividend yield is 2.1%. Calculate the no-arbitrage price of a 140-day forward contract on the index.

Answer:

$$FP = 1,140 \times e^{(0.046 - 0.021) \times (140/365)} = 1,151$$

0.025 ×

For the continuous time case, the **value of the forward contract on an equity index** is calculated as follows:

$$V_t\left(\text{of the long position}\right) = \left(\frac{S_t}{e^{\delta^c \times (T-t)}}\right) - \left(\frac{FP}{e^{R_f^c \times (T-t)}}\right)$$

Example: Calculating the value of a forward contract on an equity index

After 95 days, the value of the index in the previous example is 1,025. Calculate the value to the long position of the forward contract on the index, assuming the continuously compounded risk-free rate is 4.6% and the continuous dividend yield is 2.1%.

Answer:

After 95 days there are 45 days remaining on the original forward contract:

$$V_{95}\left(\text{of the long position}\right)=\left(\frac{1,025}{e^{0.021\times\left(45/365\right)}}\right)-\left(\frac{1,151}{e^{0.046\times\left(45/365\right)}}\right)=-122.14$$

LOS 58.c: Calculate and interpret the price and the value of 1) a forward contract on a fixed-income security, 2) a forward rate agreement (FRA), and 3) a forward contract on a currency.

In order to calculate the no-arbitrage **forward price on a coupon-paying bond**, we can use the same formula as we used for a dividend-paying stock or portfolio, simply substituting the present value of the expected coupon payments (PVC) *over the life of the contract* for PVD, or the future value of the coupon payments (FVC) for FVD, to get the following formulas:

$$FP\left(\text{on a fixed income security}\right)=\left(S_0-PVC\right)\times\left(1+R_f\right)^T$$
$$\text{or}$$
$$=S_0\times\left(1+R_f\right)^T-FVC$$

The value of the forward contract prior to expiration is as follows:

$$V_t\left(\text{long position}\right)=\left[S_t-PVC_t\right]-\left[\frac{FP}{\left(1+R_f\right)^{\left(T-t\right)}}\right]$$

In our examples, we assume that the spot price on the underlying coupon-paying bond includes accrued interest. For fixed income contracts, use a 365-day basis to calculate T if the contract maturity is given in days.

Example: Calculating the price of a forward on a fixed income security

Calculate the price of a 250-day forward contract on a 7% U.S. Treasury bond with a spot price of $1,050 (including accrued interest) that has just paid a coupon and will make another coupon payment in 182 days. The annual risk-free rate is 6%.

Answer:

Remember that U.S. Treasury bonds make semiannual coupon payments, so:

$$C=\frac{\$1,000\times0.07}{2}=\$35.00$$

$$PVC=\frac{\$35.00}{1.06^{182/365}}=\$34.00$$

The forward price of the contract is therefore:

$$FP\left(\text{on a fixed income security}\right)=\left(\$1,050-\$34.00\right)\times1.06^{250/365}=\$1,057.37$$

Example: Calculating the value of a forward on a fixed income security

After 100 days, the value of the bond in the previous example is $1,090. Calculate the value of the forward contract on the bond to the long position, assuming the risk-free rate is 6.0%.

Answer:

There is only one coupon remaining (in 82 days) before the contract matures (in 150 days), so:

$$PVC = \frac{\$35.00}{1.06^{82/365}} = \$34.54$$

$$V_{100}\left(\text{long position}\right) = \$1,090 - \$34.54 - \left(\frac{\$1,057.37}{1.06^{150/365}}\right) = \$23.11$$

WARM-UP: LIBOR-BASED LOANS AND FORWARD RATE AGREEMENTS

Eurodollar deposit is the term for deposits in large banks outside the United States denominated in U.S. dollars. The lending rate on dollar-denominated loans between banks is called the London Interbank Offered Rate (LIBOR). It is quoted as an annualized rate based on a 360-day year. In contrast to T-bill discount yields, LIBOR is an add-on rate, like a yield quote on a short-term certificate of deposit. LIBOR is used as a reference rate for floating rate U.S. dollar-denominated loans worldwide.

Example: LIBOR-based loans

Compute the amount that must be repaid on a $1 million loan for 30 days if 30-day LIBOR is quoted at 6%.

Answer:

The add-on interest is calculated as $1 million × 0.06 × (30 / 360) = $5,000. The borrower would repay $1,000,000 + $5,000 = $1,005,000 at the end of 30 days.

LIBOR is published daily by the British Banker's Association and is compiled from quotes from a number of large banks; some are large multinational banks based in other countries that have London offices. There is also an equivalent euro lending rate called **Euribor**, or Europe Interbank Offered Rate. Euribor, established in Frankfurt, is published by the European Central Bank.

The long position in a **forward rate agreement** (FRA) is the party that would borrow the money (long the loan with the contract price being the interest rate on the loan). If the floating rate at contract expiration (LIBOR for U.S. dollar deposits and Euribor for euro deposits) is above the rate specified in the forward agreement, the long position in the contract can be viewed as the right to borrow at below market rates and the long will receive a payment. If rates at the expiration date are below the then-current market rates, the short will receive a cash payment from the long. (The right to lend at *above* market rates would have a positive value.)

> *Professor's Note: We say "can be viewed as" because an FRA is settled in cash, so there is no requirement to lend or borrow the amount stated in the contract. For this reason the creditworthiness of the long position is not a factor in the interest rate on the FRA. However, to understand the pricing and calculation of value for an FRA, viewing the contract as a commitment to lend or borrow at a certain interest rate at a future date is helpful.*

The notation for FRAs is unique. There are two numbers associated with an FRA: the number of months until the contract expires and the number of months until the underlying loan is settled. The difference between these two is the maturity of the underlying loan. For example, a 2 × 3 FRA is a contract that expires in two months (60 days), and the underlying loan is settled in three months (90 days). The underlying rate is 1-month (30-day) LIBOR on a 30-day loan in 60 days. See Figure 4.

Figure 4: Illustration of a 2 × 3 FRA

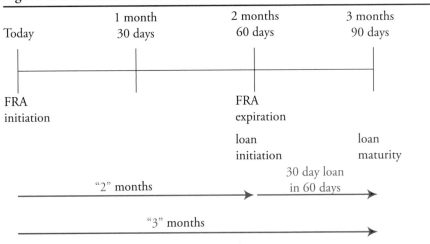

Pricing FRAs

There are three important things to remember about FRAs when we're pricing and valuing them:

1. LIBOR rates in the Eurodollar market are add-on rates and are always quoted on a 30/360 day basis in annual terms. For example, if the LIBOR quote on a 30-day loan is 6%, the actual unannualized monthly rate is 6% × (30/360) = 0.5%

2. The long position in an FRA, in effect, is long the rate and wins when the rate increases.

3. Although the interest on the underlying loan won't be paid until the end of the loan (e.g., in three months in Figure 4), the payoff on the FRA occurs at the expiration of the FRA (e.g., in two months). Therefore, the payoff on the FRA is the present value of the interest savings on the loan (e.g., discounted one month in Figure 4).

The forward "price" in an FRA is actually a forward interest rate. The calculation of a forward interest rate is presented in Level 1 as the computation of forward rates from spot rates. We will illustrate this calculation with an example.

Example: Calculating the price of an FRA

Calculate the price of a 1 × 4 FRA (i.e., a 90-day loan, 30 days from now). The current 30-day LIBOR is 4% and the 120-day LIBOR is 5%.

Answer:

The actual (unannualized) rate on the 30-day loan is:

$$R30 = 0.04 \times \frac{30}{360} = 0.00333$$

The actual (unannualized) rate on the 120-day loan is:

$$R120 = 0.05 \times \frac{120}{360} = 0.01667$$

We wish to calculate the actual rate on a 90-day loan from day 30 to day 120:

$$\text{price of 1} \times \text{4 FRA} = \frac{1 + R120}{1 + R30} - 1 = \frac{1.01667}{1.00333} - 1 = 0.0133$$

We can annualize this rate as:

$$0.0133 \times \frac{360}{90} = 0.0532 = 5.32\%$$

This is the no-arbitrage forward rate, the forward rate that will make the values of the long and the short positions in the FRA both zero at the initiation of the contract.

The time line is the following figure.

Pricing a 1 × 4 FRA

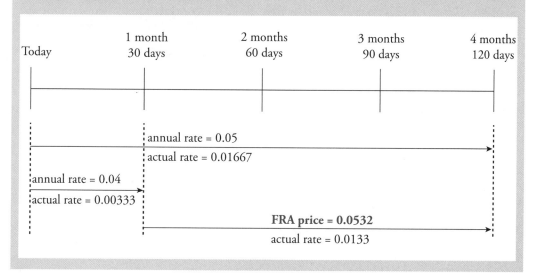

Valuing an FRA at Maturity

To understand the calculation of the value of the FRA *after the initiation of the contract*, recall that in the previous example the long in the FRA has the "right" to borrow money 30 days from inception for a period of 90 days at the forward rate. If interest rates increase (specifically the 90-day forward contract rate), the long will profit as the contract has fixed a borrowing rate below the now-current market rate. These "savings" will come at the end of the loan term, so to value the FRA we need to take the present value of these savings. An example incorporating this fact will illustrate the cash settlement value of an FRA at expiration.

Example: Calculating value of an FRA at maturity (i.e., cash payment at settlement)

Continuing the prior example for a 1 × 4 FRA, assume a notional principal of $1 million and that, at contract expiration, the 90-day rate has increased to 6%, which is above the contract rate of 5.32%. Calculate the value of the FRA at maturity, which is equal to the cash payment at settlement.

Answer:

The interest savings at the end of the loan term (compared to the market rate of 6%) will be:

$$\left[\left(0.0600 \times \frac{90}{360}\right) - \left(0.0532 \times \frac{90}{360}\right)\right] \times \$1,000,000 = \$1,700$$

The present value of this amount at the FRA settlement date (90 days prior to the end of the loan term) discounted at the current rate of 6% is:

$$\frac{\$1,700}{1 + \left(0.06 \times \dfrac{90}{360}\right)} = \$1,674.88$$

This will be the cash settlement payment from the short to the long at the expiration of the contract. Note that we have discounted the savings in interest at the end of the loan term by the *market* rate of 6% that prevails at the contract settlement date for a 90-day term, as shown in the following figure.

Valuing a 1 × 4 FRA at Maturity

Valuing an FRA Prior to Maturity

To value an FRA prior to the settlement date, we need to know the number of days that have passed since the initiation of the contract. For example, let's suppose we want to value the same 1 × 4 FRA ten days after initiation. Originally it was a 1 × 4 FRA, which means the FRA now expires in 20 days. The calculation of the "savings" on the loan will be the same as in our previous example, except that we need to use the "new" FRA price that would be quoted on a contract covering the same period as the original "loan." In this case the "new" FRA price is the now-current market forward rate for a 90-day loan made at the settlement date, 20 days in the future. Also, we need to discount the interest savings implicit in the FRA back an extra 20 days, or 110 days, instead of 90 days as we did for the value at the settlement date.

Example: Calculating value of an FRA prior to settlement

Value a 5.32% 1 × 4 FRA with a principal amount of $1 million 10 days after initiation if 110-day LIBOR is 5.9% and 20-day LIBOR is 5.7%.

Answer:

Step 1: Find the "new" FRA price on a 90-day loan 20 days from today. This is the current 90-day forward rate at the settlement date, 20 days from now.

$$\left[\frac{1 + \left(0.059 \times \frac{110}{360}\right)}{1 + \left(0.057 \times \frac{20}{360}\right)} - 1 \right] \times \frac{360}{90} = 0.0592568$$

Step 2: Calculate the interest difference on a $1 million, 90-day loan made 20 days from now at the forward rate calculated previously compared to the FRA rate of 5.32%.

$$\left[\left(0.0592568\times\frac{90}{360}\right)-\left(0.0532\times\frac{90}{360}\right)\right]\times\$1,000,000=\$1,514.20$$

Step 3: Discount this amount at the current 110-day rate.

$$\frac{\$1,514.20}{1+\left(0.059\times\frac{110}{360}\right)}=\$1,487.39$$

Valuing a 1 × 4 FRA Prior to Settlement

Professor's Note: I have tried to explain these calculations in such a way that you can value an FRA at any date from initiation to settlement using basic tools that you already know. Once you understand where the value of an FRA comes from (the interest savings on a loan to be made at the settlement date) and when this value is to be received (at the end of the loan), you can calculate the present value of these savings even under somewhat stressful test conditions. Just remember that if the rate in the future is less than the FRA rate, the long is "obligated to borrow" at above-market rates and will have to make a payment to the short. If the rate is greater than the FRA rate, the long will receive a payment from the short.

Pricing Currency Forward Contracts

The **price and value of a currency forward contract** is refreshingly straightforward after that last bit of mental exercise. The calculation of the currency forward rate is just an application of covered interest parity from the topic review of foreign exchange parity relations in Study Session 4.

Recall that the interest rate parity result is based on an assumption that you should make the same amount when you lend at the riskless rate in your home country as you would if you bought *one unit* of the foreign currency at the current spot rate, S_0, invested it at the foreign risk-free rate, and entered into a forward contract to exchange the proceeds of the investment at maturity for the home currency at the forward rate of F_T (both the forward and the spot rates are quoted as the price in the home currency for one unit of the foreign currency).

Covered interest rate parity gives us the no-arbitrage forward price of a unit of foreign currency in terms of the home currency for a currency forward contract of length T in years:

$$F_T \left(\text{currency forward contract} \right) = S_0 \times \frac{\left(1 + R_{DC}\right)^T}{\left(1 + R_{FC}\right)^T}$$

where:
F and S are quoted in domestic currency per unit of foreign currency
R_{DC} = domestic currency interest rate
R_{FC} = foreign currency interest rate

For foreign currency contracts use a 365-day basis to calculate T if the maturity is given in days.

Professor's Note: This is different from the way we expressed interest rate parity back in Study Session 4, in which F and S were quoted in terms of foreign currency per unit of domestic currency. The key is to remember our numerator/ denominator rule: if the spot and forward quotes are in currency A per unit of currency B, the currency A interest rate should be on top and the currency B interest rate should be on the bottom. For example, if S and F are in euros per Swiss franc, put the European interest rate on the top and the Swiss interest rate on the bottom.

Example: Calculating the price of a currency forward contract

The risk-free rates are 6% in the United States and 8% in Mexico. The current spot exchange rate is $0.0845 per Mexican peso (MXN). Calculate the forward exchange rate for a 180-day forward contract.

Answer:

$$F_T \left(\text{currency forward contract} \right) = \$0.0845 \times \frac{1.06^{180/365}}{1.08^{180/365}} = \$0.0837$$

Valuing Currency Forward Contracts

At any time prior to maturity, the value of a currency forward contract to the long will depend on the spot rate at time t, S_t, and can be calculated as:

$$V_t \left(\text{currency forward contract} \right) = \left[\frac{S_t}{\left(1 + R_{FC}\right)^{(T-t)}} \right] - \left[\frac{F_T}{\left(1 + R_{DC}\right)^{(T-t)}} \right]$$

Example: Calculating the value of a currency forward contract

Calculate the value of the forward contract in the previous example if, after 15 days, the spot rate is $0.0980 per MXN.

Answer:

$$V_{15} \left(\text{currency forward contract} \right) = \left(\frac{\$0.0980}{1.08^{165/365}} \right) - \left(\frac{\$0.0837}{1.06^{165/365}} \right) = \$0.0131$$

The continuous time price and value formulas for currency forward contracts are:

$$F_T = \left(\text{currency forward contract} \right) = S_0 \times e^{\left(R^c_{DC} - R^c_{FC} \right) \times T}$$

$$V_t \left(\text{currency forward contract} \right) = \left[\frac{S_t}{e^{R^c_{FC} \times (T-t)}} \right] - \left[\frac{F_T}{e^{R^c_{DC} \times (T-t)}} \right]$$

V_t in both cases is the value in domestic currency units for a contract covering one unit of the foreign currency. For the settlement payment in the home currency on a contract, simply multiply this amount by the notional amount of the foreign currency covered in the contract.

LOS 58.d: Evaluate credit risk in a forward contract and explain how market value is a measure of the credit risk to a party in a forward contract.

At any date after initiation of a forward contract, it is likely to have positive value to either the long or the short. Recall that this value is the amount that would be paid to settle the contract in cash at that point in time. The party with the position that has positive value has credit risk in this amount because the other party would owe them that amount if the contract were terminated. The contract value and, therefore, the credit risk, may increase, decrease, or even change sign over the remaining term of the contract. However, at any point in time, the market values of forward contracts, as we have calculated them, are a measure of the credit risk currently borne by the party to which a cash payment would be made to settle the contract at that point. One way to reduce the credit risk in a forward contract is to mark-to-market partway through.

KEY CONCEPTS

LOS 58.a

The theoretical forward contract price for any asset is the price which would prevent a riskless arbitrage transaction under the assumption of no transactions costs, no credit risk, and unlimited borrowing and lending at the risk-free rate:

$$FP = S_0 \times \left(1 + R_f\right)^T \ \text{ or } \ S_0 = \frac{FP}{\left(1 + R_f\right)^T}$$

The value of the long position in a forward contract on an asset that makes no periodic payment during the term of the contract is the spot price of the asset minus the present value of the forward price. This can be positive or negative:

$$V_0\left(\text{of long position at initiation}\right) = S_0 - \left[\frac{FP}{\left(1 + R_f\right)^T}\right]$$

LOS 58.b

The calculation of the forward price for an equity forward contract is different because the periodic dividend payments affect the no-arbitrage price calculation. The forward price is reduced by the future value of the expected dividend payments; alternatively, the spot price is reduced by the present value of the dividends.

$$FP\left(\text{on an equity security}\right) = \left(S_0 - PVD\right) \times \left(1 + R_f\right)^T = \left[S_0 \times \left(1 + R_f\right)^T\right] - FVD$$

The value of an equity forward contract to the long is the spot equity price minus the present value of the forward price minus the present value of any dividends expected over the term of the contract:

$$V_t\left(\text{long position}\right) = \left[S_t - PVD_t\right] - \left[\frac{FP}{\left(1 + R_f\right)^{(T-t)}}\right]$$

We typically use the continuous time versions to calculate the price and value of a forward contract on an equity index using a continuously compounded dividend yield.

$$FP\left(\text{on an equity index}\right) = S_0 \times e^{\left(R_f^c - \delta^c\right) \times T} = \left(S_0 \times e^{-\delta^c \times T}\right) \times e^{R_f^c \times T}$$

$$V_t\left(\text{of the long position}\right) = \left(\frac{S_t}{e^{\delta^c \times (T-t)}}\right) - \left(\frac{FP}{e^{R_f^c \times (T-t)}}\right)$$

LOS 58.c

For forwards on coupon-paying bonds, the price is calculated as the spot price minus the present value of the coupons times the quantity one plus the risk-free rate.

$$FP\left(\text{on a fixed income security}\right) = \left(S_0 - PVC\right) \times \left(1 + R_f\right)^T = S_0 \times \left(1 + R_f\right)^T - FVC$$

The value of a forward on a coupon-paying bond t years after inception is the spot bond price minus the present value of the forward price minus the present value of any coupon payments expected over the term of the contract:

$$V_t \left(\text{long position} \right) = \left[S_t - PVC_t \right] - \left[\frac{FP}{\left(1 + R_f \right)^{(T-t)}} \right]$$

The "price" of an FRA is the implied forward rate for the period beginning when the FRA expires to the maturity of the underlying "loan."

The value of an FRA at maturity is the interest savings to be realized at maturity of the underlying "loan" discounted back to the date of the expiration of the FRA at the current LIBOR. The value of an FRA prior to maturity is the interest savings estimated by the implied forward rate discounted back to the valuation date at the current LIBOR.

For a currency forward, the price is the exchange rate implied by covered interest rate parity. The value at settlement is the gain or loss to the long from making a currency exchange in the amounts required by the contract at the contract exchange rate, rather than at the prevailing market rate:

$$F_T \left(\text{currency forward contract} \right) = S_0 \times \frac{\left(1 + R_{DC} \right)^T}{\left(1 + R_{FC} \right)^T}$$

where:
F and S are quoted in domestic currency per unit of foreign currency

Prior to settlement, the value of a currency forward is the present value of any gain or loss to the long from making a currency exchange in the amounts required by the contract at the contract exchange rate, compared to an exchange at the prevailing forward exchange rate at the settlement date.

$$V_t \left(\text{currency forward contract} \right) = \left[\frac{S_t}{\left(1 + R_{FC} \right)^{(T-t)}} \right] - \left[\frac{F_T}{\left(1 + R_{DC} \right)^{(T-t)}} \right]$$

The continuous time price and value formulas for a currency forward contract are:

$$F_T \left(\text{currency forward contract} \right) = S_0 \times e^{\left(R_{DC}^c - R_{FC}^c \right) \times T}$$

$$V_t \left(\text{currency forward contract} \right) = \left[\frac{S_t}{e^{R_{FC}^c \times (T-t)}} \right] - \left[\frac{F_T}{e^{R_{DC}^c \times (T-t)}} \right]$$

LOS 58.d

Credit risk is the risk that the counterparty will not pay when a positive amount is owed at settlement. The larger is the value or the forward to one party, the greater the credit (default) risk to that party.

CONCEPT CHECKERS

1. A stock is currently priced at $30 and is expected to pay a dividend of $0.30
    20 days and 65 days from now. The contract price for a 60-day forward contract
    when the interest rate is 5% is *closest* to:
    A. $29.46.
    B. $29.70.
    C. $29.94.

2. After 37 days, the stock in Question 1 is priced at $21 and the risk-free rate is
    still 5%. The value of the forward contract on the stock to the short position is:
    A. −$8.85.
    B. +$8.85.
    C. +$9.00.

3. The contract rate (annualized) for a 3 × 5 FRA if the current 60-day rate is 4%,
    the current 90-day rate is 5%, and the current 150-day rate is 6%, is *closest* to:
    A. 6.0%.
    B. 6.9%.
    C. 7.4%.

4. A 6% Treasury bond is trading at $1,044 (including accrued interest) per $1,000
    of face value. It will make a coupon payment 98 days from now. The yield curve
    is flat at 5% over the next 150 days. The forward price per $1,000 of face value
    for a 120-day forward contract, is *closest* to:
    A. $1,014.52.
    B. $1,030.79.
    C. $1,037.13.

5. The forward price of a 200-day stock index futures contract when the spot
    index is 540, the continuous dividend yield is 1.8%, and the continuously
    compounded risk-free rate is 7% (with a flat yield curve) is *closest* to:
    A. 545.72.
    B. 555.61.
    C. 568.08.

6. An analyst who mistakenly ignores the dividends when valuing a short position
    in a forward contract on a stock that pays dividends will *most likely*:
    A. overvalue the position by the present value of the dividends.
    B. undervalue the position by the present value of the dividends.
    C. overvalue the position by the future value of the dividends.

CHALLENGE PROBLEMS

7. A portfolio manager owns Macrogrow, Inc., which is currently trading at $35 per share. She plans to sell the stock in 120 days, but is concerned about a possible price decline. She decides to take a short position in a 120-day forward contract on the stock. The stock will pay a $0.50 per share dividend in 35 days and $0.50 again in 125 days. The risk-free rate is 4%. The value of the trader's position in the forward contract in 45 days, assuming in 45 days the stock price is $27.50 and the risk-free rate has not changed, is *closest* to:
    A. $7.17.
    B. $7.50.
    C. $7.92.

8. A portfolio manager expects to receive $5,000,000 from a new client in 30 days. These assets are to be invested in a basket of equities. He decides to take a long position in a 30-day forward contract on the S&P 500 stock index to hedge against an increase in equity prices. The index is currently at 1,057. The continuously compounded dividend yield is 1.50%, and the discrete risk-free rate is 4%. Fifteen days later the index value is 1,103. The value of the forward contract after 15 days, assuming no change in the risk-free rate or the dividend yield, is *closest* to:
    A. $41.58.
    B. $43.04.
    C. $44.93.

9. The CFO of Yellow River Company received a report from the economics department which states that short-term rates are expected to increase 50 basis points in the next 90 days. As a floating rate borrower (typically against 90-day LIBOR), the CFO recognizes that he must hedge against an increase in future borrowing costs over the next 90 days because of a potential increase in short-term interest rates. He considers many options, but decides on entering into a long forward rate agreement (FRA). The 30-day LIBOR is 4.5%, 90-day LIBOR is 4.7%, and 180-day LIBOR is 4.9%. To *best* hedge this risk, Yellow River should enter into a:
    A. 3 × 3 FRA at a rate of 4.48%.
    B. 3 × 6 FRA at a rate of 4.48%.
    C. 3 × 6 FRA at a rate of 5.02%.

10. Consider a U.K.-based company that exports goods to the EU. The U.K. company expects to receive payment on a shipment of goods in 60 days. Because the payment will be in euros, the U.K. company wants to hedge against a decline in the value of the euro against the pound over the next 60 days. The U.K. risk-free rate is 3% and the EU risk-free rate is 4%. No change is expected in these rates over the next 60 days. The current spot rate is 0.9230 £ per €. To hedge the currency risk, the U.K. company should take a short position in a Euro contract at a forward price of:
    A. 0.9205.
    B. 0.9215.
    C. 0.9244.

11. The most important measure of credit risk in a forward contract is:
    A. time to maturity.
    B. OAS.
    C. market value.

ANSWERS – CONCEPT CHECKERS

1. **C** The dividend in 65 days occurs after the contract has matured, so it's not relevant to computing the forward price.

$$PVD = \frac{\$0.30}{1.05^{20/365}} = \$0.2992$$

$$FP = (\$30.00 - \$0.2992) \times 1.05^{60/365} = \$29.94$$

2. **B**

$$V(\text{long position}) = \$21.00 - \left[\frac{\$29.94}{1.05^{23/365}}\right] = -\$8.85$$

$$V(\text{short position}) = +\$8.85$$

3. **C** The actual (unannualized) rate on the 90-day loan is:

$$R90 = 0.05 \times \frac{90}{360} = 0.0125$$

The actual rate on the 150-day loan is:

$$R150 = 0.06 \times \frac{150}{360} = 0.025$$

The price of the 3 × 5 FRA (the 60-day forward rate in 90 days) is:

$$\left(\frac{1.025}{1.0125} - 1\right) \times \frac{360}{60} = 0.074 = 7.4\%$$

4. **B** Remember that U.S. Treasury bonds make semiannual coupon payments, so:

$$C = \frac{\$1,000 \times 0.06}{2} = \$30.00$$

$$PVC = \frac{\$30.00}{1.05^{98/365}} = \$29.61$$

The forward price of the contract is therefore:

$$FP(\text{on a fixed income security}) = (\$1,044 - \$29.61) \times (1.05)^{120/365} = \$1,030.79$$

5. **B** Use the dividend rate as a continuously compounded rate to get:

$$FP = 540 \times e^{(0.07 - 0.018) \times (200/365)} = 555.61$$

6. **B** The value of the long position in a forward contract on a stock at time t is:

$$V_t \left(\text{long position}\right) = \left[S_t - PVD_t\right] - \left[\frac{FP}{\left(1 + R_f\right)^{(T-t)}}\right]$$

If the dividends are ignored, the *long* position will be overvalued by the present value of the dividends; that means the *short* position (which is what the question asks for) will be undervalued by the same amount.

ANSWERS – CHALLENGE PROBLEMS

7. **A** The dividend in 125 days is irrelevant because it occurs after the forward contract matures.

$$PVD = \frac{\$0.50}{1.04^{35/365}} = \$0.4981$$

$$FP = \left(\$35 - \$0.4981\right) \times 1.04^{120/365} = \$34.95$$

$$V_{45} \left(\text{short position}\right) = -\left(\$27.50 - \frac{\$34.95}{1.04^{75/365}}\right) = \$7.17$$

8. **C** The discrete risk-free rate is given in the problem, so the first thing to do is calculate the continuously compounded risk-free rate and the forward price at initiation:

$$\text{continuously compounded risk-free rate} = \ln(1.04) = 0.0392$$
$$FP\left(\text{on an equity index}\right) = 1,057 \times e^{(0.0392 - 0.015) \times (30/365)} = 1,059.10$$

The value after 15 days is:

$$V_{15} = \left(\frac{1,103}{e^{0.015 \times (15/365)}}\right) - \left(\frac{1059.10}{e^{0.0392 \times (15/365)}}\right) = \$44.93$$

9. **C** A 3 × 6 FRA expires in 90 days and is based on 90-day LIBOR, so it is the appropriate hedge for 90-day LIBOR 90 days from today. The rate is calculated as:

$$R90 = 0.047 \times \frac{90}{360} = 0.0118$$
$$R180 = 0.049 \times \frac{180}{360} = 0.0245$$
$$\text{price of } 3 \times 6 \text{ FRA} = \left(\frac{1.0245}{1.0118} - 1\right) \times \frac{360}{90} = 0.0502 = 5.02\%$$

10. **B** The U.K. company will be receiving euros in 60 days, so it should short the 60-day forward on the euro as a hedge. The no-arbitrage forward price is:

$$F_T = £0.923 \times \frac{1.03^{60/365}}{1.04^{60/365}} = 0.9215$$

11. **C** The primary element of credit risk for a forward is the market value of the contract.

FUTURES MARKETS AND CONTRACTS

EXAM FOCUS

This topic review focuses on the no-arbitrage pricing relationships for futures contracts. The pricing of futures is quite similar, and in some cases identical, to the pricing of forwards. You should understand the basic futures pricing relation and how it is adjusted for assets that have storage costs or positive cash flows.

WARM-UP: FUTURES CONTRACTS

Futures contracts are very much like the forward contracts we learned about in the previous topic review. They are similar in that:

- Deliverable contracts obligate the long to buy and the short to sell a certain quantity of an asset for a certain price on a specified future date.
- Cash settlement contracts are settled by paying the contract value in cash on the expiration date.
- Both forwards and futures are priced to have zero value at the time the investor enters into the contract.

There are important differences, including:

- Futures are marked to market at the end of every trading day. Forward contracts are not marked to market.
- Forwards are private contracts and do not trade on organized exchanges. Futures contracts trade on organized exchanges.
- Forwards are customized contracts satisfying the needs of the parties involved. Futures contracts are highly standardized.
- Forwards are contracts with the originating counterparty; a specialized entity called a clearinghouse is the counterparty to all futures contracts.
- Forward contracts are usually not regulated. The government having legal jurisdiction regulates futures markets.

LOS 59.a: Explain why the futures price must converge to the spot price at expiration.

The **spot (cash) price** of a commodity or financial asset is the price for immediate delivery. The **futures price** is the price today for delivery at some future point in time (the maturity date). The **basis** is the difference between the spot price and the futures price.

> basis = spot price – futures price

As the maturity date nears, the basis converges toward zero. At expiration, the spot price must equal the futures price because the futures price has become the price today for delivery today, which is the same as the spot. Arbitrage will force the prices to be the same at contract expiration.

Example: Why the futures price must equal the spot price at expiration

Suppose the current spot price of silver is $4.65. Demonstrate by arbitrage that the futures price of a futures silver contract that expires in one minute must equal the spot price.

Answer:

Suppose the futures price was $4.70. We could buy the silver at the spot price of $4.65, sell the futures contract, and deliver the silver under the contract at $4.70. Our profit would be $4.70 – $4.65 = $0.05. Because the contract matures in one minute, there is virtually no risk to this arbitrage trade.

Suppose instead the futures price was $4.61. Now we would buy the silver contract, take delivery of the silver by paying $4.61, and then sell the silver at the spot price of $4.65. Our profit is $4.65 – $4.61 = $0.04. Once again, this is a riskless arbitrage trade.

Therefore, in order to prevent arbitrage, the futures price at the maturity of the contract must be equal to the spot price of $4.65.

WARM-UP: FUTURES MARGINS AND MARKING TO MARKET

Each exchange has a clearinghouse. The clearinghouse guarantees that traders in the futures market will honor their obligations. The clearinghouse does this by splitting each trade once it is made and acting as the opposite side of each position. To safeguard the clearinghouse, the exchange requires both sides of the trade to post margin and settle their accounts on a daily basis. Thus the margin in the futures markets is a performance guarantee.

Marking to market is the process of adjusting the margin balance in a futures account each day for the change in the value of the contract from the previous trading day, based on the settlement price. The futures exchanges can require a mark to market more frequently (than daily) under extraordinary circumstances.

LOS 59.b: Determine the value of a futures contract.

Like forward contracts, futures contracts have no value at contract initiation. Unlike forward contracts, futures contracts do not accumulate value changes over the term of the contract. Since futures accounts are marked to market daily, the value after the margin deposit has been adjusted for the day's gains and losses in contract value is always zero. The futures price at any point in time is the price that makes the value of a new contract equal to zero. The value of a futures contract strays from zero only during the trading periods between the times at which the account is marked to market:

value of futures contract = current futures price – previous mark-to-market price

If the futures price increases, the value of the long position increases. The value is set back to zero by the mark to market at the end of the mark-to-market period.

LOS 59.c: Explain how forward and futures prices differ.

The no-arbitrage price of a futures contract should be the same as that of a forward contract that was presented in the previous topic review:

$$FP = S_0 \times (1 + R_f)^T$$

where:
FP $=$ futures price
S_0 $=$ spot price at inception of the contract $(t = 0)$
R_f $=$ annual risk-free rate
T $=$ futures contract term in years

However, there are a number of "real-world" complications that will cause futures and forward prices to be different. If investors prefer the mark-to-market feature of futures, futures prices will be higher than forward prices. If investors would rather hold a forward contract in order to avoid the marking to market of a futures contract, the forward price would be higher than the futures price. From a technical standpoint, the differences between the theoretical (no-arbitrage) prices of futures and forwards center on the correlation between interest rates and the mark-to-market cash flows of futures:

- Higher reinvestment rates for gains and lower borrowing costs to fund losses lead to a preference for the mark-to-market feature of futures, and higher prices for futures than forwards, when interest rates and asset values are positively correlated.
- A preference to avoid the mark-to-market cash flows will lead to a higher price for the forward relative to the future if interest rates and asset values are negatively correlated.

A preference for the mark-to-market feature will arise from a positive correlation between interest rates and the price of the contract asset. When the value of the underlying asset increases and the mark to market generates cash, reinvestment opportunities tend to be better due to the positive correlation of asset values with higher interest rates. When the value of the underlying asset decreases and the mark to market requires cash, borrowing costs tend to be lower due to the positive correlation.

The opposite result will occur when the correlation between the price of the underlying asset and interest rates is negative. Consider forwards and futures contracts on fixed income prices. Fixed income values fall when interest rates rise, so rates and values are negatively correlated. Borrowing costs are higher when funds are needed and reinvestment rates are lower when funds are generated by the mark to market of the futures contracts. Figure 1 summarizes these results.

Figure 1: Prices of Futures versus Forward Contracts

If the correlation between the underlying asset value and interest rates is...	Investors will...
Positive	Prefer to go long in a **futures contract**, and the futures price will be greater than the price of an otherwise comparable forward contract
Zero	Have no preference
Negative	Prefer to go long in a **forward contract**, and the forward price will be greater than the price of an otherwise comparable futures contract

FUTURES ARBITRAGE

Professor's Note: The trades necessary to conduct futures arbitrage are the same as those for forward arbitrage that we outlined in the previous topic review. The only difference is that now we are going long or short in the futures contract.

A **cash-and-carry arbitrage** consists of buying the asset, storing/holding the asset, and selling the asset at the futures price when the contract expires. The steps in a cash-and-carry arbitrage are as follows.

At the initiation of the contract:

- Borrow money for the term of the contract at market interest rates.
- Buy the underlying asset at the spot price.
- Sell (go short) a futures contract at the current futures price.

At contract expiration:

- Deliver the asset and receive the futures contract price.
- Repay the loan plus interest.

If the futures contract is overpriced, this 5-step transaction will generate a riskless profit. The futures contract is overpriced if the actual market price is greater than the no-arbitrage price.

Example: Futures cash and carry arbitrage

Assume the spot price of gold is $900/oz., that the 1-year futures price is $975/oz., and that an investor can borrow or lend funds at 7%. Ignore transaction and storage costs. Calculate the arbitrage profit.

Answer:

The futures price, according to the no-arbitrage principle, should be:

$$FP = \$900 \times 1.07 = \$963$$

Instead, it's trading at $975. That means the futures contract is overpriced, so we should conduct cash and carry arbitrage by going short in the futures contract, buying gold in the spot market, and borrowing money to pay for the purchase. If we borrow $900 to fund the purchase of gold, we must repay $900 × 1.07 = $963.

Today		1 Year from Today	
Spot price of gold	$900		
Futures price of gold	$975		
Transaction	*Cash Flow*	*Transaction*	*Cash Flow*
Short futures	$0	Settle short position by delivering gold	$975
Buy gold in spot market	−$900		
Borrow at 7%	+$900	Repay loan	−$963
Total cash flow	$0	Total cash flow = arbitrage profit	+$12

The riskless profit is equal to the difference between the futures contract proceeds and the loan payoff, or $975 − $963 = $12. Notice that this profit is equal to the difference between the actual futures price of $975 and the no-arbitrage price of $963.

If the futures price is too low (which presents a profitable arbitrage opportunity), the opposite of each step should be executed to earn a riskless profit.

This is **reverse cash-and-carry arbitrage**. The steps in reverse cash-and-carry arbitrage are as follows.

At the initiation of the contract:

- Sell asset short.
- Lend short sale proceeds at market interest rates.
- Buy (go long) futures contract at market price.

Study Sess

Cross-Reference to CFA Institute Assigned Reading #59 – Futures Markets and Co...

At contract expiration:

- Collect loan proceeds.
- Take delivery of the asset for the futures price and cover the short sale commitment.

Example: Futures reverse cash and carry arbitrage

Assume gold is priced at $900/oz., that the 1-year futures price is $945/oz., and that an investor can borrow or lend funds at 7%. Ignore transaction and storage costs. Calculate the profits from arbitrage.

Answer:

The futures price, according to the no-arbitrage principle, should be:

$$FP = \$900 \times 1.07 = \$963$$

Instead, it's trading at $945. That means the futures contract is underpriced, so we should conduct reverse cash and carry arbitrage by going long in the futures contract, shorting gold, and investing the short-sale proceeds.

Today		1 Year from Today	
Spot price of gold	$900		
Futures price of gold	$945		
Transaction	*Cash Flow*	*Transaction*	*Cash Flow*
Long futures	$0	Settle long position by buying gold	−$945
Short gold	+$900	Deliver gold to close short position	
Invest short-sale proceeds at 7%	−$900	Receive investment proceeds	+ $963
Total cash flow	$0	Total cash flow = arbitrage profit	+$18

The riskless profit is equal to the loan proceeds less the futures contract payment, or $963 − $945 = $18.

Professor's Note: It may help to remember "buy low, sell high." If the futures price is "too high," sell the future and buy the spot. If the futures price is "too low," buy the future and sell the spot.

LOS 59.d: Describe the monetary and nonmonetary benefits and costs associated with holding the underlying asset, and explain how they affect the futures price.

Any positive costs associated with storing or holding the asset in a cash and carry arbitrage will increase the no-arbitrage futures price because it is costly to buy, store, and deliver the asset. Many commodities have storage costs (e.g., corn, live cattle, and gold). There also is risk of loss from spoilage (corn), disease (cattle), and fire (oil or gas). Insuring or bearing these risks adds to the cost of holding these assets.

With *financial* assets there may be a significant benefit to holding the underlying asset, but there are no storage costs other than the opportunity cost of the funds. For example, holders of dividend-paying stocks, coupon bonds, and currencies will earn dividends, coupon payments, and interest, respectively. A monetary benefit from holding the asset will *decrease* the no-arbitrage futures price since the net cost of holding the asset is reduced.

There may also be non-monetary benefits from holding an asset in short supply. For a manufacturing firm, for example, this may be the benefit of having a ready supply so that a temporary shortage of their primary input will not disrupt their operations. The return from these non-monetary benefits is called the **convenience yield**.

Recall the pricing relation we developed for spot and forward prices when there is no cost or benefit to holding the underlying asset:

$$FP = S_0 \times (1 + R_f)^T$$

If we define the net cost of holding the asset as the costs net of any non-monetary benefits, we have:

net costs (NC) = storage costs − convenience yield

The generalized no-arbitrage futures price is now:

$$FP = S_0 \times (1 + R_f)^T + FV(NC)$$

where:
$FV(NC)$ = future value, at contract expiration, of the net costs of holding the asset

Positive net costs of holding the asset increase the futures price.

When the asset generates cash flows, the net costs are negative (a net benefit), and the futures price is decreased. We can define the net benefit of holding an asset as:

NB = yield on the asset + convenience yield

In that case, the no-arbitrage futures price is:

$$FP = S_0 \times (1 + R_f)^T - FV(NB)$$

where:
$FV(NB)$ = future value, at contract expiration, of the net benefits of holding the asset

The futures price will be *lower* when the dividend or coupon yield on the underlying asset is *higher* or when the non-monetary benefits of holding the asset are higher.

LOS 59.e: Describe backwardation and contango.

Backwardation refers to a situation where the futures price is below the spot price. For this to occur, there must be a significant benefit to holding the asset, either monetary or non-monetary. Backwardation might occur if there are benefits to holding the asset that offset the opportunity cost of holding the asset (the risk-free rate) and additional net holding costs.

Contango refers to a situation where the futures price is above the spot price. If there are no benefits to holding the asset (e.g., dividends, coupons, or convenience yield), the futures price will be $FP = S_0(1 + R_f)^T + FV(NC)$, and contango will occur because the futures price will be greater than the spot price.

LOS 59.f: Discuss whether futures prices equal expected spot prices.

If both parties to a futures transaction are hedging existing risk, the futures price may be equal to expected future spot prices. In markets of hedgers, the futures price might be temporarily above or below expected future spot prices, but it would be an unbiased predictor of future spot rates.

If we view a futures contract as a transfer of risk from an asset holder to the buyer of the contract, we would expect the futures price to be lower than the expected price in the future to compensate the future buyer for accepting asset price risk. This situation is called **normal backwardation**. If the futures price is greater than the expected spot price, it is called **normal contango**.

The most likely situation in financial markets is one in which futures prices are biased predictors of spot rates (i.e., futures prices do not equal expected spot prices) and, more specifically, futures prices are less than expected spot prices (normal backwardation).

 Professor's Note: In LOS 59.e, we're comparing the current futures price and the current spot price. In LOS 59.f, we're comparing the current futures price and the expected future spot price.

WARM-UP: EURODOLLAR, TREASURY BOND, STOCK INDEX, AND CURRENCY FUTURES

Eurodollar futures are based on 90-day LIBOR, which is an add-on yield. By convention, however, the price quotes are calculated as (100 − annualized LIBOR in percent). These contracts settle in cash, and the minimum price change is one "tick," which is a price change of 0.0001 = 0.01%, or $25 per $1 million contract.

Treasury bond (T-bond) futures are traded for T-bonds with a maturity of 15 years or more. The contract is deliverable with a face value of $100,000. T-bond futures are quoted as a percent and fractions of 1% (measured in 1/32nds) of face value.

The short in a T-bond futures contract has the option to deliver any of several bonds which will satisfy the delivery terms of the contract. This is called a delivery option and is valuable to the short. Each bond is given a conversion factor that is used to adjust the long's payment at delivery so the more valuable bonds receive a larger payment. These factors are multipliers for the futures price at settlement. The long pays the futures price at expiration multiplied by the conversion factor.

Stock index futures are based on the level of an equity index. The most popular stock index future is the S&P 500 Index Future that trades in Chicago. Settlement is in cash and is based on a multiplier of 250. The value of a contract is 250 times the level of the index stated in the contract. With an index level of 1000, the value of each contract is $250,000. Each index point in the futures price represents a gain or loss of $250 per contract. A smaller contract on the same index has a multiplier of 50.

The **currency futures market** is smaller in volume than the forward market we described in the previous topic review. In the United States, currency contracts trade on the euro, Mexican peso, and yen, among others. Contracts are set in units of the foreign currency, and the price is stated in U.S. dollars per unit of foreign currency.

WARM-UP: TREASURY BILL FUTURES PRICING

Treasury bill (T-bill) futures contracts are based on a $1 million face value 90-day (13-week) T-bill, and they settle in cash. The price quotes are 100 minus the annualized discount in percent on the T-bills. For example, a price quote of 98.52 represents an annualized discount of 1.48%, an actual discount from face of 0.0148(90 / 360) = 0.0037, and a "delivery" price of (1 − 0.0037) × $1 million = $996,300. Each change of 0.01 in the price of a T-bill futures contract is worth $25. If you took a long position at 98.52 and the price fell to 98.50, your loss is $50 per contract.

T-bill futures are priced using the no-arbitrage principle. The key to understanding the pricing of T-bill futures is to recognize that the underlying asset is a 90-day T-bill *at the maturity of the futures contract.*

For example, suppose we want to price a 77-day T-bill future. If we bought a 167-day T-bill, we could deliver it in 77 days to satisfy a short position in a 90-day T-bill futures contract. In other words, in 77 days the 167-day T-bill will be a 90-day T-bill. If the borrowing cost of the 77-day loan to finance the purchase is equal to the gains from selling the T-bill in 77 days at the futures price, there is no arbitrage opportunity.

Since a T-bill is a pure discount security, there are no cash flow benefits to consider, and we have the familiar (by now) relation:

$$FP = S_0 \times (1 + R_f)^T$$

Remember, for an asset without cash flows or storage costs, the right-hand side of this equation is the cost of buying and holding the asset for a period of T years. The holding costs here are simply the interest costs at R_f over the term of the futures contract.

Example: Calculating the price of a T-bill futures contract

A 60-day T-bill is quoted at 6%, and a 150-day bill is priced at 6.5%. Calculate the no-arbitrage price of a 90-day future.

Answer:

The T-bill prices as a percentage of face value are:

$$B_{60} = 1 - \left(0.060 \times \frac{60}{360} \right) = 0.9900$$

$$B_{150} = 1 - \left(0.065 \times \frac{150}{360} \right) = 0.9729$$

The cost of holding the 150-day bill for 60 days is the 60-day risk-free rate, which is the yield (not the discount) on the 60-day bill. In effect, for 60 days we're borrowing 0.99 and repaying 1.00, so the yield is the 0.01 "interest" divided by the original amount:

$$\text{60-day risk-free yield} = \frac{1.00 - 0.99}{0.99} = 0.0101$$

The 150-day T-bill is, in effect, the spot asset, since in 60 days it will be a 90-day T-bill. We calculate the no-arbitrage futures price using the price of the 150-day bill:

$$FP = S_0 \times (1 + R_f)^T = 0.9729 \times 1.0101 = 0.9827$$

Note that we used the 60-day yield from the T-bill directly—we didn't annualize it to R_f because we needed the effective rate for a 60-day loan to calculate *FP*.

An alternative way to get the futures price is to divide the price of the deliverable bill by the price of one that matures at contract expiration. In this example, we get the same result:

$$FP = \frac{0.9729}{0.9900} = 0.9827$$

LOS 59.g: Describe the difficulties in pricing Eurodollar futures and creating a pure arbitrage opportunity.

Eurodollar Futures

With T-bills, the arbitrage strategy that creates the pricing bounds is straightforward. If we sell a 77-day future on a 90-day bill, and buy a 167-day bill, we have an arbitrage. In 77 days, the bill will be a 90-day bill and its value should be equal to that of the (identical) bill covered by the contract.

Eurodollar futures do not allow such an arbitrage. The Eurodollar futures are priced as a discount yield and LIBOR is subtracted from 100 to get the quote. Every basis point (0.01%) move in (annualized) 90-day LIBOR represents a $25 gain or loss on the contract, just as with the T-bill contract.

LIBOR, however, is actually an add-on yield, the rate you would earn on the face amount of a deposit. An add-on yield account for 167 days that pays $1 at maturity can be valued at expiration (77 days later) using 90-day LIBOR 77 days from now ($L90_{t=77}$) as:

$$\frac{\$1}{1 + L90_{t=77}}$$

Prior to contract expiration, it will be worth the present value of the expectation of this value. This is important because the value of the deposit will not change $25 for every one basis point change in expected 90-day LIBOR in 77 days as the value of the futures contract does. The asset value is not perfectly hedged by the contract value as it is with the T-bill contract. While no riskless arbitrage relation exists for the Eurodollar futures contract, it is still a very useful, and widely used, hedging instrument for exposure to LIBOR.

LOS 59.h: Calculate and interpret the price of Treasury bond futures, stock index futures, and currency futures.

Treasury Bond Futures

In order to calculate the no-arbitrage futures price for a T-bond contract, we must take account of the value of the coupon payments in constructing an arbitrage relation. To adjust the futures price for the expected coupon payments, we subtract the future value of the coupon payments (FVC) from the no-arbitrage futures price on a bond with no coupon payments.

$$FP = \text{bond price} \times (1 + R_f)^T - FVC$$

Since the cost to hold the asset is reduced by the asset cash flows, the futures price that insures that a cash-and-carry arbitrage would provide no profit is lower than without the cash flows. It is cheaper to buy, hold, and deliver the asset because of the coupon payments.

Example: Calculating the price of a Treasury bond futures contract

Calculate the no-arbitrage futures price of a 1.2 year futures contract calling for the delivery of a specific bond, a 7% T-bond with exactly 10 years to maturity and a price of $1,040, when the annual risk-free rate is 5%.

Answer:

The semiannual coupon on a single, $1,000 face-value 7% bond is $35. A bondholder will receive one payment 0.5 years from now (when there are 0.7 years left to maturity of the futures contract) and one payment 1 year from now (when there are 0.2 years until maturity). The future value of these coupons at the end of 1.2 years (the expiration date) is:

$$FVC = \left(\$35 \times 1.05^{0.7}\right) + \left(\$35 \times 1.05^{0.2}\right) = \$71.56$$

The futures price is then:

$$FP = \left(\$1,040 \times 1.05^{1.2}\right) - \$71.56 = \$1,031.15$$

The short on the T-bond contract has the option of delivering any one of a number of different bonds. Each bond is assigned a **conversion factor** (CF), a multiplier for the futures price on the "contract" bond, to adjust the settlement payment for delivery for higher or lower coupon bonds (with identical face value). The conversion factor is used to adjust the no-arbitrage price for the "cheapest to deliver" of all the permitted bonds.

The adjustment to the futures price we calculated is:

$$FP = \left[\text{bond price} \times \left(1 + R_f\right)^T - FVC\right] \times \frac{1}{CF}$$

Example: Pricing a T-Bond futures contract with a delivery option

Suppose the futures contract from the previous example allows many different bonds to be delivered. The conversion factor of the 10-year 7% T-bond is 1.13. Calculate the appropriate no-arbitrage futures price.

Answer:

The no-arbitrage futures price is now equal to the futures price calculated from the previous example, adjusted by the conversion factor of 1.13.

$$FP = \frac{\$1,031.15}{1.13} = \$912.52$$

An arbitrage involving the cheapest to deliver bond may not be risk-free because the cheapest to deliver bond may change during the term of the contract. This offers an advantage to an arbitrageur who is short the future because the short holds the delivery option, not the long.

Stock Futures

A futures contract on an individual stock may have expected dividend payments over the life of the futures contract. In order to price such a contract, we must adjust for the future value of the expected dividends. The no-arbitrage futures price adjusted for the future value of the dividends (FVD) or present value of the dividends (PVD) can be written as:

$$FP(\text{on an individual stock}) = S_0 \times (1 + R_f)^T - FVD = (S_0 - PVD) \times (1 + R_f)^T$$

> ### Example: Calculating the price of a stock futures contract
>
> Calculate the no-arbitrage price for a 120-day future on a stock that is currently priced at $30 and is expected to pay a dividend of $0.40 in 15 days and $0.40 in 105 days. Assume the annual risk-free rate is 5% and the yield curve is flat.
>
> *30.485 = .39920   39.39*
>
> **Answer:**
>
> The first dividend can be reinvested for 105 days and the second for 15 days, so that:
>
> $$FVD = \left(\$0.40 \times 1.05^{105/365}\right) + \left(\$0.40 \times 1.05^{15/365}\right) = \$0.8065$$
>
> $$FP = \left(\$30.00 \times 1.05^{120/365}\right) - \$0.8065 = \$29.68$$

Equity Index Futures

For an index contract, rather than take the present value of each dividend on (possibly) hundreds of stocks, we can make the calculation as if the dividends are paid continuously (rather than at discrete times) at the continuous time equivalent of the dividend yield rate on the index.

Using continuous time discounting, we get a no-arbitrage futures price of:

$$FP(\text{on an equity index}) = S_0 \times e^{\left(R_f^c - \delta^c\right) \times T}$$

where:

R_f^c = continuously compounded risk-free rate

δ^c = continuously compounded dividend yield

Example: Calculating the value of a futures contract on an equity index

The current value of the Nasdaq index is 1,780. The continuous dividend yield is 1.1%, and the continuously compounded risk-free rate is 3.7%. Calculate the no-arbitrage futures price of an 87-day futures contract on the Nasdaq index.

Answer:

$$FP = 1{,}780 \times e^{(0.037-0.011) \times (87/365)} = 1{,}791.06$$

Currency Futures

The price of a currency future is derived exactly as we did for forwards. Recall that R_{FC} and R_{DC} are the risk-free returns in the two different currencies, S_0 is the spot exchange rate, and F_T is the price of a futures contract of T years duration, with both the spot and futures price quoted in units of domestic currency per one unit of foreign currency.

$$F_T \left(\text{currency futures contract}\right) = S_0 \times \frac{\left(1 + R_{DC}\right)^T}{\left(1 + R_{FC}\right)^T}$$

where:
DC = domestic currency
FC = foreign currency

 Professor's Note: You should recognize this as the equation of interest rate parity from Study Session 4. The key to applying this formula correctly is to remember our numerator/denominator rule from Study Session 4: if the spot and forward quotes are in Currency A/Currency B, the Currency A interest rate should be on top and the Currency B interest rate should be on the bottom. For example, if S and F are in euro per Swiss franc, put the European interest rate on the top and the Swiss interest rate on the bottom.

The continuous time version with continuously compounded interest rates is:

$$F_T = \left(\text{currency futures contract}\right) = S_0 \times e^{\left(R_{DC}^c - R_{FC}^c\right) \times T}$$

Example: Calculate the price of a currency futures contract

The risk-free rates are 5% in U.S. dollars ($) and 6.5% in British pounds (£). The current spot exchange rate is $1.7301/£. Calculate the no-arbitrage $ price of a 6-month £ futures contract.

Answer:

With higher short-term rates in Great Britain, the £ is expected to depreciate relative to the $.

$$F_{0.5} = \$1.7301 \times \frac{1.05^{0.5}}{1.065^{0.5}} = \$1.7179 \text{ per } £$$

(.0247

 Professor's Note: For details on how to exploit arbitrage opportunities when interest rate parity doesn't hold by conducting covered interest arbitrage, see LOS 18.h in Study Session 4.

KEY CONCEPTS

LOS 59.a

At expiration of a futures contract, the spot price must equal the futures price because the futures price has become the price today for delivery today, which is the same as the spot. Arbitrage will force the prices to be the same at contract expiration.

LOS 59.b

Since futures accounts are marked to market daily, the value after the margin deposit has been adjusted for the day's gains and losses in contract value is always zero. The futures price at any point in time is the price that makes the value of a new contract equal to zero.

The futures price is a no-arbitrage price. For a future of term T on an asset with no storage costs or expected cash flows over the term of the contract, the futures price is:

$$FP = S_0 \times (1 + R_f)^T$$

LOS 59.c

When interest rates and asset values are positively correlated, higher reinvestment rates for gains and lower borrowing costs to fund losses lead to a preference for the mark to market feature of futures, and higher prices for futures than forwards. If interest rates and asset values are negatively correlated, a preference to avoid the mark-to-market cash flows will lead to a higher price for the forward relative to the future.

LOS 59.d

Futures prices are affected by the monetary costs and benefits of holding the underlying asset. Storage and insurance are costs, while any cash flows from the asset are a benefit:

$$FP = S_0 \times (1 + R_f)^T + FV(NC)$$

There can also be non-monetary benefits from holding assets and having the use of them. This non-monetary return is termed a convenience yield. In that case, the no-arbitrage futures price is:

$$FP = S_0 \times (1 + R_f)^T - FV(NB)$$

LOS 59.e

Backwardation refers to a situation where the futures price is below the spot price. For this to occur, there must be a significant benefit to holding the asset, either monetary or non-monetary. Contango refers to a situation where the futures price is above the spot price.

LOS 59.f

If the futures market is made up of a balance of short and long hedgers, futures prices may be unbiased predictors of future spot rates. If the market is characterized as a transfer of asset price risk from asset holders to futures buyers, futures prices may be less than expected future spot rates. This is called normal backwardation. If the futures price is greater than the expected spot price, it is called normal contango.

LOS 59.g

Eurodollar futures are priced as a discount yield, and LIBOR-based deposits are priced as an add-on yield. The result is that the deposit value is not perfectly hedged by the Eurodollar contract, so Eurodollar futures can't be priced using the standard no-arbitrage framework.

LOS 59.h

Futures prices on coupon bonds must be adjusted for the future value of the expected coupons. For any T-bond:

$$FP = \text{bond price} \times (1 + R_f)^T - FVC$$

T-bond futures prices must be adjusted to conform to the price for the bond that is cheapest to deliver, using its conversion factor (CF):

$$FP = \left[\text{bond price} \times (1 + R_f)^T - FVC \right] \times \frac{1}{CF}$$

Stock index futures prices are adjusted for the future value of expected dividends:

$$FP = S_0 \times (1 + R_f)^T - FVD$$

In continuous time with a dividend yield on the index of δ, the calculation is:

$$FP(\text{on an equity index}) = S_0 \times e^{\left(R_f^c - \delta^c \right) \times T}$$

The price of currency futures is calculated as:

$$F_T (\text{currency futures contract}) = S_0 \times \frac{(1 + R_{DC})^T}{(1 + R_{FC})^T}$$

where :
F and S are quoted in domestic currency per unit of foreign currency

In continuous time it is $F_T = (\text{currency futures contract}) = S_0 \times e^{\left(R_{DC}^c - R_{FC}^c \right) \times T}$

CONCEPT CHECKERS

1. At the maturity of the futures contract, arbitrage guarantees that the:
    A. futures price is equal to the spot price.
    B. basis is greater than zero if backwardation occurs.
    C. basis is less than zero if contango occurs.

2. To initiate an arbitrage trade if the futures contract is overpriced, the trader should:
    A. borrow at the risk-free rate, short the asset, and sell the futures.
    B. short the asset, invest at the risk-free rate, and buy the futures.
    C. borrow at the risk-free rate, buy the asset, and sell the futures.

3. Backwardation refers to a situation where:
    A. spot prices are above futures prices.
    B. spot prices are below futures prices.
    C. expected future spot prices are above futures prices.

4. Forward prices are likely to be lower than futures prices when:
    A. interest rates are low.
    B. asset values are positively correlated with short rates.
    C. asset values are negatively correlated with short rates.

5. A stock index is at 965, the continuous dividend yield is 1%, and the continuous risk-free rate is 3%. The fair value for a 270-day future is *closest* to:
    A. 978.42.
    B. 979.38.
    C. 984.30.

6. A 9% Treasury bond with exactly five years to maturity is priced at $1,135. If the current risk-free rate is 5%, the no-arbitrage price of a 1.4-year futures is *closest* to:
    A. $1,122.33.
    B. $1,188.87.
    C. $1,193.33.

7. An 8-year $1,000 par Treasury bond pays a 7% semiannual coupon. The bond has a conversion factor of 1.025. The risk-free rate is 6%, and the annual yield on the bond is 7%. The bond just made a coupon payment. The price of a 15-month futures contract on this bond is *closest* to:
    A. $979.00.
    B. $1,003.47.
    C. $1,049.32.

CHALLENGE PROBLEMS

8.   The discrete risk-free rates are 5.25% in the United States and 6.25% in the U.K. The spot exchange rate is $1.6500 per pound and the market price of a 75-day futures contract on the pound is $1.6498. The appropriate arbitrage strategy is to go:
   A. short in the pound futures contract at the futures price of $1.6498.
   B. short in the pound in the spot market at the spot price of $1.6468.
   C. long in the pound futures contract at the futures price of $1.6446.

9.   Assuming the futures contract is trading at the no-arbitrage price, for a futures contract on an equity index with a positive dividend yield:
   A. backwardation will occur if the dividend yield is greater than the risk-free rate.
   B. contango will occur if the dividend yield is greater than the risk-free rate.
   C. contango will occur if the risk-free rate is positive.

10. An analyst has been given the following currency exchange rates and interest rates.

Country	Yield	1-year Futures Rate (USD per CAD)	Spot Exchange Rate (USD per CAD)
U.S.	6%	---	---
Canada	8%	0.70	0.72

The profitable arbitrage is to:
   A. sell the futures at the futures price of $0.7067.
   B. sell the futures at the futures price of $0.7336.
   C. buy the futures at the futures price of $0.7000.

11. Liz Potter is analyzing futures markets in the nation of Subservia for the first time. She has noted various historical time periods with a high volume of normal backwardation trading, and other periods of time with a high volume of normal contango trading. Currently, most of the trading volume evidences normal contango pricing. Futures prices in Subservia are *most likely*:
   A. biased predictors of expected spot rates.
   B. unbiased predictors of expected spot rates.
   C. lower than expected spot rates.

ANSWERS – CONCEPT CHECKERS

1. **A**   The spot price of a commodity or financial instrument is the current cash price or the price for immediate delivery. The futures price represents the price today for delivery at some future point in time (the maturity date). As the maturity date nears, the pricing differential between the spot and futures (the basis) must converge toward zero. On the maturity date, the spot price must equal the futures price because the futures price has become the price today for delivery today—the same as the spot.

2. **C**   If the actual futures price is too high relative to the no-arbitrage price, sell futures, borrow at the risk-free rate, and buy the asset that can be delivered against your futures sale. At futures maturity, deliver the asset, receive the futures price, repay debt, and keep the profit.

3. **A**   Backwardation refers to a situation where spot prices are higher than futures prices—significant monetary benefits of the asset or a relatively high convenience yield can lead to this result.

4. **B**   When interest rates and asset values are positively correlated, higher reinvestment rates for gains and lower borrowing costs to fund losses lead to a preference for the mark-to-market feature of futures, and higher prices for futures than forwards.

5. **B** $FP = 965 \times e^{(0.03-0.01) \times (270/365)} = 979.38$

6. **A**   The semiannual coupon on a single, \$1,000 face-value 9% bond is \$45. A bondholder will receive one payment 0.5 years from now and one payment 1 year from now. The future value of these coupons at the end of 1.4 years (the expiration date):

$$FVC = \left(\$45 \times 1.05^{0.9}\right) + \left(\$45 \times 1.05^{0.4}\right) = \$92.91$$

The futures price is then:

$$FP = \left(\$1,135 \times 1.05^{1.4}\right) - \$92.91 = \$1,122.33$$

7. **A**   The semiannual coupon on a \$1,000 face value, 7% bond is \$35. The bond will make two more coupon payments before the futures contracts matures: one in 6 months (0.5 years), and another in 12 months (1 year). The future value of these coupons at the end of 15 months (1.25 years) is:

$$FVC = \left(\$35 \times 1.06^{0.75}\right) + \left(\$35 \times 1.06^{0.25}\right) = \$72.08$$

The bond is trading at par because the coupon rate is equal to the annual yield, so the spot price is \$1,000. The futures price (including the conversion factor of 1.025) is:

$$\begin{aligned}
FP &= \left[\left(\$1,000 \times 1.06^{1.25}\right) - \$72.08\right] \times \frac{1}{1.025} \\
&= \$1,003.47 \times \frac{1}{1.025} \\
&= \$979.00
\end{aligned}$$

ANSWERS – CHALLENGE PROBLEMS

8. **A** First calculate the continuously compounded rates:

$$R_\$^c = \ln(1.0525) = 0.0512 = 5.12\%$$
$$R_£^c = \ln(1.0625) = 0.0606 = 6.06\%$$

The no-arbitrage price of the contract is:

$$F_{75} = \$1.6500 \times e^{(0.0512 - 0.0606) \times (75/365)} = \$1.6468$$

Notice that you get the same (rounded) answer by using the discrete interest rates and the discrete formula:

$$F_{75} = \$1.6500 \times \frac{1.0525^{75/365}}{1.0625^{75/365}} = \$1.6468$$

The futures contract is overpriced because the market price of $1.6498 is larger than the no arbitrage price of $1.6468. Therefore, the appropriate arbitrage strategy is to short the futures contract and go long in the pound in the spot market.

9. **A** The price of a futures contract on an equity index is:

$$FP = S_0 \times e^{\left(R_f^c - \delta\right) \times T}$$

FP will be less than S_0 (i.e., backwardation will occur) if the dividend yield (δ) is greater than the continuously compounded risk-free rate $\left(R_f^c\right)$.

10. **C** Canada: no arbitrage F = 0.72 (1.06 / 1.08) = 0.7067. The futures rate of 0.70 is "too low" (0.70 < 0.7067), so we buy the future (borrow spot CAD at 8%). Remember: "buy low, sell high."

11. **A** Based on the evidence presented, the most likely situation in the financial markets is one in which futures prices are biased predictors of spot rates. During periods of normal backwardation, the futures price is less than the expected spot prices, suggesting the presence of a positive risk premium for futures buyers.

The following is a review of the Derivatives: Options, Swaps, and Interest Rate and Credit Derivatives principles designed to address the learning outcome statements set forth by CFA Institute®. This topic is also covered in:

OPTION MARKETS AND CONTRACTS

EXAM FOCUS

This topic review covers the pricing of options. You should know how to use the binomial model to price options on stocks, equity indices, fixed income securities, and caps and floors. You should also know how to use the Black-Scholes-Merton model to value equity options.

WARM-UP: PUT-CALL PARITY FOR EUROPEAN OPTIONS

A **fiduciary call** is a portfolio consisting of:

- A long position in a European call option with an exercise price of X that matures in T years on a stock (with a price at time t of S_t).
- A long position in a pure-discount riskless bond that pays X in T years.

The cost of a fiduciary call is the cost of the call (C_0) plus the cost of the bond (the present value of X). The payoff to a fiduciary call will be X if the call is out-of-the-money and S_T if the call is in-the-money, as shown in Figure 1.

Figure 1: Payoff to a Fiduciary Call

	$S_T \leq X$ *Call is out-of- or at-the-money*	$S_T > X$ *Call is in-the-money*
Long call payoff	0	$S_T - X$
Long bond payoff	X	X
Total payoff	X	S_T

A **protective put** is a portfolio consisting of:

- A long position in a European put option with an exercise price of X that matures in T years.
- A long position in the underlying stock.

The cost of a protective put is the cost of the put option (P_0) plus the cost of the stock (S_0). The payoff to a protective put is X if the put is in-the-money and S_T if the put is out-of-the-money.

Figure 2: Payoff to a Protective Put

	$S_T < X$ *Put is in-the-money*	$S_T \geq X$ *Put is out-of- or at-the-money*
Long put payoff	$X - S_T$	0
Long stock payoff	S_T	S_T
Total payoff	X	S_T

Notice that the payoff to a fiduciary call is the same as the payoff to a protective put. Arbitrage ensures that the two should have the same cost, which leads us to **put-call parity for European options**:

$$C_0 + \left[\frac{X}{\left(1 + R_f\right)^T}\right] = P_0 + S_0$$

LOS 60.a: Calculate and interpret the prices of a synthetic call option, synthetic put option, synthetic bond, and synthetic underlying stock, and infer why an investor would want to create such instruments.

Put-call parity is very useful because it tells us how to create a synthetic position in any one of the four instruments by combining the other three. For example, if we solve for the value of the call option, we get:

$$C_0 = P_0 + S_0 - \left[\frac{X}{\left(1 + R_f\right)^T}\right]$$

Interpret the plus signs as a long position in the security and the negative signs as short positions. That means we can create a **synthetic European call option** by:

*   Buying a European put option on the same stock with the same exercise price (*X*) and the same maturity (*T*).
*   Buying the stock.
*   Shorting (i.e., borrowing) the present value of *X* worth of a pure-discount riskless bond.

A **synthetic European put option** is formed by:

*   Buying a European call option.
*   Shorting the stock.
*   Buying (i.e., investing in) the discount bond.

A **synthetic stock position** is formed by:

*   Buying a European call option.
*   Shorting (i.e., writing) a European put option.
*   Buying (i.e., investing in) the discount bond.

A **synthetic pure-discount riskless bond** is created by:

- Buying a European put option.
- Buying the stock.
- Shorting (i.e., writing) a European call option.

Example: Using put-call parity

A 1-year call option on Cross Reef Inc. with an exercise price of $60 is trading for $8. The current stock price is $62. The risk-free rate is 4%. Calculate the price of the synthetic put option implied by put-call parity.

Answer:

According to put-call parity, the price of the synthetic put option is:

$$P_0 = C_0 - S_0 + \left[\frac{X}{\left(1+R_f\right)^T} \right]$$

$$= \$8 - \$62 + \frac{\$60}{1.04}$$

$$= \$3.69$$

There are two reasons investors might want to create synthetic positions in the securities:

1. To price options by using combinations of other instruments with known prices.

2. To earn arbitrage profits by exploiting relative mispricing among the four securities. If put-call parity doesn't hold, an arbitrage profit is available, as discussed in the next section.

USING PUT-CALL PARITY FOR ARBITRAGE

As with all arbitrage trades, you want to "buy low and sell high." If put-call parity doesn't hold (if the cost of a fiduciary call does not equal the cost of a protective put), then you buy (go long in) the underpriced position and sell (go short) in the overpriced position.

Example: Exploiting violations of put-call parity

The stock of ArbCity Inc. is trading for $75. A 3-month call option with an exercise price of $75 is selling for $4.50, and a 3-month put at $75 is selling for $3.80. The risk-free rate is 5%. Calculate the no-arbitrage price of the put option, and illustrate how the violation of put-call parity can be exploited to earn arbitrage profits.

Answer:

First, calculate what the put option should be selling for, given the other prices:

$$P_0 = C_0 - S_0 + \left[\frac{X}{\left(1 + R_f\right)^T} \right] = \$4.50 - \$75.00 + \left[\frac{\$75}{1.05^{0.25}} \right]$$

$$= \$4.50 - \$75.00 + \$74.09 = \$3.59$$

Put-call parity doesn't hold because the actual market price of the put is \$3.80, not the no-arbitrage price of \$3.59:

$$C_0 + \left[\frac{X}{\left(1 + R_f\right)^T} \right] \neq P_0 + S_0$$

$$\$4.50 + \$74.09 \neq \$3.80 + \$75$$

$$\$78.59 \neq \$78.80$$

The fiduciary call (the left-hand side of the equation) is relatively underpriced, and the protective put (the right-hand side) is relatively overpriced. Therefore, the arbitrage strategy is to buy the fiduciary call (and pay \$78.59) and short sell the protective put (and receive \$78.80). The arbitrage profits from this trade are \$78.80 – \$78.59, or \$0.21 per share. The net cash flow at maturity will be zero, so we've produced cash flow of \$0.21 today with no cash outflow obligation in the future—that's what we call an arbitrage profit. The cash flows are shown in the following table.

Today		Three Months from Today			
		If Stock Price < $75		If Stock Price > $75	
Transaction	Cash Flow	Transaction	Cash Flow	Transaction	Cash Flow
Long call option	−$4.50			Exercise call and buy stock	−$75.00
Invest in zero coupon bond	−$74.09	Proceeds from bond	+$75.00	Proceeds from bond	+$75.00
Cost of fiduciary call	−$78.59				
Short put option	+$3.80	Put exercised, obligation to buy stock	−$75.00		
Short stock	+$75.00				
Proceeds from protective put	+$78.80	Settle short position by delivering stock	$0.00	Settle short position by delivering stock	$0.00
Total cash flow = arbitrage profit	$0.21	Total cash flow	$0.00	Total cash flow	$0.00

In a frictionless market, these violations will be eliminated very quickly as arbitrageurs jump in to exploit them.

LOS 60.b: Calculate and interpret prices of interest rate options and options on assets using one- and two-period binomial models.

A **binomial model** is based on the idea that, over the next period, some value will change to one of two possible values (binomial). In order to construct a binomial model, we need to know the beginning asset value, the size of the two possible changes, and the probabilities of each of these changes occurring.

One-Period Binomial Model

Assume that a share of stock is currently priced at $30. The size of the possible price changes, and the probability of these changes occurring, are as follows:

$$U = \text{size of up move} = 1.333$$

$$D = \text{size of down move} = \frac{1}{U} = \frac{1}{1.333} = 0.75$$

$$\pi_U = \text{probability of an up-move} = 0.55$$

$$\pi_D = \text{probability of a down-move} = 1 - \pi_U = 1 - 0.55 = 0.45$$

Note that the down-move factor is the reciprocal of the up-move factor, and the probability of an up-move is one minus the probability of a down-move. The one-period binomial tree for the stock is shown in Figure 3. The beginning stock value of $30 is to the left, and to the right are the two possible paths the stock can take, based on the starting point and the size of an up- and down-move. If the stock increases by a factor of 1.333 (a return of 33.3%), it ends up at $40.00; if it falls by a factor of 0.75 (a return of −25%), it ends up at $22.50.

Figure 3: One-Period Binomial Tree

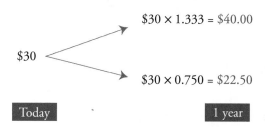

$30 × 1.333 = $40.00

$30

$30 × 0.750 = $22.50

Today

1 year

The probabilities of an up-move and a down-move are calculated based on the size of the moves and the risk-free rate as:

$$\pi_U = \text{risk-neutral probability of an up-move} = \frac{1 + R_f - D}{U - D}$$

$$\pi_D = \text{risk-neutral probability of a down-move} = 1 - \pi_U$$

where :
R_f = risk-free rate
U = size of an up-move
D = size of a down-move

Professor's Note: These two probabilities are not the actual probability of an up- or down-move. They are risk-neutral pseudo probabilities that are consistent with investor risk-neutrality. The distinction between actual probabilities and risk-neutral probabilities is not part of the Level 2 curriculum, so you don't need to worry about it for the exam.

We can calculate the value of an option on the stock by:

* Calculating the payoff of the option at maturity in both the up-move and down-move states.
* Calculating the expected value of the option in one year as the probability-weighted average of the payoffs in each state.
* Discounting the expected value back to today at the risk-free rate.

Example: Calculating call option value with a one-period binomial tree

Use the binomial tree in Figure 3 to calculate the value today of a one-period call option on the stock with an exercise price of $30. Assume the risk-free rate is 7%, the current value of the stock is $30, and the size of an up-move is 1.333.

Answer:

First we have to calculate the parameters—the size of a down-move and the probabilities:

$$D = \text{size of a down-move} = \frac{1}{U} = \frac{1}{1.333} = 0.75$$

$$\pi_U = \text{risk-neutral probability of an up-move} = \frac{1 + 0.07 - 0.75}{1.333 - 0.75} = 0.55$$

$$\pi_D = \text{risk-neutral probability of a down-move} = 1 - 0.55 = 0.45$$

Next determine the payoffs to the option in each state. If the stock moves up to $40, a call option with an exercise price of $30 will pay off $10. If the stock moves down to $22.50, the call option will be worthless. The option payoffs are illustrated in the following figure.

©2009 Kaplan, Inc.

Let the stock values for the up-move and down-move be S_1^+ and S_1^- and for the call values, C_1^+ and C_1^-.

One-Period Call Option with X = $30

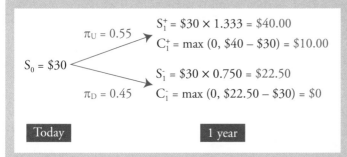

$\pi_U = 0.55$

$S_1^+ = \$30 \times 1.333 = \$40.00$
$C_1^+ = \max(0, \$40 - \$30) = \$10.00$

$S_0 = \$30$

$S_1^- = \$30 \times 0.750 = \$22.50$
$C_1^- = \max(0, \$22.50 - \$30) = \$0$

$\pi_D = 0.45$

Today   1 year

The expected value of the option in one period is:

E(call option value in 1 year) = ($10 × 0.55) + ($0 × 0.45) = $5.50

The value of the option today, discounted at the risk-free rate of 7%, is:

$$C_0 = \frac{\$5.50}{1.07} = \$5.14$$

We can use the same basic framework to **value a one-period put option**. The only difference is that the payoff to the put option will be different from the call payoffs.

Example: Valuing a one-period put option on a stock

Use the information in the previous two examples to calculate the value of a put option on the stock with an exercise price of $30.

Answer:

If the stock moves up to $40, a put option with an exercise price of $30 will be worthless. If the stock moves down to $22.50, the put option will be worth $7.50.

The risk-neutral probabilities are 0.55 and 0.45 for an up- and down-move, respectively. The expected value of the put option in one period is:

E(put option value in 1 year) = ($0 × 0.55) + ($7.50 × 0.45) = $3.375

The value of the option today, discounted at the risk-free rate of 7%, is:

$$P_0 = \frac{\$3.375}{1.07} = \$3.154$$

Study Session 17

ARBITRAGE WITH A ONE-PERIOD BINOMIAL MODEL

If the price of the one-period $30 call option from the previous example is not $5.14, there is an arbitrage opportunity. This arbitrage will involve the call option and shares of stock. If the option is overpriced, we would short the option and buy a fractional share of the stock for each option we shorted. If the option is underpriced, we would purchase the option and short a fractional share of stock for each option share.

The fractional share of stock in the arbitrage trade (commonly referred to as the hedge ratio) for each option traded is derived from the option's delta, which is calculated in the one-period model as:

$$\text{Delta} = \frac{C_1^+ - C_1^-}{S_1^+ - S_1^-}$$

The concept of delta will be explained more fully later on in this topic review. For now, the main point is that delta provides you with the information required to calculate a hedge ratio.

Example: Calculating arbitrage profit

Assume the option in the previous example is actually selling for $6.50. Illustrate how this arbitrage opportunity can be exploited to earn an arbitrage profit. Assume we trade 100 call options.

Answer:

Because the option is overpriced, we will short 100 options and purchase a certain number of shares of stock determined by the hedge ratio:

$$\text{Delta} = \frac{\$10 - \$0}{\$40 - \$22.50} = 0.5714 \text{ shares per option}$$

$$\text{total shares of stock to purchase} = 100 \times 0.5714 = 57.14$$

A portfolio that is long 57.14 shares of stock at $30 per share and short 100 calls at $6.50 per call has a net cost of:

net portfolio cost = (57.14 × $30) − (100 × $6.50) = $1,064

The values of this portfolio at maturity if the stock moves up to $40 or down to $22.50 are:

portfolio value in up-move = (57.14 × $40) − (100 × $10) = $1,286

portfolio value in down-move = (57.14 × $22.50) −(100 × $0) = $1,286

The return on the portfolio in either state is:

$$\text{portfolio return} = \frac{\$1,286}{\$1,064} - 1 = 0.209 = 20.9\%$$

This is a true arbitrage opportunity! We've created a portfolio that earns a return of 20.9% no matter what happens next period. That means it's risk free. The actual risk-free rate in the market is 7%. The profitable arbitrage trades are to:

- Borrow $1,064 at 7% for one year. In one year, we'll owe $1,064 × 1.07 = $1,138.48.
- Buy the hedged portfolio for $1,064.
- In one year, collect the $1,286, repay the loan at $1,138.48, and keep the arbitrage profits of $147.52.

Two-Period Binomial Model

Valuing an option using a **two-period binomial model** requires a little more work, but the basic steps are still the same:

- Calculate the stock values at the end of two periods (there are three possible outcomes because an up-then-down move gets you to the same place as a down-then-up move).
- Calculate option payoffs at the end of two periods.
- Calculate expected values at the end of two periods using the up- and down-move probabilities.
- Discount these back one period at the risk-free rate to find the option values at the end of the first period.
- Discount this back one period to find the option value today.
- Calculate expected value at the end of period one using the up- and down-move probabilities.

Example: Valuing a call option on a stock with a two-period model

Suppose you have a stock currently priced at $50, and a two-period European call option is available with a strike price of $45. The size of an up-move is 1.25. The risk-free rate per period is 7%. Compute the value of the call option using a two-period binomial model.

Answer:

First compute the size and probability of up- and down-moves, and then compute the theoretical value of the stock in each period:

$$D = \frac{1}{1.25} = 0.80$$

$$\pi_U = \frac{1.07 - 0.80}{1.25 - 0.80} = 0.6$$

$$\pi_D = 1 - 0.6 = 0.4$$

The two-period binomial tree for the stock is shown in the following figure.

Two-Period Binomial Tree for Stock Price

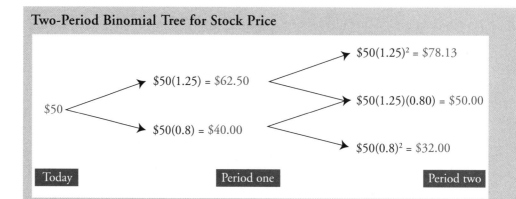

We know the value of the option at expiration in each state is equal to max (0, stock price – exercise price):

$$C_2^{++} = \max(0, \$78.13 - \$45.00) = \$33.13$$

$$C_2^{-+} = \max(0, \$50.00 - \$45.00) = \$5.00$$

$$C_2^{+-} = \max(0, \$50.00 - \$45.00) = \$5.00$$

$$C_2^{--} = \max(0, \$32.00 - \$45.00) = \$0$$

We will approach this problem by using the single-period binomial model and applying this model to each period. Using this method, we can compute the value of the call option in the up-state in period one as follows:

$$C_1^+ = \frac{\left(\pi_U \times C_2^{++}\right) + \left(\pi_D \times C_2^{+-}\right)}{1 + R_f} = \frac{E\left(\text{call option value}\right)}{1 + R_f}$$

$$= \frac{\left(0.6 \times \$33.13\right) + \left(0.4 \times \$5.00\right)}{1.07}$$

$$= \frac{\$21.88}{1.07} = \$20.45$$

The value of the call in the down-state in period one is computed as:

$$C_1^- = \frac{\left(\pi_U \times C_2^{-+}\right) + \left(\pi_D \times C_2^{--}\right)}{1 + R_f} = \frac{E\left(\text{call option value}\right)}{1 + R_f}$$

$$= \frac{\left(0.6 \times \$5.00\right) + \left(0.4 \times \$0.00\right)}{1.07}$$

$$= \frac{\$3.00}{1.07} = \$2.80$$

Now we know the value of the option in both the up-state (C_1^+) and the down-state (C_1^-) one period from now. To get the value of the option today, we simply apply our methodology one more time. Therefore, bringing (C_1^+) and (C_1^-) back one more period to the present, the *value of the call option today* is:

$$C_0 = \frac{\left(\pi_U \times C^+\right) + \left(\pi_D \times C^-\right)}{1 + R_f} = \frac{E\left(\text{call option value}\right)}{1 + R_f}$$

$$= \frac{\left(0.6 \times \$20.45\right) + \left(0.4 \times \$2.80\right)}{1.07}$$

$$= \frac{\$13.39}{1.07} = \$12.51$$

The binomial tree for the call option is shown below.

Two-Period Binomial Tree for Option Price

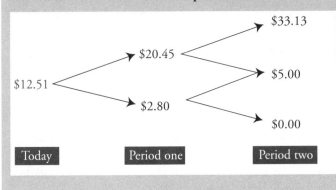

WARM-UP: BINOMIAL INTEREST RATE TREES

An interest rate model makes assumptions about interest rate volatility along with a set of paths that interest rates may follow over time. This set of possible interest rate paths is referred to as an interest rate tree. The possible interest rate paths that are used to value bonds with a binomial model is called a **binomial interest rate tree**. The diagram in Figure 4 depicts a two-period binomial interest rate tree.

Figure 4: Two-Period Binomial Interest Rate Tree

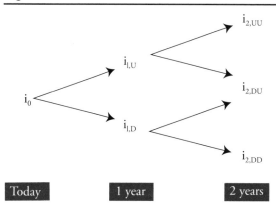

A node is a point in time when interest rates can take one of two possible paths: an upper path, U, or a lower path, D. Now consider the node on the right side of the diagram where the interest rate $i_{2,DU}$ appears. This is the rate that will occur if the initial rate, i_0, follows the lower path from Node 0 to Node 1 to become $i_{1,D}$, then follows the upper of the two possible paths to Node 2, where it takes on the value $i_{2,DU}$. At the risk of stating the obvious, the upper path from a given node leads to a higher rate than the lower path. Notice also that an upward move followed by a downward move gets us to the same place on the tree as a down-then-up move, so $i_{2,DU} = i_{2,UD}$.

The interest rates at each node in this interest rate tree are one-period forward rates corresponding to the nodal period. Beyond the root of the tree, there is more than one one-period forward rate for each nodal period (i.e., at year 1, we have two 1-year forward rates, $i_{1,U}$ and $i_{1,D}$). The relationship among the set of rates associated with each individual nodal period is a function of the interest rate volatility assumption of the model being employed to generate the tree. A change in the assumed interest rate volatility will affect the rates at every node in the tree.

The construction of an interest rate tree, binomial or otherwise, is a tedious process, one you will not have to do on the exam. In practice, the interest rate tree is usually generated using specialized computer software. There is one underlying rule governing the construction of an interest rate tree—*the values for on-the-run issues generated using an interest rate tree should prohibit arbitrage opportunities.* This means that the value of an on-the-run issue produced by the interest tree must equal the value of its market price. It should be noted that in accomplishing this, the interest rate tree must maintain the interest rate volatility assumption of the underlying model.

Options on Fixed Income Securities

To price options on bonds, we need a binomial interest rate tree that shows possible future one-period interest rates. We can then calculate the payoffs for a bond or an interest rate option using the interest rate outcomes. Once we have payments for each node, we can take the probability-weighted present value of these payments, just as we did in the stock call example.

The difference here is that the risk-free rate is not constant. Interest rate trees are straight-forward when interest rates are fixed. Since the tree gives us a series of one-period rates, we need to discount the payments by one or more of these rates, depending on how many periods the payoff is out (to the right) on the tree.

There are three basic steps to valuing an option on a fixed-income instrument using a binomial tree:

Step 1: Price the bond at each node using the projected interest rates.
Step 2: Calculate the intrinsic value of the option at each node at the maturity of the option.
Step 3: Bring the terminal option values determined in Step 2 back to today.

The risk-neutral probability of an up- and down-move in the interest rate tree is always 50%, unlike with equity options, where the probabilities depend on the risk-free rate and the size of the up- and down-moves.

Example: Calculating value of a call option on a coupon bond

You want to value a European call option with two years to expiration and a strike price of $100.00. The underlying bond is a $100 par value, 7% annual coupon bond with three years to maturity. The figure below represents the first two years of the binomial tree for valuing the underlying bond.

Fill in the missing data in the binomial tree, and calculate the value of the European call option (note that because the option is European, it can only be exercised at the end of year 2).

Two-Period Binomial Tree for Option Price

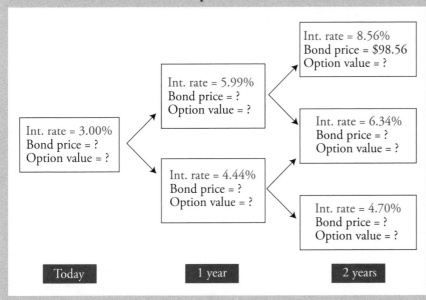

Answer:

Step 1: *Calculate the bond prices* at each node using the backward induction methodology.

At the middle node in year 2, the price is $100.62. You can calculate this using your calculator by noting that at the end of year 2, the bond has one year left to maturity:

$$N = 1; I/Y = 6.34; PMT = 7; FV = 100; CPT \rightarrow PV = 100.62$$

At the bottom node in year 2, the price is $102.20, calculated as follows:

$$N = 1; I/Y = 4.70; PMT = 7; FV = 100; CPT \rightarrow PV = 102.20$$

At the top node in year 1, the price is $100.57, calculated as follows:

$$price = \frac{[(\$98.56 + \$7) \times 0.5] + [(\$100.62 + \$7) \times 0.5]}{1.0599} = \$100.57$$

Note: Don't forget the coupon payment ($7 in this example).

At the bottom node in year 1, the price is $103.80, calculated as follows:

$$price = \frac{[(\$100.62 + \$7) \times 0.5] + [(\$102.20 + \$7) \times 0.5]}{1.0444} = \$103.80$$

Today the price is $106.00, calculated as follows:

$$price = \frac{[(\$100.57 + \$7) \times 0.5] + [(\$103.80 + \$7) \times 0.5]}{1.03} = \$106.00$$

As shown here, the price at a given node is the average of the present value of the cash flows associated with the two nodes that "feed" into the given node. The discount rate applied is the prevailing interest rate at the given node. Note that since this is a European option, you really only need the bond prices at the maturity date of the option (end of year 2) if you are given the arbitrage-free interest rate tree. However, it is good practice to compute all the bond prices.

Step 2: *Determine the intrinsic value of the option* at maturity in each node. For example, the intrinsic value of the option at the bottom node at the end of year 2 is $2.20 (= $102.20 – $100.00). At the top node in year 2, the intrinsic value of the option is zero since the bond price is less than the call price.

Step 3: Calculate the option value at each node prior to expiration. For example, at the top node for year 1, the option price is $0.29, calculated as follows:

$$price = \frac{(\$0.00 \times 0.5) + (\$0.62 \times 0.5)}{1.0599} = \$0.29$$

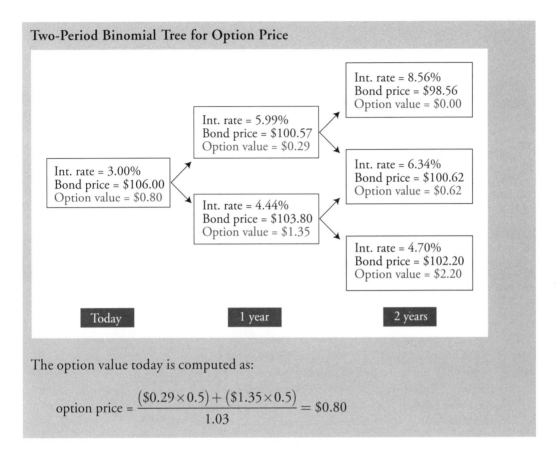

Two-Period Binomial Tree for Option Price

The option value today is computed as:

$$\text{option price} = \frac{(\$0.29 \times 0.5) + (\$1.35 \times 0.5)}{1.03} = \$0.80$$

If this were an American option, we would have to check to make sure that the option value at each node was not less than the intrinsic value of the option. For example, the lowest node at year 1 shows an option value of $1.35. However, the intrinsic value of the option at that node (if the option were exercisable) is $3.80 (= 103.80 − 100). Hence, if the option were American style, arbitrage would be possible (i.e., buy the option for $1.35, and exercise immediately for a profit of $3.80 − $1.35 = $2.45). Challenge Problem 15 at the end of this topic asks you to value this same option assuming it is an American option. If you need to value an American option, the value at any node will be equal to the greater of the present value of the future payoffs or the current intrinsic value.

Options on Interest Rates: Caps and Floors

Interest rate caps and floors are just bundles of European-style options on interest rates, called **caplets** and **floorlets**. The value of a cap or floor is the sum of the values of the individual caplets or floorlets.

An interest rate caplet is similar to a call option on interest rates. The value of a caplet is:

$$\text{expiration value of caplet} = \frac{\max\ \{0,\ [(\text{one-year rate} - \text{cap rate}) \times \text{notional principal}]\}}{1 + \text{one-year rate}}$$

Likewise, an interest rate floorlet is equivalent to a put option on interest rates:

$$\text{expiration value of floorlet} = \frac{\max\ \{0,\ [(\text{floor rate} - \text{one-year rate}) \times \text{notional principal}]\}}{1 + \text{one-year rate}}$$

In order to value a cap (floor), you simply value each caplet (floorlet) and then add them up.

 Professor's Note: Caps and floors pay in arrears: the payoff occurs one period after the expiration of the cap or floor. The basics of caps and floors are discussed in the next topic review.

Example: Valuing an interest rate cap

Suppose you purchase a 2-year cap with annual reset and a strike rate of 5.0% on a notional principal of $25 million. This represents a bundle containing a 1-year option and a 2-year option. Fill in the binomial trees, and calculate the value of the 2-year caplet, the 1-year caplet, and the 2-year cap.

2-Year Caplet

1-Year Caplet

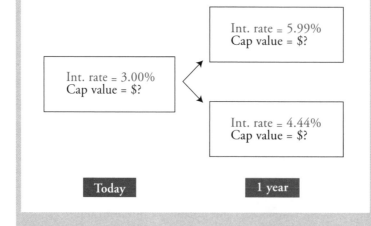

Answer:

The value of the 2-year caplet is $333,094, as shown in the figure.

Value of a 2-Year Caplet

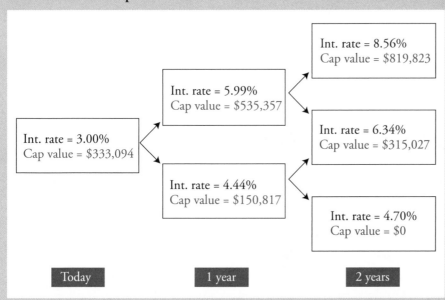

Here are the steps that can be followed to see how the values in the boxes were obtained:

Step 1: Determine the value of each caplet at expiration. Since this is a 2-year option, this means at the end of year 2. For example, the caplet value in the middle box at the end of year 2 was determined as follows:

$$\text{caplet value} = \frac{\max\left\{0,\left[\$25{,}000{,}000\times\left(0.0634\ -\ 0.0500\right)\right]\right\}}{1.0634} =$$

$$\frac{\$335{,}000}{1.0634} = \$315{,}027$$

Step 2: Calculate option prices at all prior nodes (note that since the option is European style we do not need to compare our calculated value with the intrinsic value at each node). For the top node at the end of year 1, this was calculated as:

$$\text{value} = \frac{\left(\$819{,}823\times0.5\right)+\left(\$315{,}027\times0.5\right)}{1.0599} = \$535{,}357$$

$$\text{2-year caplet} = \frac{\left(\$535{,}357\times0.5\right)+\left(\$150{,}817\times0.5\right)}{1.0300} = \$333{,}094$$

Step 3: Replicate the above procedure for the 1-year caplet.

Value of a 1-Year Caplet

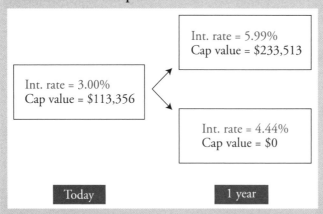

For example, the caplet value in the top box at the end of year 1 was determined as follows:

$$\text{caplet value} = \frac{\max\left\{0, \left[\$25{,}000{,}000 \times (0.0599 - 0.0500)\right]\right\}}{1.0599} = \frac{\$247{,}500}{1.0599} = \$233{,}513$$

$$\text{1-year caplet} = \frac{(\$233{,}513 \times 0.5) + (\$0 \times 0.5)}{1.0300} = \$113{,}356$$

Step 4: Add the two values together to get the value of the cap:

$$\text{value of 2-year cap} = \$113{,}356 + \$333{,}094 = \$446{,}450$$

The procedure for the valuation of a floor is identical, except that the expiration value of each floorlet is:

$$\text{expiration value of floorlet} = \frac{\max\left\{0, \left[(\text{floor rate} - \text{one-year rate}) \times \text{notional principal}\right]\right\}}{1 + \text{one-year rate}}$$

LOS 60.c: Explain the assumptions underlying the Black-Scholes-Merton model and their limitations.

The **Black-Scholes-Merton** (BSM) **model** values options in continuous time and is derived from the same no-arbitrage assumption used to value options with the binomial model. In the binomial model, the hedge portfolio is riskless over the next period, and the no-arbitrage option price is the one that guarantees that the hedge portfolio will yield the risk-free rate. To derive the BSM model, an "instantaneously" riskless portfolio (one that is riskless over the next instant) is used to solve for the option price based on the same logic.

The assumptions underlying the Black-Scholes-Merton model and the model's limitations are shown in Figure 5.

Figure 5: Black-Scholes-Merton Model Assumptions and Limitations

Assumption	Limitation
*The price of the underlying asset follows a lognormal distribution.**	Not applicable.
The (continuous) risk-free rate is constant and known.	The BSM model is not useful for pricing options on bond prices and interest rates. In those cases interest rate volatility is a key factor in determining the value of the option.
The volatility of the underlying asset is constant and known. Option values depend on the volatility of the price of the underlying asset or interest rate.	In practice the volatility is not known and must be estimated. The bigger problem is that volatility is often not constant over time and the BSM model is not useful in these situations. More sophisticated models have been developed to handle this issue, but fortunately for us they are not part of the Level 2 curriculum.
Markets are "frictionless." There are no taxes, no transactions costs, and no restrictions on short sales or the use of short-sale proceeds.	Model is less realistic and less useful. More sophisticated models developed to address this issue are outside the scope of the Level 2 curriculum.
The underlying asset has no cash flow, such as dividends or coupon payments.	The BSM model can be easily altered if we relax the assumption of no cash flows on the underlying asset.
The options valued are European options, which can only be exercised at maturity.	The model does not correctly price American options. Binomial option pricing models are more appropriate for pricing American options.

*A variable that is lognormally distributed is one where the logs of the values (in this case, the continuous returns) are normally distributed. It has a minimum of zero and conforms to prices better than the normal distribution (which would produce negative prices).

Professor's Note: It appears as though the candidate is no longer responsible for using the BSM model to actually price a call option. That means you don't have to memorize the formula. We have presented the formula anyway so that you are familiar with it and recognize it if you see it.

The formula for the BSM model is:

$$C_0 = \left[S_0 \times N(d_1)\right] - \left[X \times e^{-R_f^c \times T} \times N(d_2)\right]$$

where :

$$d_1 = \frac{\ln\left(\dfrac{S_0}{X}\right) + \left[R_f^c + \left(0.5 \times \sigma^2\right)\right] \times T}{\sigma \times \sqrt{T}}$$

$$d_2 = d_1 - \left(\sigma \times \sqrt{T}\right)$$

T = time to maturity (as % of a 365-day year)

S_0 = asset price

X = exercise price

R_f^c = continuously compounded risk-free rate

σ = volatility of continuously compounded returns on the stock

$N(\bullet)$ = cumulative normal probability of value in parentheses

We've given you the formulas for the call value. However, remember that you can always use put-call parity (with continuously compounded interest rates) to calculate the put value:

$$P_0 = C_0 - S_0 + \left(X \times e^{-R_f^c \times T}\right)$$

LOS 60.d: Explain how an option price, as represented by the Black-Scholes-Merton model, is affected by each of the input values (the option Greeks).

There are five inputs to the BSM model: asset price, exercise price, asset price volatility, time to expiration, and the risk-free rate. The relationship between each input and the option price (except exercise price) is captured by a sensitivity factor designated as one of the "Greeks."

Delta describes the relationship between asset price and option price. Call option deltas are positive because as the underlying asset price increases, call option value also increases. In contrast, the delta of a put option is negative because the put value falls as the asset price increases. See Figure 6.

Figure 6: Call and Put Delta: The Relationship Between Option Price and Underlying Asset Price

Vega measures the sensitivity of the option price to changes in the volatility of returns on the underlying asset, as shown in Figure 7. Both call and put options are more valuable, all else equal, the higher the volatility, so vega is positive for calls and puts. Volatility is a very important input to any option valuation model (and *vega is an important sensitivity measure*) because option values are very sensitive to changes in volatility.

Figure 7: Call and Put Vega: The Relationship Between Option Price and Volatility

Rho measures the sensitivity of the option price to changes in the risk-free rate, as shown in Figure 8. The price of a European call or put option does not change much if we use different inputs for the risk-free rate, so rho is not a very important sensitivity measure. Call options increase in value as the risk-free rate increases (the rho of a call option is positive). You can see this by looking at the BSM model. As the risk-free rate increases, the second term decreases, and the value of the call option increases.

$$C_0 = \left[S_0 \times N(d_1)\right] - \left[X \times e^{-R_f^c \times T} \times N(d_2)\right]$$

Put options decrease in value as the risk-free rate increases (the rho of a put option is negative).

Figure 8: Call and Put Rho: The Relationship Between Option Price and the Risk-Free Rate

Theta measures the sensitivity of the option price to the passage of time, as shown in Figure 9. As time passes and a call option approaches maturity, its value declines, all else equal. This is called "time decay." This is also true for *most* put options (deep in-the-money put options close to maturity may actually increase in value as time passes).

Notice that because it is described as a measure of "time decay," *theta is less than zero*: as time passes and the option approaches the maturity date, its value decreases.

Figure 9: Call and Put Theta: The Relationship Between Option Price and the Time to Expiration

Professor's Note: The statement that theta is less than zero is counterintuitive to many Level 2 candidates because there are two ways to state the relationship between time and option value:

- *The relationship between option value and **time to maturity** is positive: all else equal, shorter maturity options have lower values.*
- *The relationship between option value and the **passage of time** is negative: all else equal, as time passes and the option approaches maturity, the value of the option decays.*

The key to understanding why theta is less than zero is to recognize that it is capturing the intuition of the second statement.

Figure 10: Direction of BSM European Option Prices for a Change in the Five Model Inputs

Sensitivity Factor ("Greek")	Input	Calls	Puts
Delta	Asset price (S)	Positively related Delta > 0	Negatively related Delta < 0
Vega	Volatility (σ)	Positively related Vega > 0	Positively related Vega > 0
Rho	Risk-free rate (r)	Positively related Rho > 0	Negatively related Rho < 0
Theta	Time to expiration (T)	Value → \$0 as call → maturity Theta < 0	Value usually →\$0 as put → maturity Theta <0*
	Exercise price (X)	Negatively related	Positively related

* There is an exception to the general rule that European put option thetas are negative. The put value may increase as the option approaches maturity if the option is deep in-the-money and close to maturity.

Professor's Note: Remember that these relationships are for European options on assets with no cash flows (e.g., dividends).

LOS 60.e: Explain the delta of an option and demonstrate how it is used in dynamic hedging.

Delta is the change in the price of an option for a one-unit change in the price of the underlying security:

$$delta_{call} = \frac{C_1 - C_0}{S_1 - S_0} = \frac{\Delta C}{\Delta S}$$

where:
ΔC = *change in* the price of the call over a short time interval
ΔS = *change in* the price of the underlying stock over a short time interval

> **Example: Calculating delta**
>
> During the last ten minutes of trading, call options on Commart Inc. common stock have risen from $1.20 to $1.60. Shares of the underlying stock have risen from $51.30 to $52.05 during the same time interval. Calculate the delta of the call option.
>
> **Answer:**
>
> The call option delta can be estimated as:
>
> $$delta_{call} = \frac{\$1.60 - \$1.20}{\$52.05 - \$51.30} = \frac{\$0.40}{\$0.75} = 0.533$$

Usually, however, we want to estimate the change in the value of the call given the change in the value of the stock and the option's delta. The BSM model helps us out here because a call option's delta for small changes in S is $N(d_1)$ from the BSM model, while a put option's delta is $N(d_1) - 1$. However, because we're now using a linear relationship to estimate a non-linear change, the following relationships are only approximations:

$$\Delta C \approx N(d_1) \times \Delta S$$

$$\Delta P \approx [N(d_1) - 1] \times \Delta S$$

where:
ΔP = change in put price

The approximations are close for small changes in stock price, but the approximation gets worse as the ΔS gets larger. Notice that $N(d_1)$ is less than 1, so $N(d_1) - 1$, the put option delta, must be less than zero.

Example: Calculating change in option price

$N(d_1)$ from the BSM model is 0.58. Calculate the approximate change in the price of a call option on the stock if the stock price increased by $0.75.

Answer:

$$\Delta C \approx 0.58 \times \$0.75 = \$0.435$$

Interpreting Delta

The payoff diagrams for a European call option before and at expiration are shown in Figure 11. The "at expiration" diagram represents the call option's intrinsic value:

- Zero when the call option is out-of-the-money.
- Stock price minus exercise price when the option is in-the-money.

Prior to expiration the option also has time value, so the prior-to-expiration curve lies above the at-expiration diagram by the amount of the time value.

Figure 11: European Call Option Payoff Diagrams

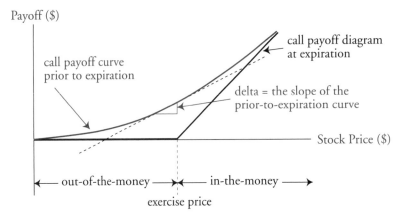

The slope of the "prior-to-expiration" curve is the change in call price per unit change in stock price. Sound familiar? It should—that's also the definition of delta. That means *delta is the slope of the prior-to-expiration curve*. The delta of the put option is also the slope of the *prior-to-expiration* put curve.

Let's review some basic facts about call and put options:

- The value of a call option increases as the underlying stock price increases. This means the delta of a call option is greater than zero.
- The value of a put option decreases as the underlying stock price increases. This means the delta of a put option is less than zero.

We know that an option's delta is equal to the *slope* of the prior-to-expiration curve (see Figure 11). You can see that the slope of the call option curve is positive. This is consistent with our observations. You can also see why delta approximates the change in call price only for small changes in stock price. As the change in stock price increases, the dotted line gets further away from the "call payoff curve prior to expiration."

Take a closer look at Figure 11. When the call option is deep out-of-the-money, the slope of the at-expiration curve is close to zero, which means the call delta will be close to zero. For deep out-of-the-money call options (when the stock price is low), the option price does not change much for a given change in the underlying stock. When the call option is in-the-money (when the stock price is high), the slope of the at-expiration curve is close to 45 degrees, which means the call delta is close to one. In this case, the call option price will change almost one-for-one given a change in the underlying stock price.

The bottom line is that *a call option's delta will increase from 0 to +1 as stock price increases*.

For a put option, the put delta is close to zero when the put is out-of-the-money (when the stock price is high). When the put option is in-the-money (the stock price is close to zero), the put delta is close to –1.

The bottom line is that *a put option's delta will increase from –1 to 0 as stock price increases*.

Example: Interpreting call and put deltas

The current stock price of Com.Net is $60. Call and put options with exercise prices of $100 are currently trading. Compare and contrast the change in the price of each option for a $1 increase in the stock price.

Answer:

The call option is deep out-of-the-money and must have a delta close to zero. The put option is deep in-the-money and will have a delta close to –1. Therefore, the value of the out-of-the-money call will *increase* by a very small amount, and the value of the in-the-money put will *decrease* by close to $1. The put price will fall by more than the call price will increase.

We can also discuss what happens to delta as the option approaches maturity, even if the underlying stock price doesn't change. The effects for call and put options are different and depend on whether the options are in or out-of-the-money.

Remember that a call option delta is between 0 and 1. If the call option is:

- **Out-of-the-money** (stock price is less than exercise price), the call delta **moves closer to 0** as time passes, assuming the underlying stock price doesn't change.
- **In-the-money** (stock price is greater than exercise price), the call delta **moves closer to 1** as time passes, assuming the underlying stock price doesn't change.

Remember that a put option delta is between −1 and 0. If the put option is:

- **Out-of-the-money** (stock price is greater than exercise price), the put delta **moves closer to 0** as time passes, assuming the underlying stock price doesn't change.
- **In-the-money** (stock price is less than exercise price), the put delta **moves closer to −1** as time passes, assuming the underlying stock price doesn't change.

Dynamic Hedging

The goal of a **delta-neutral portfolio (or delta-neutral hedge)** is to combine a long position in a stock with a short position in a call option so that the value of the portfolio does not change when the value of the stock changes. A delta-neutral portfolio is a risk-free combination of a long stock position and short calls where the number of calls to sell is equal to:

$$\textit{number of options} \text{ needed to delta hedge} = \frac{\textit{number of shares} \text{ hedged}}{\textit{delta} \text{ of call option}}$$

Delta neutral portfolios are best illustrated with an example.

Example: Hedging with call options, part 1

You own 60,000 shares of Arthurall Company common stock that is currently selling for $50. A call option on Arthurall with a strike price of $50 is selling at $4 and has a delta of 0.60. Determine the number of call options necessary to create a delta-neutral hedge.

Answer:

In order to determine the number of call options necessary to hedge against instantaneous movements in Arthurall's stock price, we calculate:

$$\text{number of options needed to delta hedge} = \frac{60,000}{0.60}$$

$$= 100,000 \text{ options, or } 1,000 \text{ option contracts}$$

Because we are long the stock, we need to short the options.

Example: Hedging with call options, part 2

Calculate the effect on portfolio value of a $1.00 increase in the price of Arthurall stock.

Answer:

Assuming the price of Arthurall stock increased instantly by $1.00, the value of the call options would decrease by $0.60 because you're *short* (or have sold) the call option contracts. Recall that when you're short an asset, as the underlying price rises, you lose, and when the price falls, you win. Therefore, the net impact of the price change would be zero:

total value of increase in stock position 60,000 × $1 = $60,000

total value of decrease in option position = 100,000 × –$0.60 = –$60,000

total change in portfolio value = $60,000 – $60,000 = $0

A key consideration in delta-neutral hedging is that the delta-neutral position only holds for very small changes in the value of the underlying stock. Hence, the delta-neutral portfolio must be continually rebalanced to maintain the hedge. This is called a dynamic hedge. As the underlying stock price changes, so does the delta of the call option. As the delta changes, the number of calls that need to be sold to maintain a risk-free position changes. Hence, continuously maintaining a delta-neutral position can be very costly in terms of transaction costs.

LOS 60.f: Explain the gamma effect on an option's price and delta and how gamma can affect a delta hedge.

Gamma measures the *rate of change in delta* as the underlying stock price changes. Call and put options on the same underlying asset with the same exercise price and time to maturity will have equal gammas. Long positions in calls and puts have positive gammas.

For example, a gamma of 0.04 implies that a $1.00 increase in the price of the underlying stock will cause a call option's delta to increase by 0.04, making the call option more sensitive to changes in the stock price.

Gamma is largest when a call or put option is at-the-money and close to expiration, as shown in Figure 12. In other words, delta is very sensitive to changes in the underlying stock price when call and put options are at-the-money and close to expiration. If the option is either deep in- or deep out-of-the-money, gamma approaches zero because changes in the underlying stock price do not have a significant effect on delta.

Figure 12: Call and Put Gamma

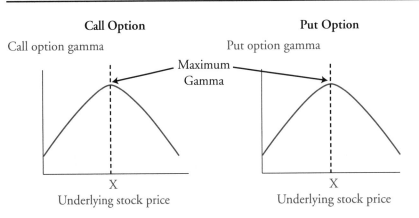

In this context, gamma can be viewed as a measure of how poorly a dynamic hedge will perform when it is not rebalanced in response to a change in the asset price. Hedges with at-the-money options will have higher gammas, and consequently small changes in stock price will lead to large changes in delta and frequent rebalancing. In contrast, hedges with deep in- or deep out-of-the money options will have small gammas, and stock price changes will not affect the delta of the hedge significantly. This lowers rebalancing and transaction costs.

LOS 60.g: Discuss the effect of the underlying asset's cash flows on the price of an option.

All else equal, the existence of cash flows on the underlying asset will:

- Decrease the value of a call option.
- Increase the value of a put option.

For example, consider an option on a stock that generates cash flows (i.e., dividends). The Gordon growth model (expected return equals dividend yield plus growth rate) suggests that a higher dividend yield for the stock will reduce the growth rate in the stock price (all else equal). Because option values are based on the change in the stock price, and a lower stock price decreases the value of a call and increases the value of a put, dividends will make call options less valuable and put options more valuable, all else equal.

We can see this by looking at the BSM Model. Just as we subtracted the present value of cash flows expected to occur during the option's life from the asset price when valuing forwards and futures, we can subtract it from the asset price in the BSM model. Since the BSM model is in continuous time, in practice $S_0 \times e^{-\delta T}$ is substituted for S_0 in the BSM formula, where δ is equal to the continuously compounded rate of dividend payment. Over time, the asset price is discounted by a greater amount to account for the greater amount of cash flows.

We can also revise put-call parity for options on underlying assets with cash flows by adjusting S for the present value of the cash flows (PVCF):

$$C_0 + \frac{X}{\left(1 + R_F\right)^T} = P_0 + \left(S_0 - PVCF\right)$$

LOS 60.h: Demonstrate the methods for estimating the future volatility of the underlying asset (i.e., the historical volatility and the implied volatility methods).

The steps in computing **historical volatility** for use as an input in the BSM continuous-time options pricing model are:

Step 1: Convert a time series of N prices to returns:

$$R_i = \frac{P_i - P_{i-1}}{P_{i-1}}, i = 1 \text{ to } N$$

Step 2: Convert the returns to continuously compounded returns:

$$R_i^c = \ln(1 + R_i), i = 1 \text{ to } N$$

Step 3: Calculate the variance and standard deviation of the continuously compounded returns:

$$\sigma^2 = \frac{\sum_{i=1}^{N}\left(R_i^c - \overline{R}_i^c\right)^2}{N-1}$$

$$\sigma = \sqrt{\sigma^2}$$

Implied volatility is the value for standard deviation of continuously compounded rates of return that is "implied" by the market price of the option. Of the five inputs into the BSM model, four are observable: stock price, exercise price, risk-free rate, and time to maturity. If we use these four inputs in the formula and set the BSM formula equal to market price, we can solve for the volatility that satisfies the equality.

Volatility enters into the equation in a complex way, and there is no closed-form solution for the volatility that will satisfy the equation. Rather, it must be found by iteration (trial and error). If a value for volatility makes the value of a call calculated from the BSM model lower than the market price, it needs to be increased (and vice versa) until the model value equals market price (remember, option value and volatility are positively related).

LOS 60.i: Illustrate how put-call parity for options on forwards (or futures) is established.

 Professor's Note: The LOS says to "illustrate," which means to derive put-call parity, but don't let this intimidate you. We're going to use a no-arbitrage argument by forming two portfolios that have the same payoffs and arguing that they must have the same cost to prevent arbitrage.

We will use the method of equivalent portfolios to get an equality that establishes **put-call parity for options on forwards (or futures)**.

The first portfolio (Portfolio 1) consists of:

- A call option on the forward contract with an exercise price of X that matures at time T on a forward contract at F_T (the price of a forward on the asset at time T).
- A pure-discount bond that pays $(X - F_T)$ at time T.

The cost of this portfolio is:

$$C_0 + \frac{X - F_T}{\left(1 + R_f\right)^T}$$

The payoff for this portfolio at expiration will depend on whether the option is in- or out-of-the-money; the bond will always pay $(X - F_T)$:

- If the call option is out-of-the-money $(S_T \leq X)$, the payoff will just be from the bond $(X - F_T)$:

  Portfolio1 payoff if call is out-of-the-money $= X - F_T$

- If the call option is in-the-money $(S_T > X)$, the option will be worth $(S_T - X)$, and the bond will be worth $(X - F_T)$:

  Portfolio 1 payoff if call is in-the-money $= (S_T - X) + (X - F_T) = S_T - F_T$

An equivalent portfolio (Portfolio 2) can be constructed by combining:

- A put option on the forward contract with an exercise price of X.
- A long position in the forward contract.

The cost of this portfolio is P_0, the cost of the option, because it's costless to enter into a forward contract.

The payoff for this portfolio at the expiration will depend on whether the option is in- or out-of-the-money; the long position in the forward contract will always pay $(S_T - F_T)$:

- If the put option is in-the-money $(S_T < X)$, the option will be worth $(X - S_T)$, and the forward contract will be worth $(S_T - F_T)$:

  Portfolio 2 payoff if put is in-the-money $= (X - S_T) + (S_T - F_T) = X - F_T$

- If the put option is out-of-the-money $(S_T \geq X)$, the payoff will just be from the forward contract:

  Portfolio 2 payoff if put is out-of-the-money $= S_T - F_T$

Since the call is in-the-money when the put is out-of-the-money, and vice versa, the payoffs to the two positions are identical. A portfolio that is long one and short the other must have a zero up-front cost, which means the cost of Portfolio 1 must equal the cost of Portfolio 2:

$$C_0 + \frac{X - F_T}{(1 + R_f)^T} = P_0$$

or

$$C_0 + \frac{X - F_T}{(1 + R_f)^T} - P_0 = 0$$

or

$$F_T = (C_0 - P_0)(1 + R_f)^T + X$$

For an asset with no cash flows or storage costs, the forward contract price is:

$$F_T = S_0 (1 + R_f)^T$$

Substituting in the parity relation, we get the familiar put-call parity for all options:

$$C_0 + \frac{X}{(1 + R_f)^T} = P_0 + S_0$$

Professor's Note: Since the forward price in relation to the spot price is $F_T = S_0 (1+R)^T$, it is also true that $S_0 = F_T / (1+R_f)^T$. Replacing S_0 with $F_T / (1+R_f)^T$ in option put-call parity produces a parity relation for options on forwards that includes the price of the forward at time 0. If you need only the forward parity relation, this would be a quicker way to get it than the equivalent portfolio derivation.

LOS 60.j: Compare and contrast American options on forwards and futures with European options on forwards and futures, and identify the appropriate pricing model for European options.

There is a benefit to early exercise of *options on futures* when they are deep in-the-money. Exercising the option (either a put or call) early will generate cash from the mark to market. This cash can earn interest, while the futures position will gain or lose from movements in the futures price. These price movements between early exercise and option expiration will mirror those of the deep in-the-money option. For this reason, *American options on futures are more valuable than comparable European options.*

Since there is no mark to market on forwards, early exercise does not accelerate the payment of any gains. With no reason for early exercise, *the value of American and European options on forwards are the same.*

THE BLACK MODEL

The Black model can be used to price European options on forwards and futures:

$$C_0 = e^{-R_f^c \times T}\left[F_T \times N(d_1) - X \times N(d_2)\right]$$

$$d_1 = \frac{\ln\left(F_T / X\right) + \left(\dfrac{\sigma^2}{2}\right)T}{\sigma\sqrt{T}}$$

$$d_2 = d_1 - \sigma\sqrt{T}$$

where :

σ = standard deviation of returns on the futures contract

F_T = futures price

The Black model is just the BSM model with $e^{-R_f^c \times T}F_T$ substituted for S_0. In fact, the price of a European option on a forward or futures contract is equal to an option on the underlying asset if the options and the forward/futures contract expire at the same time.

KEY CONCEPTS

LOS 60.a

Put-call parity for European options says that the cost of a fiduciary call must be equal to the cost of a protective put:

$$C_0 + \frac{X}{\left(1 + R_f\right)^T} = P_0 + S_0$$

Put-call parity can be used to demonstrate how to create synthetic instruments. For example, a synthetic call is a long put, a long stock position, and a short position in a pure-discount risk-free bond. Investors create these synthetic securities to exploit relative mispricing among the four securities.

LOS 60.b

To value an option using a two-period binomial model:

- Calculate the stock values at the end of two periods (there are three possible outcomes because an up-down move gets you to the same place as a down-up move).
- Calculate option payoffs at the end of two periods.
- Calculate expected values at the end of two periods using the up- and down-move probabilities. Discount these back one period at the risk-free rate to find the option values at the end of the first period.
- Calculate expected value at the end of period one using the up- and down-move probabilities. Discount this back one period to find the option value today.

To price an option on a bond using a binomial tree, (1) price the bond at each node using projected interest rates, (2) calculate the intrinsic value of the option at each node at maturity of the option, and (3) calculate the value of the option today.

The value of an interest rate cap or floor is the sum of the values of the individual caplets or floorlets.

$$\text{expiration value of caplet} = \frac{\max\left\{0, \left[\left(\text{one-year rate} - \text{cap rate}\right) \times \text{notional principal}\right]\right\}}{1 + \text{one-year rate}}$$

$$\text{expiration value of floorlet} = \frac{\max\left\{0, \left[\left(\text{floor rate} - \text{one-year rate}\right) \times \text{notional principal}\right]\right\}}{1 + \text{one-year rate}}$$

As the period covered by a binomial model is divided into arbitrarily small, discrete time periods, the model results converge to those of the continuous-time model.

LOS 60.c

The assumptions underlying the BSM model are:
- The price of the underlying asset follows a lognormal distribution.
- The (continuous) risk-free rate is constant and known.
- The volatility of the underlying asset is constant and known.
- Markets are "frictionless."
- The underlying asset generates no cash flows.
- The options are European.

Because of the limitations of its assumptions, the BSM model is not appropriate:
- For valuing interest rate options because the assumption of a constant and known risk-free rate is violated.
- When the assumption of a constant and known volatility of underlying asset returns is violated.
- In cases where taxes and transactions costs are significant.
- For pricing American options.

LOS 60.d

Direction of BSM option price for an increase in the five model inputs:

Sensitivity Factor ("Greek")	Input	Calls	Puts
Delta	Asset price (S)	Positively related Delta > 0	Negatively related Delta < 0
Vega	Volatility (σ)	Positively related Vega > 0	Positively related Vega > 0
Rho	Risk-free rate (r)	Positively related Rho > 0	Negatively related Rho < 0
Theta	Time to expiration (T)	Value $\rightarrow$ $0 as call $\rightarrow$ maturity Theta < 0	Value usually $\rightarrow$$0 as put $\rightarrow$ maturity Theta <0
	Exercise price (X)	Negatively related	Positively related

LOS 60.e

Delta is the change in the price of an option for a one-unit change in the price of the underlying security. $N(d_1)$ from the BSM model is the delta of a call option for small changes in stock price. $N(d_1) - 1$ is the put option delta. The following approximations are reasonably accurate for small changes in stock price:

$$\Delta C \approx N(d_1) \times \Delta S$$

$$\Delta P \approx [N(d_1) - 1] \times \Delta S$$

Call option deltas will increase from zero to +1 as the underlying asset price increases. Put option deltas will increase from −1 to zero as the stock price increases.

A key consideration in delta-neutral hedging is that the delta-neutral position only holds for very small changes in the value of the underlying stock. Hence, the delta-neutral portfolio must be continually rebalanced to maintain the hedge. This is called a dynamic hedge. As the underlying stock price changes, so does the delta of the call option.

LOS 60.f
Gamma measures how much delta changes as the asset price changes and, thus, offers a measure of how poorly a fixed hedge will perform as the price of the underlying asset changes.

LOS 60.g
Cash flows on the underlying asset decrease call prices and increase put prices.

LOS 60.h
Historical volatility is the standard deviation of a past series of continuously compounded returns for the underlying asset. Implied volatility is the volatility that, when used in the Black-Scholes formula, produces the current market price of the option.

LOS 60.i
Put-call parity for options on forwards and futures is as follows:

$$C_0 + \frac{X - F_T}{\left(1 + R_f\right)^T} = P_0$$

American options on futures are more valuable than European options because early exercise provides mark to market funds on the futures, which can earn interest. Americans and European options on forward contracts are equivalent because there is no mark to market.

LOS 60.j
The Black model can be used to price European options on forwards and futures.

CONCEPT CHECKERS

1. Compare the call and put prices on a stock that doesn't pay a dividend (NODIV) with comparable call and put prices on another stock (DIV) that is the same in all respects except it pays a dividend. Which of the following statements is *most accurate*? Price of:
   A. DIV call will be less than price of NODIV call.
   B. NODIV call will equal price of NODIV put.
   C. NODIV put will be greater than price of DIV put.

2. In a one-period binomial model the hedge ratio is 0.35. To construct a riskless arbitrage involving 1,000 call options if the option is "overpriced," what is the appropriate portfolio?

	Calls	Stock
A.	Buy 1,000 options	Short 350 shares
B.	Buy 1,000 options	Short 2,857 shares
C.	Sell 1,000 options	Buy 350 shares

3. Which of the following statements is *least accurate*? The value of a:
   A. call option will decrease as the risk-free rate increases.
   B. put option will decrease as the exercise price decreases.
   C. call option will decrease as the underlying stock price decreases.

4. Which of the following inputs into the Black-Scholes-Merton model is *least likely* to have opposite effects on put and call prices?
   A. Volatility.
   B. Strike price.
   C. Risk-free rate.

5. Which of the following statements is *most accurate*? Implied volatility:
   A. requires market prices.
   B. requires a series of past returns.
   C. is equal for otherwise identical options with different maturities.

6. The delta of a put is –0.43. If the price of the underlying stock increases from $40 to $44, the price of the put option:
   A. increases by approximately 4.3%.
   B. decreases by approximately 4.3%.
   C. decreases by approximately $1.72.

7. A synthetic European put option is created by:
   A. buying the discount bond, buying the call option, and short-selling the stock.
   B. buying the call option, short-selling the discount bond, and short-selling the stock.
   C. short-selling the stock, buying the discount bond, and selling the call option.

CHALLENGE PROBLEMS

8. Which of the following is not an assumption underlying the Black-Scholes-Merton options pricing model?
   A. The underlying asset does not generate cash flows.
   B. Continuously compounded returns are lognormally distributed.
   C. The option can only be exercised at maturity.

Use the following information to answer Questions 9 and 10.

Stock ABC trades for $60 and has 1-year call and put options written on it with an exercise price of $60. The annual standard deviation estimate is 10%, and the continuously compounded risk-free rate is 5%. The value of the call is $4.09.

Chefron Inc. common stock trades for $60 and has a 1-year call option written on it with an exercise price of $60. The annual standard deviation estimate is 10%, the continuous dividend yield is 1.4%, and the continuously compounded risk-free rate is 5%.

9. The value of the put on ABC stock is *closest* to:
   A. $1.16.
   B. $3.28.
   C. $4.09.

10. The value of the call on Chefron stock is *closest* to:
    A. $3.51.
    B. $4.16.
    C. $5.61.

11. The stock price is currently $80. The stock price will move up by 15% or down by a certain amount each period. The value of a two-period call option with an exercise price of $62 if the risk-free rate is 4% per period is *closest* to:
    A. $19.17.
    B. $22.99.
    C. $27.11.

12. The current stock price of Heart, Inc., is $80. Call and put options with exercise prices of $50 and 15 days to maturity are currently trading. Which of these scenarios is *most likely* to occur if the stock price falls by $1?

	Call value	Put value
A.	Decrease by $0.94	Increase by $0.08
B.	Decrease by $0.76	Increase by $0.96
C.	Decrease by $0.07	Increase by $0.89

13. A put option with an exercise price of $45 is trading for $3.50. The current stock price is $45. What is the *most likely* effect on the option's delta and gamma if the stock price increases to $50?
    A. Both delta and gamma will increase.
    B. Both delta and gamma will decrease.
    C. One will increase and the other will decrease.

14. From the Black-Scholes-Merton model, $N(d_1) = 0.42$ for a 3-month call option on Panorama Electronics common stock. If the stock price falls by $1.00, the price of the call option will:
    A. decrease by less than the increase in the price of the put option.
    B. increase by more than the decrease in the price of the put option.
    C. decrease by the same amount as the increase in the price of the put option.

15. An analyst has calculated the value of a 2-year European call option to be $0.80. The strike price of the option is 100.00, and the underlying asset is a 7% annual coupon bond with three years to maturity. The two-period binomial tree for the European option is shown in the figure.

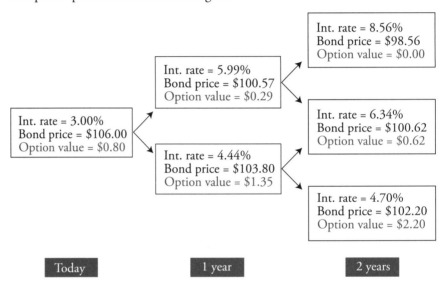

The value of the comparable 2-year American call option with a strike price of 100.00 is *closest* to:
    A. $1.56.
    B. $2.12.
    C. $3.80.

16. A CFA candidate is trying to recall the derivation of the put-call parity formula for forwards. When correctly derived, the formula is best expressed as:
    A. $F_t = (C_o - P_o)(1 + R_f)^T + X$
    B. $F_t = S_o(1 + R_f)^T - P_o - C_o$
    C. $F_t = S_o(1 + R_f)^T - P_o + C_o$

ANSWERS – CONCEPT CHECKERS

1. **A**   The dividend affects option values because if you own the option, you do not have access to the dividend. Hence, if the firm pays a dividend during the life of the option, this must be considered in the valuation formula. Dividends decrease the value of call options all else equal, and they increase the value of put options.

2. **C**   The hedge ratio in a one-period model is equivalent to a delta, the ratio of the call price change to the stock price change. We will sell the 1,000 calls since they are overpriced. Buying 350 shares of stock will produce a riskless hedge. The payoff at expiration will return more than the riskless rate on the net cost of the hedge portfolio. Borrowing to finance the hedge portfolio and earning a higher rate than the borrowing rate produces arbitrage profits.

3. **A**   The value of a call and the risk-free rate are positively related, so as the risk-free rate increases, the value of the call will increase.

4. **A**   Volatility increases will increase the values of both puts and calls.

5. **A**   Implied volatility is the volatility that produces market option prices from the BSM model. Its use for pricing options is limited because it is based on market prices. Past returns are used to calculate historical volatility.

6. **C**   The put option will decrease in value as the underlying stock price increases: $-0.43 \times \$4 = -\$1.72$.

7. **A**   A synthetic European put option is formed by:
    *   Buying a European call option.
    *   Short-selling the stock.
    *   Buying (i.e., investing) the present value of the exercise price worth of a pure-discount riskless bond.

ANSWERS – CHALLENGE PROBLEMS

8. **B**   In order to derive the BSM model, we need to assume no arbitrage is possible, and:
    *   Asset price (not returns) follows a lognormal distribution.
    *   The (continuous) risk-free rate is constant.
    *   The volatility of the underlying asset is constant.
    *   Markets are "frictionless."
    *   The asset has no cash flows.
    *   The options are European (i.e., they can only be exercised at maturity).

9. **A**   According to put/call parity, the put's value is:

$$P_0 = C_0 - S_0 + \left(X \times e^{-R_c^f \times T} \right) = \$4.09 - \$60.00 + \left[\$60.00 \times e^{-(0.05 \times 1.0)} \right] = \$1.16$$

10. **A**   ABC and Chefron stock are identical in all respects except Chefron pays a dividend. Therefore the call option on Chefron stock must be worth less than the call on ABC (i.e., less than $4.09). $3.51 is the only possible answer.

11. **B**   **Stock Tree**

Option Tree

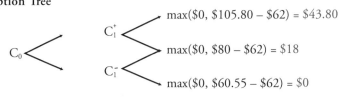

$U = 1.15$

$D = \dfrac{1}{1.15} = 0.87$

$\pi_U = \dfrac{1.04 - 0.87}{1.15 - 0.87} = 0.61$

$\pi_D = 1 - 0.61 = 0.39$

$C_2^{++} = \$43.80$

$C_2^{++} = C_2^{-+} = \$18.00$

$C_2^{--} = \$0$

$C_1^{+} = \dfrac{\left(0.61 \times \$43.80\right) + \left(0.39 \times \$18.00\right)}{1.04} = \$32.44$

$C_1^{-} = \dfrac{\left(0.61 \times \$18.00\right) + \left(0.39 \times \$0\right)}{1.04} = \$10.56$

$C_0 = \dfrac{\left(0.61 \times \$32.44\right) + \left(0.39 \times \$10.56\right)}{1.04} = \$22.99$

12. **A**   The call option is deep in-the-money and must have a delta close to one. The put option is deep out-of-the-money and will have a delta close to zero. Therefore, the value of the in-the-money call will decrease by close to $1 (e.g., $0.94), and the value of the out-of-the-money put will increase by a much smaller amount (e.g., $0.08). The call price will fall by more than the put price will increase.

13. **C**   The put option is currently at-the-money since its exercise price is equal to the stock price of $45. As stock price increases, the put option's delta (which is less than zero) will increase toward zero, becoming less negative. The put option's gamma, which measures the rate of change in delta as the stock price changes, is at a maximum when the option is at-the-money. Therefore, as the option moves out-of-the-money, its gamma will fall.

14. **A**   If $\Delta S = -\$1.00$, $\Delta C \approx 0.42 \times (-1.00) = -\$0.42$, and $\Delta P \approx (0.42 - 1) \times (-1.00) = \$0.58$.

   The call will decrease by less ($0.42) than the increase in the price of the put ($0.58).

15. **B**   In the upper node at the end of the first year the European option is worth $0.29, but the American option can be exercised and a profit of $0.57 realized (the difference between the bond price of $100.57 and the exercise price of $100).

   In the lower node at the end of the first year the European option is worth $1.35, but the American option can be exercised and a profit of $3.80 realized (the difference between the bond price of $103.80 and the exercise price of $100).

   The value of the American option today is therefore:

   $$\text{American option price} = \frac{(\$0.57 \times 0.5) + (\$3.80 \times 0.5)}{1.03} = \$2.12$$

16. **A**   The put/call parity formula for a forward is $F_t = (C_o - P_o)(1 + R_f)^T + X$. Note that you do not need to know the derivation—just the relationship to put-call parity.

The following is a review of the Derivatives: Options, Swaps, and Interest Rate and Credit Derivatives principles designed to address the learning outcome statements set forth by CFA Institute®. This topic is also covered in:

SWAP MARKETS AND CONTRACTS

EXAM FOCUS

The main focus of this topic review is describing swaps in terms of equivalent securities. You should understand how to construct and value these equivalent portfolios and the comparable swaps prior to and at expiration. In addition, pay close attention to swaptions.

LOS 61.a: Distinguish between the pricing and valuation of swaps.

The distinction between the price and the value of a swap is the same one we made for forward contracts. Remember that the price of a forward contract is the forward rate that yields a zero value for the contract at initiation. After contract initiation, as rates or prices change, the contract will likely have value to either the long or the short.

Consider a plain vanilla interest rate swap. One party agrees to pay floating (borrow at the floating rate) and receive fixed (lend at a fixed rate). At initiation of the swap, the fixed rate is selected so that the present value of the floating-rate payments is equal to the present value of the fixed-rate payments, which means the swap value is zero to both parties. This fixed rate is called the **swap rate**. Determining the swap rate is equivalent to "pricing" the swap.

As short-term rates (and expected future short-term rates) change over the term of the swap, the value of the swap to one of the parties will be positive. The swap position is an asset to that party.

If interest rates increase, the fixed-rate payer in the swap will receive higher than expected floating-rate payments. The swap will have a positive value for the fixed-rate payer. The swap contract value to the other party (receive fixed, pay floating) will be negative, a liability to the pay-floating party.

LOS 61.b: Explain the equivalence of the following swaps to combinations of other instruments: interest rate swaps to a series of off-market forward rate agreements (FRAs) and a plain vanilla swap to a combination of an interest rate call and interest rate put.

Equivalence to FRAs

It is common to view swaps as equivalent to a series of forward contracts. While this is approximately true, there are some differences. One difference is that unless the yield curve is flat, there will be a variety of fixed rates on the FRAs expiring on the swap's payment dates. If we view the swap fixed rate as a (complex) average of the fixed rates on an equivalent series of FRAs, some of the FRA rates will be above, and others below, the swap fixed rate.

Viewing the component parts of the swap in this way, we can conclude that they are (individually) off-market forwards. An *off-market forward* is one in which the forward price is different from that which gives the forward a zero value at initiation. That means an interest rate swap is a series of off-market forward rate agreements. Some of them have a positive value to the long, while others have a negative value. When the values of all the off-market FRAs are summed together as a swap, the swap has a value of zero (at initiation).

Now, let's try to show this relationship between the FRAs and swaps visually. The left side of Figure 1 represents the swap, and the diagram on the right portrays the portfolio of FRAs.

Figure 1: Equivalence of a Swap and Portfolio of FRAs

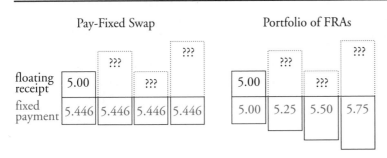

Note in the chart that the only floating-rate payment that is known today is the 5% current LIBOR rate that matures in 90 days; all other floating-rate flows are unknown as of today. However, in both the pay-fixed swap and the portfolio of FRAs, these unknown floating-rate receipts are identical. Also, all fixed-rate payments are known today in both cases. To prevent arbitrage, the present value of both alternatives must be identical. Hence, the average of the FRA rates must equal the swap fixed rate.

Another difference between a swap and a portfolio of FRAs is that, with a swap, the next payment is always known one period ahead, when the floating rate for the next period becomes known. This is not true for an FRA, since its payment is made at expiration, based on the 1-period rate for the next period.

Although some differences make the equivalence less than exact, it is appropriate to view currency swaps as a series of currency forwards and an equity swap as a series of equity forward contracts.

Equivalence to Options

A fixed-rate payer or receiver swap can be replicated with a series of put/call positions with expiration dates on the payment dates of the swap. For a fixed-rate payer swap, we need an option position that pays when floating rates increase and requires a payment to be made when rates fall. A long interest rate call and a short interest rate put would accomplish this.

A short call and a long put, at the same strike price (equal to the fixed rate on the swap), would replicate the payoffs on a receiver swap. Remember, it takes two options to create the equivalent of a forward agreement—one to mimic the gains and one to mimic the losses.

Just as a swap can be viewed as a series of FRAs, it can also be viewed as a series of long call and short put positions with the strike rates equal to the fixed rate on the swap. While there are some differences with equity and currency options, it is appropriate to view both currency and equity swaps as equivalent to a series of long call/short put combinations as well.

LOS 61.c: Calculate and interpret the fixed rate on a plain vanilla interest rate swap and the market value of the swap during its life.

Plain Vanilla Swaps as Combinations of Bonds

There is a simple bond transaction that is equivalent to an interest rate swap. The fixed-payer could gain identical exposure by issuing a fixed-coupon bond and investing the proceeds in a floating-rate bond with the same maturity and payment dates. On each payment date, a fixed coupon payment is paid and the floating-rate payment is received. This is the key insight that we will use to price interest rate swaps.

An equity swap, from the perspective of the fixed-payer, is equivalent to borrowing at a fixed rate and investing in a stock, a portfolio, or an index. The equivalence is not exact, but close enough as an explanation of the capital markets transactions to approximate the exposure of an equity-for-fixed-rate swap. We will look at the issues involved more closely in LOS 61.e in this topic review.

The exposure of a currency swap is equivalent to that of issuing a bond in one currency, exchanging the proceeds for another currency at the spot exchange rate, and purchasing a bond denominated in the other currency with the same payment and maturity dates. Either or both of the bonds can have fixed- or floating-rate payments to create equivalent portfolios to the various combinations of fixed and floating rates available in currency swaps. We will use this idea to price and value currency swaps.

Deriving the Formula for Determining the Swap Rate

We can price a plain vanilla (fixed-for-floating) interest rate swap by using the insight that the swap is equivalent to issuing a fixed-rate bond and buying an otherwise identical floating-rate note. The fixed rate must be set so that the values of the floating-rate bond and the fixed-rate bond are the same at swap initiation. By finding this rate, we can price a swap with zero value at the inception of the contract.

At issue, a floating-rate bond has a value equal to its face value. This value can change during the life of the bond, but since the rate is reset to the market rate at each payment date, the value will return to par on each of those dates.

We will use a 4-period floating-rate note with a par value of $1,000 to illustrate this method of pricing a swap. Both the fixed- and floating-rate notes must have the same par value to replicate a swap, so that the principal values match up at maturity. For the swap to have zero value at initiation, the notes must have the same market price at that point in time as well.

Our fixed-rate note must have periodic payments, C, such that:

$$\$1,000 = \frac{C}{1+R_1} + \frac{C}{1+R_2} + \frac{C}{1+R_3} + \frac{C}{1+R_4} + \frac{\$1,000}{1+R_4}$$

The discount factors $(1 + R_n)$ are the n-period discount factors at the current rates. The present value of $1 to be received n periods from now is:

$$\frac{1}{1+R_n}$$

We can also write:

$$\$1,000 = C\left[\frac{1}{1+R_1} + \frac{1}{1+R_2} + \frac{1}{1+R_3} + \frac{1}{1+R_4}\right] + \frac{\$1,000}{1+R_4}$$

and solve for C as:

$$C = \left(\frac{1-\left(\dfrac{1}{1+R_4}\right)}{\dfrac{1}{1+R_1} + \dfrac{1}{1+R_2} + \dfrac{1}{1+R_3} + \dfrac{1}{1+R_4}}\right)\$1,000$$

The answer is the fixed rate for the swap as a percentage rate, the coupon amount per dollar of principal value.

If we are given the prices of zero-coupon risk-free bonds (per $ of principal) maturing on all our payment dates, the problem is simpler. We could just substitute these in the equation as:

$$C = \frac{1-Z_4}{Z_1 + Z_2 + Z_3 + Z_4}$$

where:

$$Z_n = \frac{1}{1+R_n} = \text{price of n-period zero-coupon bond per \$ of principal}$$

The Zs are called discount factors.

For example, the present value of a $100,000 payment 180 days from today at an annual discount rate of 6% (assuming simple interest and a 360-day basis) is:

$$PV = \frac{\$100,000}{1 + 0.06\left(\dfrac{180}{360}\right)} = \frac{\$100,000}{1.03} = \$97,087$$

That is equivalent to $0.97087 per $ of face value, so the 180-day discount factor is 0.97087.

We can use this 180-day discount factor to calculate the present value of any cash flow occurring in 180 days. For example, the present value of a $15,000 payment in 180 days at 6% is:

$$PV = \$15,000(0.97087) = \$14,563$$

Calculating the Fixed Rate on a Quarterly-Pay, Plain Vanilla Swap

In practice, our payment periods will likely be quarterly and our discount rates expressed as annualized LIBOR (using 360 days), as in the following example.

Example: Calculating the fixed rate on a swap with quarterly payments

Annualized LIBOR spot rates today are:

$$R_{90\text{-day}} = 0.030$$

$$R_{180\text{-day}} = 0.035$$

$$R_{270\text{-day}} = 0.040$$

$$R_{360\text{-day}} = 0.045$$

You're analyzing a 1-year swap with quarterly payments and a notional principal amount of $5,000,000. Calculate:

- The fixed rate in percentage terms.
- The quarterly fixed payments in $.

Answer:

First calculate the discount factors. Don't forget to convert from annualized rates to per-period rates.

$$Z_{90\text{-day}} = \frac{1}{1 + \left(0.030 \times \dfrac{90}{360}\right)} = 0.99256$$

$$Z_{180\text{-day}} = \frac{1}{1 + \left(0.035 \times \dfrac{180}{360}\right)} = 0.98280$$

$$Z_{270\text{-day}} = \frac{1}{1 + \left(0.040 \times \dfrac{270}{360}\right)} = 0.97087$$

$$Z_{360\text{-day}} = \frac{1}{1 + \left(0.045 \times \dfrac{360}{360}\right)} = 0.95694$$

> *Professor's Note: It's likely that on the exam you will be given a table of discount factors to use in pricing a swap, as in the next example. We've provided the calculations here so you know where the discount factors come from.*

The quarterly fixed rate on the swap is:

$$\frac{1 - 0.95694}{0.99256 + 0.98280 + 0.97087 + 0.95694} = 0.011 = 1.1\%$$

The quarterly fixed-rate payments, assuming a notional principal of $5,000,000, are:

$$\$5,000,000 \times 0.011 = \$55,000$$

The fixed rate on the swap in annual terms is:

$$1.1\% \times \frac{360}{90} = 4.4\%$$

We have priced a swap in which one side pays quarterly LIBOR and the other side pays 4.4% fixed annually (1.1% quarterly).

Calculating the Market Value of a Swap

At any payment date, the market value of a swap (to the fixed-rate payer) is the difference between the value of a floating-rate bond and the value of a fixed-rate bond. Since the fixed-payer is essentially long a floating-rate bond and short a fixed-rate bond, this position will have positive value only when the fixed-rate bond is trading at a discount to par. This follows from the fact that the floating-rate bond will be valued at par at each payment date. Between payment dates, the floating-rate bond may be worth more or less than par.

In the following example, we will subtract the value of the fixed-rate bond from the value of the floating-rate bond to calculate the value of the swap to the fixed-rate payer after initiation and between payment dates.

Professor's Note: Keep in mind that what we are doing is valuing the interest rate swap by valuing an equivalent position in a fixed-rate bond and a floating-rate bond. I don't want you to get confused in the middle of this example and say to yourself, "Why are we worrying about principal payments when the swap doesn't require principal payments?" We calculate the value of the fixed-rate bond as the present value of the expected fixed-rate interest payments and principal payments. We calculate the value of the floating-rate bond the same way. The difference between these two values is the value of the swap. The actual swap, however, doesn't require principal payments, and interest payments are netted.

How Do We Know the Floating Rate Bond Reprices to Par at Each Settlement Date?

One of the most confusing parts of valuing a swap for Level 2 candidates is understanding how we value a floating-rate bond even though we don't know what all the upcoming coupon payments will be, since the coupon rate changes at every settlement date.

The key is to recognize that at each settlement date, the coupon rate on the floating-rate bond, which determines the coupon payment at the *next* settlement date, is set to the market rate. That means that at every settlement date the coupon rate on the bond is equal to the market rate, and you should remember from Level 1 that *if the coupon rate on a bond is equal to the market rate, the bond sells at par.*

For example, suppose we have a 2-year floating rate bond with a par value of $100 and annual payments (and annual settlement dates) based on LIBOR. When the bond is issued, the coupon rate is set to 5%, which is the current market 1-year LIBOR rate. That means in one year the bond will make a coupon payment of $5.

After six months, 6-month LIBOR is 6% annually, or 3% for six months, and we want to value the floating-rate bond. Its value will be the present value of the remaining cash flows, but it may seem to you as though we can't solve the problem because we only know the coupon payment will be $5, but we don't know what the bond will be worth at the end of the year. However, we *do* know what the bond will be worth at the end of the year: its par value of $100! Therefore, the bond will be worth ($100 + $5) / 1.03 = $101.94.

Why will the bond trade at par at the end of the year? Think about what will happen at the end of the year: the $5 coupon payment will be made and the next coupon payment (to be made at the end of the second year) will be determined. As long as the second coupon payment (received at the end of the second year) is set equal to 1-year LIBOR at the end of the first year, the bond will be worth $100.

To convince you we are not just making this up, suppose the coupon rate resets to 8% at the end of the first year, which is the 1-year LIBOR rate at the time. Then we know that at the end of the second year, when the bond matures, we will receive a payment of $108 (the $100 principal and the $8 coupon). The present value of that payment, discounted at the current market rate of 8%, is the par value:

$$\text{bond value at end of year 1 (if coupon = 8\%)} = \frac{\$108}{1.08} = \$100$$

Suppose instead that 1-year LIBOR is 15%. Then the coupon payment will be $15 and the bond will still be valued at par:

$$\text{bond value at end of year 1 (if coupon = 15\%)} = \frac{\$115}{1.15} = \$100$$

What have we shown? A floating-rate bond will always be worth its par value at every settlement date.

Example: Valuing a plain vanilla swap between payment dates

Consider a 1-year LIBOR swap with quarterly payments priced at 6.052% at initiation when 90-day LIBOR was 5.5%. The annualized LIBOR rates and discount factors 30 days later are shown in the following figure. The notional principal amount is $30,000,000. Calculate the value of the swap to the fixed-rate payer after 30 days.

LIBOR and Discount Factors for $30 Million, 1-Year Interest Rate Swap

	Rate	Present Value Factor
60-day LIBOR	6.0%	0.99010
150-day LIBOR	6.5%	0.97363
240-day LIBOR	7.0%	0.95541
330-day LIBOR	7.5%	0.93567

Answer:

The quarterly payments per $ of notional principal are:

$$0.06052 \times \frac{90}{360} = \$0.01513$$

The hypothetical fixed-rate bond will pay four coupon payments of $0.01513 in 60, 150, 240, and 330 days. It will also make a final principal payment of $1.0000 in 330 days.

The time line of the cash flows is shown in the following figure. Remember that we're valuing the swap on day 30.

Time Line for Valuing the Fixed-Rate Side of an Interest Rate Swap

We can calculate the value of the fixed-rate side of the swap as $0.993993, the present value of the expected coupon payments and the face value payment, as shown in the following figure.

Calculation of Value for the Fixed Rate Side of an Interest Rate Swap

Day	Cash Flow	Discount Factor	Present Value
90	$0.01513	0.99010	$0.014980
180	$0.01513	0.97363	$0.014731
270	$0.01513	0.95541	$0.014455
360	$1.01513	0.93567	$0.949827
		Total	$0.993993

To value the floating-rate bond at day 30, we need only note two things. First, at the payment date on day 90, the bond value will be $1.00 because the coupon rate will be reset to the current market rate. Therefore, we don't need to know what the floating-rate bond's cash flows are after day 90. Second, the first payment (per $ of notional principal) is known at inception:

$$0.055 \times \frac{90}{360} = \$0.01375$$

Since the next payment date is 60 days out, we need to discount the first floating-rate payment and the $1.00 bond value immediately after the payment is made by the current 60-day rate of 6%.

Study Ses

Cross-Reference to CFA Institute Assigned Reading #61 – Swap Markets and C...

The time line is shown below. The 60-day discount factor is 0.99010. The value of the floating-rate bond at day 30 (per $ of notional principal) is therefore $1.01375 × 0.99010 = $1.003714.

Calculation of Value for the Floating Rate Side of an Interest Rate Swap

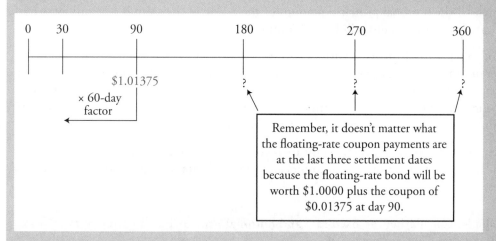

The value of the pay-fixed side of the swap is the difference between the values of the fixed and floating sides (per $ of notional principal):

swap value to fixed-rate payer = $1.003714 – $0.993993 = $0.009721

The total value of the $30,000,000 notional principal swap to the fixed-rate payer is:

swap value to fixed-rate payer = 30,000,000 × $0.009721 = $291,630

Since the relevant portion of the yield curve has shifted up, the fixed-rate liability has decreased in present value terms relative to the floating-rate asset. The reason the floating-rate bond appears to have appreciated above par value is that we have included the accrued interest by valuing the full first coupon.

LOS 61.d: Calculate and interpret the fixed rate, if applicable, and the foreign notional principal for a given domestic notional principal on a currency swap, and determine the market values of each of the different types of currency swaps during their lives.

Determining the Fixed Rate and Foreign Notional Principal

Consider two currencies, the U.S. dollar ($) and the British pound (£), where the exchange rate is currently $2 per £ or £0.5 per $. Using the method introduced earlier to price an interest rate swap, we can solve for the fixed rate that will make the present value of the fixed-rate $ payments equal to $1.00, and the fixed rate that will make the present value of the fixed-rate foreign payments equal to £1.00 in Great Britain. The interest rates in a currency swap are simply the swap rates calculated from each country's yield curve or the floating (short-term) rates in the relevant country's currency. Don't forget: With currency swaps, there are two yield curves and two swap rates, one for each currency.

The principal amounts of the fixed-rate obligations must be adjusted for the current exchange rate. We need $2.00 to equal £1.00, so these are the notional amounts, exchanged at the inception of the swap and returned at the termination of the swap. For example, if the notional principal amount of the $ side of the swap is $25 million, the £ notional principal amount will be £12.5 million.

For other than fixed-for-fixed currency swaps, we need only replace the fixed rate on either or both of the currencies with the floating rate *in the country* corresponding to the currency of the payment. A floating-rate loan that pays in £ will have a value of £1.00 at the initiation of the swap, so with our currency adjustment on the principal amounts, the fixed-for-floating currency swap will still have a zero value at initiation.

Given the yield curve information for each country and the exchange rate, we can calculate the notional principal amounts and the fixed-rate for either side of the swap, if necessary.

Example: Calculating the fixed rate and notional principal on a currency swap

In a previous example, we determined that the fixed rate on a 1-year quarterly $5,000,000 interest rate swap, given the following set of spot LIBOR rates, was 1.1% quarterly, or 4.4% on an annual basis.

$$R^{\$}_{90\text{-day}} = 0.030$$

$$R^{\$}_{180\text{-day}} = 0.035$$

$$R^{\$}_{270\text{-day}} = 0.040$$

$$R^{\$}_{360\text{-day}} = 0.045$$

The comparable set of £ rates are:

$$R^{£}_{90\text{-day}} = 0.04$$

$$R^{£}_{180\text{-day}} = 0.05$$

$$R^{£}_{270\text{-day}} = 0.06$$

$$R^{£}_{360\text{-day}} = 0.07$$

The current exchange rate is £0.50 per $. Determine the fixed rate on a 1-year £ interest rate swap. Then determine the notional £ principal amount and the quarterly cash flows on a:

- Pay $ fixed, receive £ fixed currency swap.
- Pay $ fixed, receive £ floating currency swap

Answer:

First calculate the £ discount factors. Don't forget to convert from annualized rates to per-period rates.

$$Z^{£}_{90\text{-day}} = \frac{1}{1 + \left(0.04 \times \dfrac{90}{360}\right)} = 0.99010$$

$$Z^{£}_{180\text{-day}} = \frac{1}{1 + \left(0.05 \times \dfrac{180}{360}\right)} = 0.97561$$

$$Z^{£}_{270\text{-day}} = \frac{1}{1 + \left(0.06 \times \dfrac{270}{360}\right)} = 0.95694$$

$$Z^{£}_{360\text{-day}} = \frac{1}{1 + \left(0.07 \times \dfrac{360}{360}\right)} = 0.93458$$

The quarterly fixed rate on the £ swap is:

$$\frac{1 - 0.93458}{0.99010 + 0.97561 + 0.95694 + 0.93458} = 0.017 = 1.7\%$$

The fixed rate on the £ swap in annual terms is:

$$1.7\% \times \frac{360}{90} = 6.8\%$$

Pay $ fixed, receive £ fixed currency swap.

The notional £ principal amount of the swap would be:

$5,000,000 × 0.50 = £2,500,000

At the initiation of the swap, we would exchange £2,500,000 for $5,000,000. We would pay 1.1% quarterly on the $5,000,000 notional principal ($55,000) and receive 1.7% on £2,500,000 quarterly (£42,500). At the end of one year, we would exchange the original principal amounts.

Pay $ fixed, receive £ floating currency swap.

The exchange of principal amounts at the initiation and termination of the swap would be the same as in the first example. We would still pay 1.1% quarterly on the $5,000,000. In return, we would receive the floating British rate on the £2,500,000 principal amount.

The value of a currency swap is calculated the same way as an interest rate swap. The value to any party is the present value of the cash flows they expect to receive minus the present value of the cash flows they expect to pay. There are four possible structures for a $ for £ currency swap:

- Receive $ fixed and pay £ fixed.
- Receive $ floating and pay £ fixed.
- Receive $ fixed and pay £ floating.
- Receive $ floating and pay £ floating.

Example: Calculating the value of a currency swap after initiation

Use the data on the $ and £ interest rate swaps in the previous examples to answer this question. After 300 days, the 60-day $ interest rate is 5.4%, the 60-day £ interest rate is 6.6%, and the exchange rate is £0.52 per $. The 90-day $ and £ interest rates on the last settlement date were 5.6% and 6.4%, respectively. Calculate the value of a $5,000,000 swap in which the counterparty receives $ floating and pays £ fixed.

Answer:

After 300 days, the only cash flows remaining are the last interest payments and the principal payments in 60 days. We want to find the present value of those cash flows, so we need the 60-day discount factors based on the current 60-day rates:

$$Z^{\$}_{60\text{-day}} = \frac{1}{1 + \left(0.054 \times \dfrac{60}{360}\right)} = 0.99108$$

$$Z^{\£}_{60\text{-day}} = \frac{1}{1 + \left(0.066 \times \dfrac{60}{360}\right)} = 0.98912$$

First calculate the value after 300 days of the $ floating payments. It is equivalent to the value of a $5,000,000 floating-rate bond that matures in 60 days and pays a coupon payment in 60 days of $70,000 ($5,000,000 × 0.056/4). This coupon payment was set at the beginning of the period when the $ interest rate was 5.6%. The value in $ of the $ floating side is the present value of $5,070,000 discounted using the 60-day $ discount factor of 0.99108:

value of $ floating side (in $) = 0.99108 × $5,070,000 = $5,024,776

Next calculate the value after 300 days of the £ fixed payments. Recall that the fixed £ rate was calculated in the previous example to be 6.8%. Thus, it is equivalent to the value of a 6.8% fixed rate, £2,500,000 bond that matures in 60 days and pays a coupon payment of £42,500 (£2,500,000 × 0.068/4) in 60 days. The value in £ of the £ fixed side is the present value of £2,542,500 discounted using the 60-day £ discount factor of 0.98912:

value of £ fixed side (in £) = 0.98912 × £2,542,500 = £2,514,838

©2009 Kaplan, Inc.

Convert that into $ at the current spot exchange rate of £0.52 per $ to find the value of the £ fixed side in $:

value of £ fixed side (in $) = £2,514,838 / 0.52 = $4,836,227

Finally, the value of the receive $ floating, pay £ fixed side of the swap is equal to the value of the $ floating side minus the £ fixed side, or $5,024,776 – $4,836,227 = $188,549.

 Professor's Note: It is easier to value a currency swap as we have done it here by calculating the total value of both sides (rather than calculating the value per $ of notional principal as we did in the interest rate swap valuation example). However, you should be able to do it either way.

LOS 61.e: Calculate and interpret the fixed rate, if applicable, on an equity swap and the market values of the different types of equity swaps during their lives.

To price an *N*-period pay-fixed equity swap, we can use the same formula as for a plain vanilla swap:

$$C_N = \frac{1 - Z_N}{Z_1 + Z_2 + \ldots + Z_N}$$

where:
Z_n = the present value of $1 to be received on the nth payment date of *N* dates

To value this swap after time has passed, determine the value of the equity or index portfolio and the value of the fixed-rate payments.

Example: Valuing a pay fixed, receive equity returns swap

A $10 million principal value equity swap has a fixed quarterly rate of 0.01513 and the other side pays the quarterly return on an index. The index is currently trading at 985. After 30 days have passed, the index stands at 996 and the term structure is the same as our earlier example using LIBOR annualized rates of 6%, 6.5%, 7%, and 7.5% for terms of 60, 150, 240, and 330 days. The discount factors are 0.99010, 0.97363, 0.95541, and 0.93567. The value of the pay-fixed side of the swap from that earlier example was $0.993993 per $ of notional principal. Calculate the value of the swap to the fixed-rate payer on day 30.

Answer:

We can calculate the value of the fixed-payer side of the swap by multiplying the value per $ of notional principal by the $10 million notional principal:

value of fixed-pay side = 0.993993 × $10,000,000 = $9,939,930

The value of $10,000,000 invested in the index after 30 days is:

$$\$10,000,000 \times \frac{996}{985} = \$10,111,675$$

The fixed-rate liability has decreased from its original value of $10,000,000. From the standpoint of the fixed-rate payer, the value of the swap after 30 days is:

$10,111,675 – $9,939,930 = $171,745

Professor's Note: We have not derived this result and have taken some liberties in simplifying the explanation. The LOS asks that you determine the swap rate and value an equity swap at a point in time. The analysis supplied here will accomplish this. It will work at any point during the tenor of the swap because the equity "portfolio" that is implicit in the analysis is set to the notional amount at each payment date.

If the equity swap to be valued is a floating-rate-for-equity swap, the value of the floating-rate side of the swap can be calculated just as before and compared to the value of the equity or index portfolio.

A swap of returns on two different stocks can be viewed as buying one stock (receiving the returns) and shorting an equal value of a different stock (paying the returns). There is no "pricing" at swap initiation, and we can value the swap at any point in time by taking the difference in returns (since the last payment date) times the notional principal.

Example: Valuing a receive equity return and pay different equity return swap

An investor is the Stock A returns payer (and Stock B returns receiver) in a $1million quarterly-pay swap. After one month, Stock A is up 1.3% and Stock B is down 0.8%. Calculate the value of the swap to the investor.

Answer:

The investor pays the Stock A returns and receives Stock B returns. However, the Stock B returns are negative, so he pays those as well:

value of swap = (–0.013 – 0.008) × $1,000,000 = –$21,000

LOS 61.f: Explain and interpret the characteristics and uses of swaptions, including the difference between payer and receiver swaptions.

A **swaption** is an option that gives the holder the right to enter into an interest rate swap. The notation for swaptions is similar to FRAs. For example, a swaption that matures in two years and gives the holder the right to enter into a 3-year swap at the end of the second year is a 2x5 swaption.

A **payer swaption** is the right to enter into a specific swap at some date in the future as the fixed-rate payer at a rate specified in the swaption. If swap fixed rates increase (as interest rates increase), the right to enter the pay-fixed side of a swap (a payer swaption) becomes more valuable. The holder of a European payer swaption would exercise if the market rate for fixed-rate swaps is greater than the exercise rate at maturity.

A **receiver swaption** is the right to enter into a specific swap at some date in the future as the fixed-rate receiver (i.e., the floating-rate payer) at a rate specified in the swaption. If swap fixed rates decrease (as interest rates decrease), the right to enter the receive-fixed side of a swap (a receiver swaption) becomes more valuable. The holder of a European receiver swaption would exercise at maturity if market rates are less than the exercise rate.

Swaptions can be American- or European-style options. Like any option, a swaption is purchased for a premium that depends on the strike rate (the fixed rate) specified in the swaption.

There are three primary uses of swaptions:

- *Lock in fixed rate.* If an investor anticipates a floating-rate exposure at some future date (e.g., he will be issuing bonds or getting a loan), a payer swaption would "lock in" a fixed rate and provide floating-rate payments for the loan. It would be exercised if the yield curve shifted up to give the investor (effectively) a loan at the fixed rate on the swaption.
- *Interest rate speculation.* Swaptions can be used to speculate on changes in interest rates. The investor would buy a payer swaption if he expects rate to rise, or buy a receiver swaption if he expects rates to fall.
- *Swap termination.* Swaptions can be used to terminate a swap. A fixed-rate payer on a 5-year swap could buy a 2x5 receiver swaption (at the same fixed rate as the swap). This swaption would give the investor the right to enter into an offsetting 3-year swap at the end of two years, effectively terminating the 5-year swap at the end of the second year.

LOS 61.g: Identify and calculate the possible payoffs and cash flows of an interest rate swaption.

Exercising an in-the-money swaption effectively generates an annuity over the term of the underlying swap. The amount of each annuity payment is the interest savings that result from paying a rate lower than the market rate under a payer swaption or the extra interest that results from receiving a higher rate under a receiver swaption.

For example, suppose an investor exercises a receiver swaption on a 1-year quarterly-pay LIBOR based $1 million swap with a fixed rate of 5% when the market rate on a current interest rate swap is 4%. The investor has the right to enter into a one-year swap and receive a fixed rate of 5%, while the market fixed rate for one year swaps is 4%. Therefore, the payoff to the swaption each quarter is the interest saved by receiving the higher fixed rate:

$$\text{fixed payment based on exercise rate} = 0.05 \times \frac{90}{360} \times \$1,000,000 = \$12,500$$

$$\text{fixed payment based on market rate} = 0.04 \times \frac{90}{360} \times \$1,000,000 = \$10,000$$

$$\text{extra interest per quarter} = \$12,500 - \$10,000 = \$2,500$$

We can also calculate this directly as: $(0.05 - 0.04) \times \dfrac{90}{360} \times \$1,000,000 = \$2,500$

LOS 61.h: Calculate and interpret the value of an interest rate swaption on the expiration day.

The value of an interest rate swaption at expiration is the present value of the difference between the higher fixed payments received and the lower fixed payments made (i.e., the annuity discussed in the previous LOS), ignoring transactions costs and default risk.

Example: Valuing an interest rate swaption at expiration

An investor exercises at maturity a payer swaption on a 1-year quarterly-pay LIBOR-based $10 million swap with a fixed rate of 5% when the market rate on a current interest rate swap is 6.052%. The (annual) rates and discount factors for 90-, 180-, 270-, and 360-day LIBOR are shown in the following figure. Calculate the value of the swaption at expiration.

LIBOR and Discount Rates for Payer Swaptions

	Rate	Present Value Factor
90-day LIBOR	5.5%	0.98644
180-day LIBOR	6.0%	0.97087
270-day LIBOR	6.5%	0.95352
360-day LIBOR	7.0%	0.93458

Answer:

The swaption allows the investor to take the fixed-rate payer position in the swap at 5%. The investor can also enter into a current 1-year swap as the fixed-rate receiver to get 6.052%. The floating-rate payments liability on the second swap will be offset (paid) by the floating-rate payments received on the swaption swap.

The net cash flow to the investor at each payment date will be:

$$(0.06052 - 0.05) \times \frac{90}{360} \times \$10,000,000 = \$26,300$$

The present value of these payments is $101,134, as shown in the figure.

Swaption Value at Expiration

Day	Cash Flow	Present Value Factor	Present Value
90	$26,300	0.98644	$25,943
180	$26,300	0.97087	$25,534
270	$26,300	0.95352	$25,078
360	$26,300	0.93458	$24,579
		Total	$101,134

LOS 61.i: Evaluate swap credit risk for each party and during the life of the swap, distinguish between current credit risk and potential credit risk, and illustrate how swap credit risk is reduced by both netting and marking to market.

Credit risk in a swap reflects the probability that a counterparty will default on the required payments. For example, if we are party to an interest rate swap with a positive value to us, we are subject to the credit risk of the counterparty, because if they default, we don't get paid. **Current credit risk** refers to the credit risk associated with the counterparty's default on a payment currently due. **Potential credit risk** reflects the future credit risk over the remaining term of the swap.

The credit quality of institutions in the swaps market is generally very good, so there is low credit risk at the inception of a swap contract. The credit risk is highest in the middle of the swap term because credit quality can have deteriorated and there are significant future payments remaining on the swap. Toward the end of the interest rate swap, few payments are left and credit risk is again low.

In currency swaps, principal is exchanged at termination of the swap, so the period of higher credit risk is a little later in the swap's life.

Interest payments in interest rate swaps are typically netted, so only one party pays the other the net amount due. For example, suppose at the payment date, Party A owes Party B $40,000 and Party B owes Party A $70,000. The payments would be netted and Party B would pay Party A $30,000.

Without netting, credit risk is greater. If B goes bankrupt and defaults on the $70,000 payment, it still has a claim against A of $40,000. A is obligated to pay the $40,000 and gets in line with B's other creditors for payment of A's $70,000 claim.

With netting, B's bankruptcy results in A having a claim of only the net amount, $30,000, as a bankruptcy creditor. A has no obligation to make a payment to B. Netting is usual in single swap contracts but can also be extended to cover all the swaps two parties are in together.

Marking to market involves making a payment equal to the value of the swap at periodic settlement dates and repricing the swap by resetting the swap rate. This reduces credit risk just as it does with futures contracts.

LOS 61.j: Define swap spread and relate it to credit risk.

The **swap spread** is the spread between the swap rate and the comparable maturity Treasury notes. A 2-year swap might have a (swap) spread of 40 basis points over the yield on 2-year Treasury notes.

Remember that we based the swap rate on the LIBOR curve. LIBOR is a rate for large-bank lending and is not a riskless rate. Therefore, the default premium in LIBOR is reflected in the swap rate calculated from it. The swap spread will respond to the same factors as other "quality" spreads.

KEY CONCEPTS

LOS 61.a

The "price" of a swap is the fixed rate of a fixed-for-floating swap and is set so that the swap contract has a zero value at initiation. The value of a swap is the difference between the present values of the fixed- and floating-rate payment streams. Due to shifts in the yield curve, at any point after contract initiation, the swap value may change.

LOS 61.b

A payer swap is equivalent to each of the following:
- Issuing fixed-rate debt and buying a floating-rate note.
- Entering a series of FRAs at the fixed rate.
- A combination of interest rate puts and calls with strike rates equal to the fixed rate on the swap.

A series of interest rate futures is similar to a payer swap, but futures characteristics make it difficult to match the cash flows of a swap with futures.

A swap can be thought of as a strip (or series) of FRAs with successively longer maturity dates. The swap rate is computed as the present-value average of the FRA rates. Imposing a single rate on all the FRAs means that the individual FRAs will be off-market FRAs. An off-market forward is one in which the forward price is different from that which gives the forward a zero value at initiation.

The payoffs on a payer swap are equivalent to those on a series of long call/short put interest rate options with strike prices both equal to the fixed rate on the swap. A series of short call/long put positions will mimic a receiver swap.

LOS 61.c

The fixed rate on a swap is determined by setting the present value of the fixed-rate payments equal to the present value of the expected floating-rate payments.

The value of a swap to the fixed-rate receiver at a point in time is the difference between the value of the fixed-rate bond and the floating-rate bond in the underlying equivalent position.

LOS 61.d

When a currency swap includes a fixed rate, this rate is determined using the yield curve for the relevant currency. The notional principal amounts in the two currencies are equated using current exchange rates.

LOS 61.e

The fixed-rate side of an equity swap is priced and valued just like an interest rate swap. The equity side can be valued by multiplying the notional amount of the contract by 1 + the percentage equity appreciation since the last payment date. Use the difference in values to value the swap.

LOS 61.f

A swaption is an option on a swap. A payer swaption gives the holder the right to enter into an interest rate swap as the fixed-rate payer at the exercise of the swaption. A receiver swaption gives the holder the right to enter into an interest rate swap as the fixed-rate receiver.

A swaption can be used to:
- Hedge an anticipated exposure to fixed or floating interest rate payments.
- Speculate on the direction of interest rates.
- Provide a method of exiting an existing swap prior to the normal termination date.

LOS 61.g

A payer-swaption is in-the-money if swap (fixed) rates rise. A receiver swaption is in-the-money if swap rates fall.

LOS 61.h

At expiration, the value of a payer swaption is the maximum of zero and the present value of a stream of payments equal to the fixed-rate payments on a current market rate swap minus the fixed-rate payments on the swaption swap.

LOS 61.i

Credit risk arises because of the possibility that the other party to a swap cannot or will not make the payments required by the swap contract. It is greatest in the middle of the swap term when the creditworthiness of the counterparty may have deteriorated since swap initiation and there are significant payments yet to be made over the remaining term of the swap.

Netting, within a swap or across several swaps with the same counterparty, relieves the party owed the greater amount of a separate claim for the lesser amount. Only the net payment is recognized as a debt. Marking to market can also be used to reduce credit risk.

LOS 61.j

The swap spread is the difference between the current swap (fixed) rate and the yield on a riskless (Treasury) bond of the same term as the swap. It can be interpreted as a quality or default-risk spread between a riskless security and LIBOR.

CONCEPT CHECKERS

1. The current U.S. dollar ($) to Canadian dollar (C$) exchange rate is 0.7. In a
    $1 million plain vanilla currency swap, the party that is entering the swap to
    hedge existing exposure to a C$-denominated fixed-rate liability will:
    A. receive $1 million at the termination of the swap.
    B. pay a fixed rate based on the yield curve in the United States.
    C. receive a fixed rate based on the yield curve in Canada.

2. A European-style payer swaption gives its holder the:
    A. right to enter a swap by paying the strike price at expiration of the option.
    B. right to enter a swap at expiration of the option as the fixed-rate payer.
    C. option to take either side of a swap at a certain date in the future, by making
        a current payment.

3. At what point in a swap's life is the credit risk in an interest rate swap the
    greatest?
    A. In the middle.
    B. At the end, when the largest payments are due.
    C. At the beginning, because all the payments remain.

4. Consider a 6-year plain vanilla currency swap in which we will receive LIBOR
    semiannually and pay 9% fixed semiannually in British pounds (£). The notional
    value of the swap is £50 million. The current spot rate is $1.50 per £. Which of
    the following transactions would replicate the payoffs to the pay-fixed side of the
    swap?

	Bond to issue	Bond to purchase
A.	9% fixed, £50 million	LIBOR, $33 million
B.	9% fixed, £50 million	LIBOR, $75 million
C.	LIBOR, £112 million	9% fixed, $33 million

5. Annualized LIBOR spot rates and the present value factors today are:

	Rate	Present value factor
90-day LIBOR	4.2%	0.98961
180-day LIBOR	4.8%	0.97656
270-day LIBOR	5.0%	0.96386
360-day LIBOR	5.2%	0.95057
Total		3.88060

    Based on a notional principal of $40,000,000, the annualized swap rate is *closest*
    to:
    A. 1.27%.
    B. 2.54%.
    C. 5.08%.

Use the following information to answer Questions 6 and 7.

Raul Hernandez, CFA, purchased a 1-year European receiver swaption with an exercise rate of 6% that is about to expire. The underlying is a 2-year swap with semiannual payments, and the notional principal is $10,000,000. Annualized LIBOR rates and present value factors are:

	Rate	Present value factor
180-day LIBOR	4.0%	0.9804
360-day LIBOR	4.5%	0.9569
540-day LIBOR	5.0%	0.9302
720-day LIBOR	5.5%	0.9009

6.   The receiver swaption is:
  A. out-of-the-money.
  B. at-the-money.
  C. in-the-money.

7.   The value of the receiver swaption at maturity is *closest* to:
  A. $139,431.
  B. $143,360.
  C. $148,000.

Use the following information to answer Questions 8 and 9.

Two parties enter into a 2-year fixed-for-floating interest rate swap with semiannual payments. The floating-rate payments are based on LIBOR. The 180-, 360-, 540-, and 720-day annualized LIBOR rates and present value factors are:

	Rate	Present value factor
180-day LIBOR	5.0%	0.9756
360-day LIBOR	6.0%	0.9434
540-day LIBOR	6.5%	0.9112
720-day LIBOR	7.0%	0.8772

8.   The swap rate is *closest* to:
  A. 6.62%.
  B. 6.87%.
  C. 7.03%.

9.   After 180 days, the swap is marked-to-market when the 180-, 360-, and 540-day annualized LIBOR rates are 4.5%, 5%, and 6%, respectively. The present value factors, respectively, are 0.9780, 0.9524, and 0.9174. What is the market value of the swap per $1 notional principal, and which of the two counterparties (the fixed-rate payer or the fixed-rate receiver) would make the payment to mark the swap to market?

	Market value	Payment made by
A.	$0.01166	Fixed-rate payer
B.	$0.04290	Fixed-rate payer
C.	$0.01166	Fixed-rate receiver

10.   A bank entered into a $5,000,000, 1-year equity swap with quarterly payments 300 days ago. The bank agreed to pay an annual fixed rate of 4% and receive the return on an international equity index. The index was trading at 3,000 at the end of the third quarter, 30 days ago. The current 60-day LIBOR rate is 3.6%, the discount factor is 0.9940, and the index is now at 3,150. The value of the swap to the bank is *closest* to:
        A. –$257,795.
        B. –$114,676.
        C. $230,300.

CHALLENGE PROBLEMS

11.   The equity return receiver in an equity return-for-fixed-rate equity swap receives payments that are equivalent to which of the following strategies?
        A. Buy and hold the index stocks and issue a fixed-rate bond.
        B. Issue a bond, short the index stocks, and adjust the short position value to the principal amount at each payment date.
        C. Buy the index stocks, adjust the portfolio value to the notional amount of the swap at each payment date, and issue a fixed-rate bond.

12.   Consider a receiver and payer swaption on a $1 million 1-year swap on quarterly LIBOR with a fixed rate of 6% (1.5% quarterly). The annual market swap rate at expiration is 6.6%.

        Annualized LIBOR rates:

	Rate	Discount Factor
90-day LIBOR	5.5%	0.98644
180-day LIBOR	6.0%	0.97087
270-day LIBOR	6.5%	0.95352
360-day LIBOR	7.0%	0.93458

        The difference between the payoffs at expiration to a payer swaption and a receiver swaption is *closest* to:
        A. $0.
        B. $5,768.
        C. $6,000.

13.   Consider a 2-year interest rate swap in which we pay LIBOR quarterly and receive 8% fixed semiannually. The notional value is $10 million. Assume the yield curve is flat. The receive-fixed side of this swap can be replicated with which of the following portfolios of interest rate options?

	Long position	Short position
A.	Puts at 8%	Calls at 8%
B.	Puts at 8%	Puts at 8%
C.	Calls at 8%	Puts at 8%

14. A bank entered into a 1-year currency swap with quarterly payments 200 days ago by agreeing to swap $1,000,000 for €800,000. The bank agreed to pay an annual fixed rate of 5% on the €800,000 and receive a floating rate tied to LIBOR on the $1,000,000. Current LIBOR and Euribor rates and present value factors are shown in the following table.

	Rate	Present Value Factor
70-day LIBOR	4.0%	0.9923
90-day LIBOR	4.4%	0.9891
160-day LIBOR	4.8%	0.9791
180-day LIBOR	5.2%	0.9747
70-day Euribor	5.2%	0.9900
90-day Euribor	5.6%	0.9862
160-day Euribor	6.1%	0.9736
180-day Euribor	6.3%	0.9695

The current spot exchange rate is €0.75 per $. 90-day LIBOR at the last payment date was 4.2%. The value of the swap to the bank today is *closest* to:
A. −$61,969.
B. −$42,049.
C. $42,049.

15. If interest rates increase, the value of a receiver swaption will:
A. increase, and the value of a payer swaption will decrease.
B. decrease, and the value of a payer swaption will increase.
C. decrease, and the value of a payer swaption will decrease.

ANSWERS – CONCEPT CHECKERS

1. **C**   A receive-fixed C$ position will hedge the liability risk. That party would receive $1 million at swap inception (in exchange for $\frac{1,000,000}{0.7}$ = C$1,428,571) and pay it back at termination. The fixed-rate received will be calculated using the yield curve in Canada at the initiation of the swap. Since this is a plain vanilla currency swap, the receive-fixed position will pay a floating rate based on the U.S. yield curve.

2. **B**   A payer swaption gives the holder the right to enter a swap as the fixed-rate payer at the strike rate. The strike price on the swap is the fixed rate, so there is no exercise price per se. The payment for the swaption is the premium paid for purchase, just like any other options.

3. **A**   In the middle of the swap, credit quality of one or both parties can have deteriorated over time and there are still significant payments remaining.

4. **B**   This swap can be viewed as the following set of capital market transactions:
    *   We issue a £50 million, 6-year, 9% semiannual bond denominated in pounds.
    *   Exchange our pounds proceeds from the bond issue for U.S dollars at the current spot rate: £50 million × $1.50 per pound = $75 million.
    *   We purchase a $75 million, 6-year, FRN at LIBOR denominated in $.

5. **C**   The quarterly fixed rate on the swap is:

    $$\frac{1 - 0.95057}{3.88060} = 0.0127 = 1.27\%$$

    The fixed rate on the swap in annual terms is:

    $$1.27\% \times \frac{360}{90} = 5.08\%$$

6. **C**   Calculate the swap rate:

    $$\text{semi-annual swap rate} = \frac{1 - 0.9009}{0.9804 + 0.9569 + 0.9302 + 0.9009} = 0.0263$$

    $$\text{annualized swap rate} = 0.0263 \times \frac{360}{180} = 0.0526 = 5.26\%$$

    The receiver swaption is in-the-money because the exercise rate on the swaption (6%) is greater than the current swap rate (5.26%).

7. **A**   The net cash flow to Hernandez at each payment date would be:

    $$\left(0.06 - 0.0526\right) \times \frac{180}{360} \times \$10,000,000 = \$37,000$$

    The value of the swaption is the present value of these payments:

    $$\$37,000 \times (0.9804 + 0.9569 + 0.9302 + 0.9009) = \$139,431$$

8. **A**   Calculate the swap rate:

$$\text{semi-annual swap rate} = \frac{1 - 0.8772}{0.9756 + 0.9434 + 0.9112 + 0.8772} = 0.0331$$

$$\text{swap rate} = 0.0331 \times \frac{360}{180} = 0.0662 = 6.62\%$$

9. **A** $\text{value of fixed-rate side (per \$ of notional principal)} = \left[\$0.0331 \times (0.9780 + 0.9524 + 0.9174)\right]$
$$+ \left(\$1.00 \times 0.9174\right) = \$1.01166$$

The market value of the floating-rate side is $1.0000 because we're at a payment date. The market value of the swap per $ of notional principal to the receive-fixed (and pay-floating) side is $1.01166 – $1.0000 = $0.01166. As the swap is marked to market, the pay-fixed swap holder makes a payment of $0.01166 to the receive-fixed holder for each $1 of notional principal.

10. **C** $\text{value of fixed-rate side} = 0.9940 \times \$5,050,000 = \$5,019,700$

$$\text{value of index return side} = \$5,000,000 \times \frac{3,150}{3,000} = \$5,250,000$$

$\text{value of swap to bank} = \$5,250,000 - \$5,019,700 = \$230,300$

ANSWERS – CHALLENGE PROBLEMS

11. **C**   The amount by which the portfolio value exceeds the notional principal amount is sold at each payment date to make the equity return payment. If the value has declined, the equity return receiver must make a payment in that amount, equivalent to adding funds to bring the portfolio value back up to the notional principal amount. Issuing or shorting a bond will mimic the fixed-rate liability in the swap.

12. **B**   The current market rate is 0.066 / 4 = 0.0165. The swaption swap has a fixed rate of 0.015. Since rates have increased, the payer swaption will be in-the-money. The net cash flow to the investor at each payment date will be:

$$\left(0.066 - 0.060\right) \times \frac{90}{360} \times \$1,000,000 = \$1,500$$

The present value of these payments is:

$1,500 × (0.98644 + 0.97087 + 0.95352 + 0.93458) = $5,768

A receiver swaption is out-of-the-money and no payments would be made. The difference between the two is $5,768.

13. **A**   To replicate the receive-fixed side of this swap, we would go long a series of interest rate puts with a strike rate of 8%, and short a series of interest rate calls with a strike rate of 8%. The expiration dates of the options should be the payment dates of the swap.

As interest rates rise above the swap-fixed rate of 8%, the receive-fixed party to the swap loses because he is receiving a below-market rate. This loss would be mimicked by the payoff required on the short calls. The puts would be out-of-the-money.

As interest rates fall below the swap-fixed rate of 8%, the receive-fixed party to the swap gains because she is receiving an above-market rate. This gain is mimicked by the payoff on the long interest rate puts. The calls would be out-of-the-money.

14. **A**   coupon on $ floating side = $1,000,000 × (0.042 / 4) = $10,500

value of the $ floating side = 0.9923 × $1,010,500 = $1,002,719

coupon on € fixed side = €800,000 × (0.05 / 4) = €10,000

value of € fixed side (in €) = (0.9900 × €10,000) + (0.9736 × €810,000) = €798,516

value of € fixed side (in $) = $\dfrac{798,516}{0.75} = \$1,064,688$

value of swap to bank = $1,002,719 − $1,064,688 = −$61,969

15. **B**   A receiver swaption is the right to enter into a specific swap at some date in the future as the fixed-rate receiver (i.e., the floating-rate payer) at a rate specified in the swaption. If swap fixed rates increase (as interest rates increase), the right to enter the pay-floating side of a swap (a receiver swaption) becomes less valuable.

A payer swaption is the right to enter into a specific swap at some date in the future as the fixed-rate payer at a rate specified in the swaption. If swap fixed rates increase (as interest rates increase), the right to enter the pay-fixed side of a swap (a payer swaption) becomes more valuable.

INTEREST RATE DERIVATIVE INSTRUMENTS

EXAM FOCUS

This topic review fills a few "holes" in the curriculum related to caps and floors that were not covered in prior topic reviews. Make sure you can calculate the payoff to a cap and a floor and explain how caps and floors are equivalent to packages of other securities.

LOS 62.a: Demonstrate how both a cap and a floor are packages of options on interest rates and options on fixed-income instruments.

An **interest rate cap** is an agreement in which one party agrees to pay the other at regular intervals over a certain period of time when the benchmark interest rate (e.g., LIBOR) exceeds the strike rate specified in the contract. This strike rate is called the **cap rate**. For example, the seller of a cap might agree to pay the buyer at the end of any quarter over the next two years if LIBOR is greater than a cap rate of 6%. We'll discuss the calculation of the payoff to a cap in the next LOS.

The buyer of a cap has a position similar to that of a buyer of a call on LIBOR, both of whom benefit when interest rates rise. Because an interest rate cap is a multi-period agreement, a cap is actually a portfolio of call options on LIBOR called **caplets**. For example, the 2-year cap discussed above is actually a portfolio of eight interest rate options with different maturity dates.

The cap buyer pays a premium to the seller and exercises the cap if the market rate of interest rises above the cap strike. The diagram in Figure 1 illustrates the profits of an interest rate cap at the end of one particular settlement period. It has the familiar shape of a long position in a call option.

Figure 1: Profit to a Long Cap

An **interest rate floor** is an agreement in which one party agrees to pay the other at regular intervals over a certain time period when the benchmark interest rate (e.g., LIBOR) falls below the strike rate specified in the contract. This strike rate is called the **floor rate**. For example, the seller of a floor might agree to pay the buyer at the end of any quarter over the next two years if LIBOR is less than a floor rate of 4%. We'll discuss the calculation of the payoff to a floor in the next LOS.

The buyer of a floor benefits from an interest rate decrease and, therefore, has a position that is similar to that of a buyer of a put on LIBOR, who benefits when interest rates fall and the price of the instrument rises. Once again, because a floor is a multi-period agreement, a floor is actually a portfolio of put options on LIBOR called **floorlets**.

The floor buyer pays a premium and exercises the floor if the market rate of interest falls below the floor strike. The diagram in Figure 2 illustrates the profits of an interest rate floor at the end of one particular settlement period. It has the same shape as a long put option.

Figure 2: Profit to a Long Floor

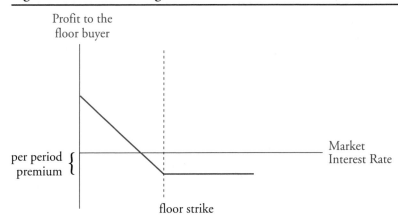

Options are traded both on *interest rates* and on *prices* of fixed-income securities. So far we've talked about options on interest rates. The values of comparable options on rates and prices respond differently to changes in interest rates because of the inverse relationship between bond yields and bond prices. Figure 3 outlines how each type of option responds to changes in yields and bond prices.

Figure 3: Options on Rate vs. Options on Prices

Option	If Rates Increase and Bond Prices Decrease	If Rates Decrease and Bond Prices Increase
Value of call on LIBOR	Increases	Decreases
Value of call on bond price	Decreases	Increases
Value of put on LIBOR	Decreases	Increases
Value of put on bond price	Increases	Decreases

We can also interpret caps and floors in terms of options on the prices of fixed-income securities:

- A long cap is equivalent to a portfolio of long put options on fixed-income security prices.
- A long floor is equivalent to a portfolio of long call options on fixed-income security prices.

LOS 62.b: Compute the payoff for a cap and a floor and explain how a collar is created.

A floating-rate borrower can use a cap to limit interest expense during the life of the cap. The payoff to the cap buyer is:

$$\text{periodic payment} = \max\left[0,\ (\text{notional principal}) \times (\text{index rate} - \text{cap strike}) \times \left(\frac{\text{actual days}}{360}\right)\right]$$

A floating-rate investor can use a floor to limit reductions in interest income during the life of the floor. The payment to the floor buyer is:

$$\text{periodic payment} = \max\left[0,\ (\text{notional principal}) \times (\text{floor strike} - \text{index rate}) \times \left(\frac{\text{actual days}}{360}\right)\right]$$

Example: Calculating the payoff for an interest rate cap

Suppose that a 1-year cap has a cap rate of 8% and a notional amount of $100 million. The frequency of settlement is quarterly, and the reference rate is 3-month LIBOR. Assume that 3-month LIBOR at the end of the next four quarters is as shown in the following figure. Calculate the payoff for each quarter.

Payoff to 8% Interest Rate Cap

Quarter	3-month LIBOR	Payoff
1	7.7%	?
2	8.0%	?
3	8.4%	?
4	8.6%	?

Answer:

The cap will have a payoff each quarter equal to:

$$\max\left[0,\ \$100{,}000{,}000 \times \left(\frac{\text{LIBOR} - 0.08}{4}\right)\right]$$

 Professor's Note: The division by 4 comes from the settlement frequency, assuming exactly 90 days per quarter.

$$\text{quarter 1 payoff} = \max\left[0,\ \$100{,}000{,}000 \times \left(\frac{0.077 - 0.08}{4}\right)\right] = \$0$$

$$\text{quarter 2 payoff} = \max\left[0,\ \$100{,}000{,}000 \times \left(\frac{0.08 - 0.08}{4}\right)\right] = \$0$$

$$\text{quarter 3 payoff} = \max\left[0,\ \$100{,}000{,}000 \times \left(\frac{0.084 - 0.08}{4}\right)\right] = \$100{,}000$$

$$\text{quarter 4 payoff} = \max\left[0,\ \$100{,}000{,}000 \times \left(\frac{0.086 - 0.08}{4}\right)\right] = \$150{,}000$$

Example: Calculating the payoff for an interest rate floor

Let's change the cap to a *floor*, keeping the other information the same. Calculate the payoff for a floor with a floor rate of 8%.

Answer:

$$\text{quarter 1 payoff} = \max\left[0,\ \$100,000,000 \times \left(\frac{0.08 - 0.077}{4}\right)\right] = \$75,000$$

$$\text{quarter 2 payoff} = \max\left[0,\ \$100,000,000 \times \left(\frac{0.08 - 0.08}{4}\right)\right] = \$0$$

$$\text{quarter 3 payoff} = \max\left[0,\ \$100,000,000 \times \left(\frac{0.08 - 0.084}{4}\right)\right] = \$0$$

$$\text{quarter 4 payoff} = \max\left[0,\ \$100,000,000 \times \left(\frac{0.08 - 0.086}{4}\right)\right] = \$0$$

As a technical note, caps and floors are usually paid in arrears, meaning that, for example, the $75,000 payoff to the floor for the first quarter will be made three months later, at the end of the second quarter.

An **interest rate collar** is a simultaneous position in a floor and a cap on the same benchmark rate over the same period with the same settlement dates. There are two types of collars:

- The first type of collar is to purchase a cap and sell a floor. For example, an investor with a LIBOR-based liability could purchase a cap on LIBOR at 8% and simultaneously sell a floor on LIBOR at 4% over the next year. The investor has now hedged the liability so that the borrowing costs will stay within the "collar" of 4% to 8%. If the cap and floor rates are set so that the premium paid from buying the cap is exactly offset by the premium received from selling the floor, the collar is called a "zero-cost" collar.
- The second type of collar is to purchase a floor and sell a cap. For example, an investor with a LIBOR-based asset could purchase a floor on LIBOR at 3% and simultaneously sell a cap at 7% over the next year. The investor has now hedged the asset so the returns will stay within the collar of 3% to 7%. The investor can create a zero-cost collar by choosing the cap and floor rates so that the premium paid on the floor offsets the premium received on the cap.

KEY CONCEPTS

LOS 62.a

An interest rate cap is an agreement in which one party agrees to pay the other at regular intervals over a certain period of time when the benchmark interest rate (e.g., LIBOR) exceeds the strike rate specified in the contract. The buyer of a cap has a position similar to that of a buyer of a call on LIBOR, both of whom benefit when interest rates rise. Because an interest rate cap is a multi-period agreement, a cap is actually a portfolio of call options on LIBOR called caplets.

An interest rate floor is an agreement in which one party agrees to pay the other at regular intervals over a certain period of time when the benchmark interest rate (e.g., LIBOR) falls below the strike rate specified in the contract. The buyer of a floor benefits from an interest rate decrease and, therefore, has a position that is similar to that of a buyer of a put on LIBOR. Because a floor is a multi-period agreement, a floor is actually a portfolio of put options on LIBOR called floorlets.

LOS 62.b

A floating-rate borrower can use a cap to limit interest expense during the life of the cap. The payoff to the cap buyer is:

$$\text{periodic payment} = \max\left[0, (\text{notional principal}) \times (\text{index rate} - \text{cap strike}) \times \left(\frac{\text{actual days}}{360}\right)\right]$$

A floating-rate investor can use a floor to limit reductions in interest income during the life of the floor. The payment to the floor buyer is:

$$\text{periodic payment} = \max\left[0, (\text{notional principal}) \times (\text{floor strike} - \text{index rate}) \times \left(\frac{\text{actual days}}{360}\right)\right]$$

An interest rate collar is a simultaneous position in a floor and a cap on the same benchmark rate over the same period with the same settlement dates. The collar investor can either buy a cap and sell a floor or buy a floor and sell a cap. If the cap and floor rates are set so that the premium paid for the long position is equal to the premium received for the short position, it is called a zero-cost collar.

CONCEPT CHECKERS

1. A 1-year cap has a cap rate of 8% and a notional amount of $10 million. The frequency of settlement is quarterly, and the reference rate is 3-month LIBOR. Assume that 3-month LIBOR for the next four quarters is as shown in the following figure.

Quarter	3-month LIBOR
1	8.7%
2	8.0%
3	7.8%
4	8.2%

    The payoff for the cap for the third quarter is *closest* to:
    A. $0.
    B. $5,000.
    C. $17,500.

2. A portfolio of put options on a benchmark interest rate like LIBOR is called an interest rate:
    A. cap.
    B. floor.
    C. collar.

3. If interest rates increase, what will *most likely* happen to the value of a long position in a:

	Call option on LIBOR?	Put option on a bond price?
A.	Increase	Increase
B.	Increase	Decrease
C.	Decrease	Increase

CHALLENGE PROBLEM

4. An interest rate floor at 7% is available from a dealer. To create an interest rate collar, an investor is *most likely* to:
    A. buy the floor and sell a 12% interest rate cap.
    B. buy the floor and sell a 7% interest rate cap.
    C. sell the floor and buy a 3% interest rate cap.

ANSWERS – CONCEPT CHECKERS

1. **A** $\text{period 1 payoff} = \max\left[0, \$10,000,000 \times \left(\frac{0.087 - 0.08}{4}\right)\right] = \$17,500$

   $\text{period 2 payoff} = \max\left[0, \$10,000,000 \times \left(\frac{0.08 - 0.08}{4}\right)\right] = \$0$

   $\text{period 3 payoff} = \max\left[0, \$10,000,000 \times \left(\frac{0.078 - 0.08}{4}\right)\right] = \$0$

   $\text{period 4 payoff} = \max\left[0, \$10,000,000 \times \left(\frac{0.082 - 0.08}{4}\right)\right] = \$5,000$

2. **B** An interest rate floor is an agreement in which one party agrees to pay the other party at regular intervals over a certain period of time when the benchmark interest rate (e.g., LIBOR) falls below the strike rate, or floor rate, specified in the contract. It is equivalent to a portfolio of put options on LIBOR. Each individual put option is called a floorlet.

3. **A** If interest rates increase, a long position in a call option on LIBOR will increase in value. An increase in interest rates will cause bond prices to fall, which will also increase the value of a long position in a put option on a bond price.

ANSWER – CHALLENGE PROBLEM

4. **A** An interest rate collar is a simultaneous position in a floor and a cap on the same benchmark rate over the same period with the same settlement dates. The strike rate on the floor must be less than the strike rate on the cap. The investor either (1) buys the floor and sells the cap, or (2) sells the floor and buys the cap. The only way to create an interest collar from the choices is to buy the floor at 7% and sell the cap at 12%.

   Buying the floor at 7% and selling the cap at 7% will result in a position similar to a short position in a forward contract on LIBOR (i.e., a forward rate agreement, or FRA). Selling the floor and buying the cap at the same rate will result in a position similar to a long position in an FRA.

The following is a review of the Derivatives: Options, Swaps, and Interest Rate and Credit Derivatives principles designed to address the learning outcome statements set forth by CFA Institute®. This topic is also covered in:

USING CREDIT DERIVATIVES TO ENHANCE RETURN AND MANAGE RISK

Study Session 17

EXAM FOCUS

This is a relatively new topic for the Level 2 curriculum. Credit derivatives and their uses in hedging and arbitrage are typically left to Level 3, and in fact, the Level 2 curriculum does not prepare the candidate for the detail in which credit default swaps are discussed in this topic review. Therefore, we suggest that you understand the basics: what a credit default swap is, how the cash flows are structured in a typical swap, and their advantages in constructing hedge and arbitrage trades. In particular, focus on how credit default swaps are used as a component of a synthetic collateralized debt obligation (CDO).

LOS 63.a: Describe the characteristics of a credit default swap, and compare and contrast a credit default swap with a corporate bond.

A **credit default swap** (CDS) is essentially an insurance contract. The **reference obligation** is the fixed income security on which the swap is written—usually a bond but potentially also a loan. If default occurs on the reference obligation, the buyer of the swap receives a payment from the seller. To obtain this coverage, the buyer of the swap pays the seller a premium that is either paid up front or over a period of time. The buyer of the swap is said to be buying protection, whereas the seller is said to be selling protection and assuming credit risk. The default swap premium is also referred to as the default swap spread.

For example, suppose a swap is written on a bond with a $10 million par value and a 3-year maturity. If the swap premium is 70 bps annually, the buyer of the swap will pay the seller $10,000,000 × 0.70% = $70,000 per year, which is usually paid on a quarterly basis. The swap will mature in three years, assuming there is no credit event.

The CDS creates a short position in the reference obligation for the buyer of the swap because the value of the CDS increases as the credit quality and market price of the reference obligation decline. The default swap becomes more valuable to the buyer when the reference obligation decreases in credit quality. The default swap could then be sold for a profit. Note that the CDS does not protect against market-wide interest rate risk, only credit risk.

From the swap seller's perspective, the default swap creates a long position in the reference obligation. If the reference obligation increases in credit quality, the default swap decreases in value below the price at which it was originally sold.

When there is a credit event, the swap will settle in cash or physical delivery, with the latter being the usual case. With physical delivery, the seller of the swap receives the

©2009 Kaplan, Inc.

reference obligation (i.e., the bond or loan) and pays the buyer of the swap the notional amount, as shown in Figure 1.

Figure 1: Physical Settlement on Credit Default Swap after a Credit Event

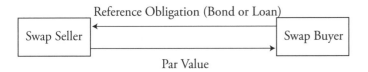

In a cash settlement, the seller of the swap would owe the buyer the net amount of the notional minus the market value as shown in Figure 2.

Figure 2: Cash Settlement on Credit Default Swap after a Credit Event

Example: Cash flows from a CDS

The Rose Foundation enters into a 2-year CDS on a notional amount of $10 million of 5-year bonds issued by the Crescent Corporation as a protection buyer. The swap specifies an annual premium of 55 basis points and cash settlement. Assume that the Crescent Corporation defaults at the end of the first year when the bonds are trading at 60 cents on the dollar. Calculate the cash flows associated with the credit default swap.

Answer:

The Rose Foundation would pay $55,000 (0.0055 × $10 million) at the beginning of the first year to the seller of the CDS. If Crescent defaults after one year, the Rose Foundation would receive a payment of $4,000,000 = (1 – 0.6) × $10 million. This represents the decline in value of the bonds.

Credit Default Swaps vs. Corporate Bonds

Credit default swaps are similar to bonds because when credit risk increases, both CDS premiums and bond yields increase.

However, a corporate bond yield spread reflects compensation over the risk-free rate for two sources of risk:

1. A spread reflecting the **interest rate risk** (also called funding risk) of the bond.

2. A spread related to **credit risk** of the issuer.

In contrast, credit default swaps only reflect the credit risk of the reference obligation, but not its interest rate risk.

LOS 63.b: Explain the advantages of using credit derivatives over other credit instruments.

Credit default swaps and other credit derivatives have a number of advantages over other credit instruments.

- *Risk management.* Credit derivatives allow credit risk to be managed separately from interest rate risk.
- *Short positions.* A short position can be taken in fixed income securities by buying a CDS or other credit derivative. In contrast, shorting the underlying credit obligation can be challenging and cost prohibitive, especially if the obligation is in high demand in the repo market.
- *Liquidity.* The credit derivative market is more liquid than the underlying cash market. Over time, trading in CDSs has increased such that 3-, 5-, 7-, and 10-year maturity swaps are fairly liquid.
- *Flexibility.* Credit derivatives facilitate credit, maturity, and currency positions not otherwise available in the underlying cash market. For example, if an investor wanted a position with a 4-year maturity, a customized contract could be devised using 3- and 5-year maturity swaps.
- *Confidentiality.* Credit derivatives are confidential, over-the-counter contracts. In contrast, in a loan, the issuer has knowledge of the contract.

LOS 63.c: Explain the use of credit derivatives by the various market participants.

As the CDS market has grown, the number of participants in credit derivatives has increased as well. The major participants are commercial banks, investment banks, hedge funds, and insurance firms. *Commercial banks* use credit derivatives to hedge their exposures arising from their loan portfolios and to satisfy regulators by buying credit protection. They are the largest participant in the market.

Investment banks act as dealers in the credit derivatives market, providing liquidity to the rest of the market. They also use credit derivatives to hedge their corporate bonds, and they have trading desks that seek to exploit mispricing.

Hedge funds now specialize in the trading of credit risk in addition to traditional convertible arbitrage and distressed debt opportunities. In their pursuit of relative value opportunities, they have become quite active and are important providers of liquidity to the market. Hedge funds represent the fastest growing segment of the credit derivatives market.

Professor's Note: Convertible arbitrage style is the name for the strategy in which the manager takes a long position in a convertible bond and sells short the associated stock. This strategy is effective if the convertible bond and the stock are mispriced relative to each other. In a distressed securities strategy, the fund manager generally takes a long position in the financial securities (bank debt, bonds, preferred stock, common stock, subordinated debt, etc.) of a financially troubled company and holds the securities through the subsequent restructuring or bankruptcy process. Distressed securities strategies may also infrequently involve short positions.

Life insurance, property and casualty insurance, reinsurers, and monoline companies take long positions in credit by selling protection.

Professor's Note: Monoline companies offer credit products without a corresponding retail banking location. Capital One is an example of such a firm.

Fund managers also use credit derivatives to exploit mispricing, and corporations use credit derivatives for hedging and income enhancement.

Structured Credit Products

Structured credit products are credit investments with various tranches of risk, with the higher-risk tranches offering higher yield. They are the fastest growing product in the credit derivatives market. In the case of a synthetic collateralized debt obligation (CDO), the exposure to a basket of CDSs is sold. The CDO can have customized or standardized terms (in the case of index products).

Insurance companies typically invest in the more senior tranches, while hedge funds pursue the higher-risk, higher-yielding subordinated tranches. Commercial banks and investment banks take positions in all the various tranches.

LOS 63.d: Discuss credit derivatives trading strategies and how they are used by hedge funds and other managers.

Credit derivatives are used in many strategies, the most common being the basis trade, curve trade, index trade, options trade, capital structure trade, and correlation trade.

Basis Trade

In a basis trade, the CDS premium is compared to the asset swap spread of the underlying bond. The latter refers to a bond's yield above a benchmark swap rate. This spread should reflect the credit risk of the bond. If it is higher than the CDS premium, the basis is negative and, to exploit the arbitrage opportunity, the investor should buy the bond and buy the CDS (in other words, buy protection against the long position).

One key drawback to this strategy is that the investor must finance the trade. Additionally, these opportunities quickly disappear, and the underlying bond might be scarce or not of the same terms as the CDS.

Example: Basis trade

A General Motors bond is at 240 basis points above LIBOR in an asset swap. The annual CDS premium is 210 basis points. Construct a basis trade to exploit the opportunity.

Answer:

The investor should go long the General Motors bond and buy the CDS, resulting in a negative basis trade strategy return of 30 basis points annually. The investor earns 240 basis points, pays 210 basis points, nets 30 basis points annually, and is protected against credit risk.

Curve Trade

In a curve trade, the investor has different opinions than the market about the long-term versus short-term prospects for a bond issuer. The trade can be a flattener or a steepener. In the flattener, the investor believes that the issuer has some short-term instability, but that its long-term prospects are sound. In this case, the investor buys a short-term CDS and sells a long-term CDS.

Example: Credit curve flattener

An investor believes that, due to an uncertain economy, the delivery firm FedEx will experience short-term volatility, but that its longer-term prospects are good. A 2-year CDS is trading at 120 bps, and a 7-year CDS is trading at 380 bps. Construct a curve trade.

Answer:

The investor should buy a 2-year CDS for 120 bps and sell a 7-year CDS for 380 bps. If FedEx does indeed experience short-term volatility, the long position in the 2-year CDS becomes more valuable.

In a credit curve steepener, the investor believes that the issuer has the ability to subsist in the short term, but that its long-term prospects are poor. The sale of the short-term CDS partially finances the purchase of the long-term CDS. The investor can either match notional principals of the opposing positions (thereby taking a position on duration) or match durations to manage the risk of these trades (thereby taking a position on default risk).

Example: Credit curve steepener

An investor believes that General Motors is unlikely to do well over the longer term but that it has sufficient cash to continue over the short term. A 2-year CDS is trading for 220 bps, and a 7-year CDS is trading for 400 bps. Construct a curve trade and take a position on duration.

Answer:

The investor should sell a 2-year CDS for 220 bps and buy a 7-year CDS for 400 bps, both with the same notional principal. The net cost of the long-term protection is 180 bps.

Index Trade

Credit indices, such as the Dow Jones iTraxx Asian and Europe indices, represent opportunities to use CDS to exploit perceived mispricing. The Dow Jones iTraxx Japan index, for example, is an equally weighted portfolio of 50 Japanese issuers.

There are numerous strategies an investor can use with credit indices.

- A short index position can be used to hedge a portfolio of credits or exploit an expected increase in market-wide credit risk.
- If an investor is bullish on a market or sector but bearish on particular issues, he could go long an index and short specific issues.
- If an investor is bearish on bonds and bullish on stocks, she could go short the credit index and long an equity index.

Options Trade

Although options on CDSs have slowly increased in popularity, CDS options markets are not as liquid as equity options markets. Options on credit indices are more liquid, but single issuer options are less liquid. There are European receiver options and payer options available in the market.

- In a receiver option, the option buyer has the right to sell a CDS (go long the underlying) at some future date. An investor with a bullish outlook would buy a receiver option in anticipation of tightening credit spreads.
- In a payer option, the option buyer has the right to buy a CDS (short the underlying) at some future date. An investor with a bearish outlook would buy a payer option in anticipation of widening of credit spreads.

These options will change in value as the value of the underlying changes. They can be used to provide leverage, hedge, take a position in volatility, create straddles, and implement other option strategies.

Capital Structure Trade

In a capital structure trade, the investor uses CDSs to exploit different views on a firm's various securities, as in the following examples:

- The investor believes that a subsidiary has less credit risk than the parent, so he sells a CDS on the subsidiary and buys a CDS on the parent.
- The investor uses his opinion on a firm's recovery rates to sell a CDS on the firm's subordinated debt and buy a cheaper CDS on the senior debt, earning the difference in the CDS premiums.
- The investor has differing views on the firm's debt and equity. For example, in a leveraged buyout, the firm's equity may increase in value while the debt decreases in value (due to the increase in leverage). An investor could exploit the opportunity by buying both a CDS and an equity call option.

If the investor's expectations are realized in any of the above strategies, he would profit from changes in the spreads for the strategy's components.

Correlation Trade

Instead of selling protection on several individual CDSs, an investor could sell protection on a basket of CDSs. One such basket is a **first-to-default swap**, where the number of CDSs in the basket is typically five. In this structure, the investor would provide protection for the first (and only the first) default. If one of the reference obligations defaults, the investor owes the basket's notional amount and receives the defaulted reference obligation.

The higher the number of CDSs in the basket, the higher the basket's premium (because there is a greater probability of one of them defaulting). Higher spreads on the individual CDSs in the basket, reflecting greater credit risk, result in higher basket premiums.

The pricing of the basket default swap also depends on the **default correlation**, which is the probability that two of the reference obligations in a basket will default concurrently. Higher default correlations result in lower premiums (the protection offered by the first-to-default basket is worth less to the protection buyer when it is likely that several of the obligations will default at the same time).

From the investor's perspective, the advantage of providing protection in a first-to-default basket (relative to providing protection in one CDS) is that the premium received is higher, as it is usually 60% to 80% of the summed premiums of the five individual CDSs. Furthermore, the investor's exposure is limited to only one reference obligation because the contract terminates after the first default.

Another type of correlation trade utilizes a delta hedge of different tranches of a synthetic CDO. For example, a position in an equity tranche could be delta hedged with a debt tranche position, thereby earning the net difference between the equity tranche yield and the debt tranche yield. The equity tranche could also be hedged with a basket of single issuer CDSs.

KEY CONCEPTS

LOS 63.a

A credit default swap provides compensation to the buyer when a credit event occurs on a referenced bond or loan. Its pricing depends on the credit risk of the reference obligation, not the interest rate risk.

CDS are similar to corporate bonds in that both provide compensation for credit risk. They differ in that CDS do not provide compensation for interest rate risk.

LOS 63.b

Relative to the underlying, credit derivatives allow credit risk to be separately managed from interest rate risk, facilitate short positions, offer greater liquidity, provide customized positions, and provide confidentiality.

LOS 63.c

Banks use credit derivatives for hedging and regulatory purposes. Investment banks act as market makers, hedge exposures, and seek mispriced situations (as do hedge funds and fund managers). Insurance firms sell protection, and corporations use them for hedging and income enhancement.

LOS 63.d

Credit derivatives can be used in a wide variety of strategies, the most common of which are: basis trade, curve trade, index trade, options trade, capital structure trade, and correlation trade.

CONCEPT CHECKERS

1. An investor would like to hedge a long position in a bond using a credit default swap (CDS). Which of the following expectations and positions would be *most appropriate*?

Expectation	Position
A. The Federal Reserve may raise interest rates	Buy a CDS
B. The Federal Reserve may raise interest rates	Sell a CDS
C. The issuer may restructure its capital structure	Buy a CDS

2. An investor would like to take a confidential, customized position in the credit markets. Which market provides the *best* availability of these features: the underlying cash market or the credit derivatives market?

Confidentiality	Customization
A. Cash market	Credit derivatives market
B. Credit derivatives market	Cash market
C. Credit derivatives market	Credit derivatives market

3. How do insurance firms typically use credit derivatives, and what is their position in the underlying asset from buying or selling protection?

Credit derivative use	Position in the underlying
A. Buy protection	Short
B. Sell protection	Long
C. Sell protection	Short

4. An investor believes that the difficulties for an airline will soon subside. What type and subcategory of credit derivative strategy will they *most likely* use?

Type of strategy	Subcategory of strategy
A. Basis trade	Flattener
B. Basis trade	Steepener
C. Curve trade	Flattener

ANSWERS – CONCEPT CHECKERS

1. **C** A credit default swap (CDS) only provides a hedge against a credit event, which is usually defined in a CDS as bankruptcy, entity default, and restructuring. If a bond investor was worried about interest rate risk, a credit default swap would not provide a useful hedge. The credit default swap would only provide a hedge against Fed action to the extent that the Fed action increased the credit risk of the issue.

   The investor should buy a CDS because this will provide the investor with compensation should the bond experience an increase in credit risk.

2. **C** The investor should use the credit derivatives market for both features. Relative to the underlying cash market, it offers greater liquidity, greater ease of creating short positions, customization of terms, and confidentiality. In addition, it allows credit risk to be separated from interest rate risk.

3. **B** Insurance firms take a long position in the underlying asset by selling protection in the credit derivatives market. For example, in the case of a sold credit default swap, they earn the premium from its sale and do not owe the counterparty compensation as long as there is not a credit event. They are thus long the underlying credit instrument.

4. **C** The investor will likely use a curve trade and, more specifically, a curve flattener. The investor buys a short-term CDS and sells a long-term CDS, because the investor believes that the issuer has some short-term instability, but that the long-term prospects are better. If the investor's expectations are realized, they would profit from relative changes in the spreads for the short-term and long-term CDS.

18 minutes

Use the following information to answer Questions 1 through 6.

Babatunde Honny, CFA, has operated his own portfolio management business for many years. Several of his clients have fixed income positions, and one of Honny's analysts has advised him that the firm can improve the performance of these portfolios through swaps. Honny has begun investigating the properties of swaps. His plan is first to establish some minor positions to gain some experience before actively using swaps on behalf of his clients.

Honny knows that the most basic type of swap is the plain vanilla swap where one counterparty pays LIBOR as the floating rate, and the other counterparty pays a fixed rate determined by the swap market. He feels this would be a good place to begin and plans to engage in a 2-year, annual-pay plain vanilla swap where he pays LIBOR and receives the fixed swap rate from the other counterparty. To get an idea regarding the swap rate he can expect on the 2-year swap, he estimates the swap rate using the corresponding spot rates for 1- and 2-year horizons, which are 5.0% and 4.6%, respectively.

He finds that when taking a swap position that there are other types of risks to consider. Honny thinks he should try to hedge some of these other types of risk the contract might have. He first focuses on credit risk. He finds it interesting that the credit risk of a swap typically varies over the time between inception and maturity. Also, there is something called potential credit risk, which also varies over the life of the swap. Sometimes current credit risk is more of a concern than potential credit risk, sometimes potential credit risk is more of a concern than current credit risk, and sometimes they are of equal concern.

As he learns more, Honny considers other possible swap positions that he might take. He is considering entering into a 4-year swap instead of a 2-year swap, but he knows this can be more risky. Instead of a 4-year swap, he investigates taking the 2-year swap position, which he first considered, and then taking a position in a derivative that will allow him to extend the horizon two more years when the 2-year swap expires. He finds that there are two appropriate varieties of derivatives that can be written on swaps that can achieve this goal: (1) swaptions and (2) forward swaps.

One of Honny's clients, George Rosen, is aware of Honny's plans to use swaps and derivatives on swaps in the management of his clients' portfolios. Rosen has a position for which he thinks a swap strategy will be appropriate. Rosen asks Honny to arrange for him a swaption that matures in three years. Honny is uncertain of the level of Rosen's familiarity with swaps and swaptions, so he wants to make sure that the derivative is appropriate for the client. He asks Rosen exactly what he intends to accomplish by entering into the swaption.

Honny realizes that more of his clients may approach him about using swaptions. He wants to be able to advise his clients about how to use them, how to close positions early, and how to settle positions at maturity. He finds that there are several ways to close a swaption position and to settle a swaption at maturity.

1. Which of the following would be the *least appropriate* alternative investments to replicate the exposure Honny will get from the 2-year, plain vanilla swap position that he plans to take?
    A. Short a series of interest rate puts and short a series of interest rate calls.
    B. Short a series of bond futures.
    C. Short a series of forward rate agreements.

2. Given the 1- and 2-year rates, the 2-year swap fixed rate would be *closest* to:
    A. 4.20%.
    B. 4.61%.
    C. 4.80%.

3. At the inception of a swap, the:
    A. potential credit risk is greater than the current credit risk.
    B. current credit risk is greater than the potential credit risk.
    C. current credit risk is equal to the potential credit risk, and both are equal to zero.

4. To have the right to extend the 2-year swap position when the swap expires, the *most appropriate* position for Honny would be to long a:
    A. payer swaption.
    B. receiver swaption.
    C. forward swap.

5. Which of the following is *least likely* a reason that Rosen might want to enter into a swaption with a maturity of three years? To:
    A. close an existing swaption position.
    B. hedge a floating rate bond that he owns with three years to maturity.
    C. have the right to terminate a 5-year swap early.

6. Which of the following is the *least likely* way the market value of a swaption at expiration can be received?
    A. As an annuity settlement.
    B. By paying the swap spread.
    C. By entering into the underlying swap.

SELF-TEST ANSWERS: DERIVATIVES

1. **B** Since Honny will pay the floating rate in the 2-year swap, he gains when the floating rate goes down and loses when it goes up (relative to expectations at inception). This exposure could be replicated with either a short position in a series of FRAs or with a series of short interest rate calls and long interest rate puts. Since short bond futures gain when floating rates increase and gain when floating rates increase, such a position would give him an exposure opposite to the floating rate payer position in a fixed-for-floating interest rate swap.

2. **B** The first step is to calculate the discount factors, based upon the 1-year and 2-year spot rates provided (note that we are assuming periods of exactly one year in length):

$$Z_{1\text{-year}} = \frac{1}{(1.05)^1} = 0.9524$$

$$Z_{2\text{-year}} = \frac{1}{(1.046)^2} = 0.9140$$

$$\text{swap fixed rate} = \frac{1 - Z_{2\text{-year}}}{Z_{1\text{-year}} + Z_{2\text{-year}}} = \frac{1 - 0.9140}{0.9524 + 0.9140} = 0.0461$$

3. **A** At the inception of a swap the expected value of the swap is zero, and there is no current credit risk. Potential credit risk always exists. Potential credit risk is typically assumed to be low at inception because of the high credit worthiness of the swap market participants. Yet, even at the beginning of a swap, there is some potential credit risk, because the counterparty may experience a change in credit worthiness during the life of the swap.

4. **B** To have the "right" to extend the swap, a swaption is the more appropriate choice. Forward swaps require both counterparties to engage in the swap (i.e., an obligation is created). A payer swaption gives the owner the right to pay the fixed rate, and a receiver swaption gives the owner the right to receive the fixed rate.

5. **B** The swaption can be used to hedge the planned issuance of a floating rate bond in the future, but the instrument would not be an effective means of hedging an existing floating rate bond that expires on or before the maturity date of the swaption. It is possible to use swaptions to achieve all of the other objectives listed.

6. **B** The swap spread refers to the difference between the fixed rate of a swap and the comparable Treasury notes and would not play a direct role in the settlement of a swaption. Entering into the underlying swap is simply the exercise of the swaption that is in-the-money. Both settlement with a spot payment or the promise of a series of payments are acceptable ways to settle the swap.

PORTFOLIO CONCEPTS

EXAM FOCUS

This is a very long, intensive topic review of a very important Level 2 topic, so expect it to be tested extensively on the exam. It will require a significant amount of time for you to master the concepts addressed in the LOS. You should focus on both the broad concepts and the particular details. Although everything in this topic review is fair game for the exam, you must have a firm grasp of the key differences among (and applications to portfolio management of) mean-variance analysis, the capital asset pricing model, the single-factor market model, the arbitrage pricing theory, macroeconomic multifactor models, and fundamental multifactor models.

LOS 64.a: Discuss mean-variance analysis and its assumptions, and calculate the expected return and the standard deviation of return for a portfolio of two or three assets.

Mean-variance analysis refers to the use of expected returns, variances, and covariances of individual investments to analyze the risk-return tradeoff of combinations (i.e., portfolios) of these assets.

Over a half century has passed since Professor Harry Markowitz established the tenets of mean-variance analysis, or capital market theory, the focal point of which is the efficient frontier. Several assumptions underlie mean-variance analysis. The assumptions establish a uniformity of investors, which greatly simplifies the analysis.

The main assumptions of mean-variance analysis can be summarized as follows:

- All investors are **risk averse**. Investors minimize risk for any given level of expected return, or, stated differently, investors demand additional compensation in exchange for additional risk. Investors may differ in their degree of risk aversion, but the key is that all investors are assumed to be risk averse to some degree.
- Expected returns, variances, and covariances are known for all assets. Investors know the future values of these parameters.
- Investors create optimal portfolios by relying solely on expected returns, variances, and covariances. No other distributional parameter is used. For example, often returns are assumed to follow a normal distribution in which skewness and kurtosis can be ignored.
- Investors face no taxes or transaction costs. Therefore, there is no difference between before-tax gross returns and after-tax net returns, placing all investors on equal footing.

Mean-variance analysis is used to identify optimal or efficient portfolios. Before we can discuss the implications of efficient portfolios, however, we must first be able to understand and calculate portfolio expected returns and standard deviations.

EXPECTED RETURN AND STANDARD DEVIATION FOR A TWO-ASSET PORTFOLIO

The **expected return** on a portfolio is a weighted average of the expected returns on the individual assets that are included in the portfolio. For example, for a two-asset portfolio:

$$E(R_p) = w_1 E(R_1) + w_2 E(R_2)$$

where:
$E(R_p)$ = expected return on Portfolio P
w_i = proportion ("weight") of the portfolio allocated to Asset i
$E(R_i)$ = expected return on Asset i

The weights (w_1 and w_2) must sum to 100% for a two-asset portfolio.

The variance of a two-asset portfolio equals:

$$\sigma_P^2 = w_1^2 \sigma_1^2 + w_2^2 \sigma_2^2 + 2 w_1 w_2 \text{Cov}_{1,2}$$

where:
σ_p^2 = variance of the returns for Portfolio P
σ_1^2 = variance of the returns for Asset 1
σ_2^2 = variance of the returns for Asset 2
w_i = proportion (weight) of the portfolio allocated to Asset i
$\text{Cov}_{1,2}$ = covariance between the returns of the two assets

The covariance, $\text{Cov}_{1,2}$, measures the strength of the relationship between the returns earned on assets 1 and 2. The covariance is unbounded (ranges from negative infinity to positive infinity), and, therefore, is not a very useful measure of the strength of the relationship between two asset's returns. Instead, we often scale the covariance by the standard deviations of the two assets to derive the **correlation**, $\rho_{1,2}$:

$$\rho_{1,2} = \frac{\text{Cov}_{1,2}}{\sigma_1 \sigma_2}$$

From the previous equation, notice that the covariance equals $\rho_{1,2} \sigma_1 \sigma_2$, where $\rho_{1,2}$ is the correlation of returns between the two assets. Therefore, the variance of the two-asset portfolio can be written:

$$\sigma_P^2 = w_1^2 \sigma_1^2 + w_2^2 \sigma_2^2 + 2 w_1 w_2 \rho_{1,2} \sigma_1 \sigma_2$$

Example: Expected return and standard deviation for a two-asset portfolio

Using the information in the following figure, calculate the expected return and standard deviation of the two-asset portfolio.

Characteristics for a Two-Stock Portfolio

	Caffeine Plus	*Sparklin'*
Amount invested	$40,000	$60,000
Expected return	11%	25%
Standard deviation	15%	20%
Correlation	0.30	

Answer:

First, determine the **weight** of each stock relative to the entire portfolio. Since the investments are $40,000 and $60,000, we know the total value of the portfolio is $100,000:

w_c = investment/portfolio value = $40,000/$100,000 = 0.40

w_s = investment/portfolio value = $60,000/$100,000 = 0.60

Next, we determine the **expected return** on the portfolio:

$$E(R_p) = w_c E(R_c) + w_s E(R_s)$$

$$E(R_p) = (0.40)(0.11) + (0.60)(0.25) = 0.1940 = 19.40\%$$

Then, we calculate the **variance** of the portfolio:

$$\sigma_p^2 = w_c^2 \sigma_c^2 + w_s^2 \sigma_s^2 + 2 w_c w_s \rho_{cs} \sigma_c \sigma_s$$
$$= (0.40)^2 (0.15)^2 + (0.60)^2 (0.20)^2 + 2(0.40)(0.60)(0.30)(0.15)(0.20)$$
$$= 0.02232$$

And, finally, the **standard deviation** of the portfolio:

$$\sigma_p = \sqrt{\sigma_p^2} = \sqrt{0.02232} = 0.1494 = 14.94\%$$

In the Caffeine Plus and Sparklin' example, we calculated the expected return and standard deviation of one possible combination: 40% in Caffeine Plus and 60% in Sparklin'. An infinite number of combinations of the two stocks are possible, however. We can plot these combinations on a graph with expected return on the *y*-axis and standard deviation on the *x*-axis, commonly referred to as plotting in risk/return "space." Figure 1 shows some of these combinations.

Figure 1: Portfolio Returns for Various Weights of Two Assets

$w_{Caffeine\ Plus}$	100%	80%	60%	40%	20%	0%
$w_{Sparklin'}$	0%	20%	40%	60%	80%	100%
$\hat{R}_p$	11.00%	13.80%	16.60%	19.40%	22.20%	25.00%
σ_p	15.00%	13.74%	13.72%	14.94%	17.10%	20.00%

The plot in Figure 2 represents all possible expected return and standard deviation combinations attainable by investing in varying amounts of Caffeine Plus and Sparklin'.

Figure 2: Expected Return and Standard Deviation Combinations

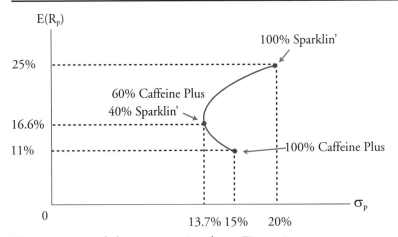

There are several things to notice about Figure 2:

- If 100% of the portfolio is allocated to Caffeine Plus, the portfolio will have the expected return and standard deviation of Caffeine Plus (i.e., Caffeine Plus *is* the portfolio), and the investment return and risk combination is at the lower end of the curve.

- As the investment in Caffeine Plus is decreased and the investment in Sparklin' is increased, the investment moves up the curve to the point where the portfolio's expected return is 16.6% and its standard deviation is 13.72% (labeled 60% Caffeine Plus/40% Sparklin').

- Finally, if 100% of the portfolio is allocated to Sparklin', the portfolio will have the expected return and standard deviation of Sparklin', and the investment return and risk combination is at the upper end of the curve (e.g., higher risk and higher expected return).

Three-Asset Portfolio

Just as in the two-asset case, the **expected return** on a portfolio of *three* assets is the weighted average of the returns on the individual assets:

$$E(R_P) = w_1 E(R_1) + w_2 E(R_2) + w_3 E(R_3)$$

where:
$$w_1 + w_2 + w_3 = 100\%$$

The standard deviation of a portfolio of three assets is calculated similarly to that for the two-asset portfolio, except that there are three new terms: a weighted variance term (for the third asset) and two more covariance terms (for assets 1 and 3 and assets 2 and 3).

$$\sigma_P^2 = w_1^2\sigma_1^2 + w_2^2\sigma_2^2 + \left[w_3^2\sigma_3^2\right] + 2w_1w_2\,cov_{1,2} + \left[2w_1w_3\,cov_{1,3} + 2w_2w_3\,cov_{2,3}\right]$$

$$\sigma_P^2 = w_1^2\sigma_1^2 + w_2^2\sigma_2^2 + w_3^2\sigma_3^2 + 2w_1w_2\rho_{1,2}\sigma_1\sigma_2 + 2w_1w_3\rho_{1,3}\sigma_1\sigma_3 + 2w_2w_3\rho_{2,3}\sigma_2\sigma_3$$

$$\sigma_P = \sqrt{\sigma_P^2}$$

Example: Three-asset portfolio

Calculate the expected return and standard deviation of the three-asset portfolio shown in the following figure.

Expected Returns and Standard Deviations for Three Stocks

	Caffeine Plus	*Sparklin'*	*Golo*
Amount invested	$40,000	$25,000	$35,000
Expected return	11%	25%	30%
Standard deviation	15%	20%	25%
	Correlations		
Caffeine Plus and Sparklin'	0.30		
Caffeine Plus and Golo	0.10		
Sparklin' and Golo	0.50		

Answer:

First, determine the **weight** of each stock in the portfolio:

$$w_c = \$40,000/\$100,000 = 0.40$$

$$w_s = \$25,000/\$100,000 = 0.25$$

$$w_g = \$35,000/\$100,000 = 0.35$$

Next, calculate the **expected return** of the portfolio:

$$E(R_p) = w_c E(R_c) = w_s E(R_s) + w_g E(R_g)$$
$$= (0.40)(0.11) + (0.25)(0.25) + (0.35)(0.30) = 0.2115 = 21.15\%$$

Now, calculate the **variance** and **standard deviation** of the portfolio:

Portfolio variance:

$$= (0.40)^2 (0.15)^2 + (0.25)^2 (0.20)^2 + (0.35)^2 (0.25)^2$$
$$+ 2(0.40)(0.25)(0.30)(0.15)(0.20) + 2(0.40)(0.35)(0.10)(0.15)(0.25)$$
$$+ 2(0.25)(0.35)(0.50)(0.20)(0.25)$$
$$= 0.02098$$

Porfolio standard deviation $= \sqrt{0.020981} = 0.14485 = 14.485\%$

LOS 64.b: Explain the minimum-variance and efficient frontiers, and discuss the steps to solve for the minimum-variance frontier.

The Minimum-Variance Frontier

A **minimum-variance portfolio** is one that has the smallest variance among all portfolios with identical expected return. For instance, assume we wish to earn a return equal to 25% on a portfolio comprising Caffeine Plus, Sparklin', and Golo from the three-asset example above. Many different portfolio combinations of the three stocks provide an expected return of 25%. One possibility is simply to invest 100% of the portfolio in Sparklin' stock. The expected return on the portfolio will equal 25% and the variance will equal $(0.20)^2 = 0.04 = 4\%$. But, we can achieve a 25% expected return on our portfolio with smaller variance by forming a portfolio of the three stocks. In this example, the minimum-variance portfolio is the one that provides a 25% expected return with the smallest possible variance among all portfolios that provide a 25% expected return.

Figure 3 illustrates the portfolio possibilities all of which are constrained to have a 25% expected return. All portfolios with an expected return of 25% lie on the horizontal line, but the portfolios have different variances (risk). All the portfolios comprise the identical set of three assets, but with different weightings. Portfolios to the left on the horizontal line have smaller variance (lower risk). If faced with these portfolio possibilities, any risk-averse investor will prefer the portfolio lying farthest to the left (the minimum-variance Portfolio E).

Figure 3: Minimum-Variance Portfolio

 Professor's Note: The mathematical solution for the minimum-variance portfolio is beyond the scope of analysis here. Instead, be sure to understand the general steps that are followed when deriving each minimum-variance portfolio.

The **minimum-variance frontier** is a graph of the expected return/variance combinations for all minimum-variance portfolios. The shape of the minimum-variance frontier for many assets (stocks) will look similar to that for two assets (e.g., Figure 2), but constructing it is considerably more complicated. Here are the steps in the process:

1. *Estimation step*: Estimate the expected return and variance for each individual asset and the correlation of each pair of assets. Historical standard deviations and correlations provide unbiased estimates of their future measures, but we need good forecasts of the future.

2. *Optimization step*: Solve for the weights that minimize the portfolio variance subject to the following constraints:
   - The portfolio expected return equals a pre-specified target return, τ:

$$\sum_{i=1}^{n} w_i E(R_i) = \tau$$

   - The portfolio weights sum to 100%: $\sum_{i=1}^{n} w_i = 100\% = 1$

Repeat Step 2 for many different values of τ. We would not want to solve this problem by hand! Fortunately, Step 2 usually is accomplished with the aid of a computer.

The optimization step solves for the weights, w_i^*, that minimize the portfolio variance subject to the two constraints (the asterisk signifies that the values determined for the weights are the ones that guarantee that the portfolio variance has been minimized).

3. *Calculation step*: Calculate the expected returns and variances for all the minimum-variance portfolios determined in Step 2. The graph of the expected return and variance combinations from Step 2 is the minimum-variance frontier.

For instance, for one of the portfolio expected return choices in Step 2, assume we select a target portfolio expected return of 10% ($t = 10\%$). After the weights have been determined in Step 2, we then let the computer calculate the variance for the portfolio, using the minimum-variance weights. The optimized portfolio, P^*, will have the smallest possible variance among all portfolios that have an expected return equal to 10%.

For example, suppose the results in Figure 4 have been derived from the estimation, optimization, and calculation steps discussed previously.

Figure 4: Expected Return/Variance Combinations

Portfolio	Expected Return	Variance
A	0.02	0.05
B	0.04	0.02
C	0.06	0.01
D	0.08	0.02
E	0.10	0.05
F	0.12	0.10
G	0.14	0.17

Portfolio A has the smallest possible variance among all portfolios with an expected return of 2%, Portfolio B has the smallest possible variance among all portfolios with an expected return of 4%, and so on. All seven portfolios are *minimum-variance portfolios* (i.e., derived from the estimation, optimization, and calculations steps described previously).

Portfolio C, in the previous example, is the **global minimum-variance portfolio**—the portfolio with the smallest variance among all possible portfolios.

The graph of the minimum-variance frontier using the data in Figure 4 is provided in Figure 5 (the minimum-variance frontier is the curve from Point A to Point G).

Figure 5: Minimum-Variance Frontier: Expected Return vs. Variance

In practice, the minimum-variance frontier is plotted in expected return, standard deviation space. The standard deviation is easier to work with than variance because it is measured in the same units (single percentage units, rather than squared percentage units provided by the variance) as expected return.

Notice that the minimum-variance frontier in Figure 5 includes some portfolios that no rational investor would select. All portfolios lying on the convex portion (negatively sloped portion, from A to C) of the minimum-variance frontier are inferior to portfolios lying on the concave portion (positively sloped portion, from C to G) of the minimum-variance frontier. For example, portfolios A and E have identical risk, but Portfolio E has a much higher expected return, and a similar contrast exists for Portfolio D versus Portfolio B. All rational investors would prefer Portfolio D over Portfolio B and Portfolio E over Portfolio A.

The Efficient Frontier

Portfolios such as D and E in Figure 5 are called **efficient portfolios**, which are portfolios that have:

- Minimum risk of all portfolios with the same expected return.
- Maximum expected return for all portfolios with the same risk.

 Professor's Note: Another way to say this is that Portfolio D "dominates" Portfolio B and Portfolio E "dominates" Portfolio A.

This brings us to one of the most important concepts in portfolio theory—the **efficient frontier**, developed by Professor Harry Markowitz in 1952 (for which he was awarded the 1990 Nobel Prize in Economics). The *efficient frontier* is a plot of the expected return and risk combinations of all efficient portfolios, all of which lie along the upper portion of the minimum-variance frontier (from Point C to Point G in Figure 5).

The efficient frontier is an extremely useful portfolio management tool. Once the investor's risk tolerance is determined and quantified in terms of variance or standard deviation, the optimal portfolio for the investor can be easily identified. For example, the best portfolio for an investor willing to accept variance equal to 0.02 is Portfolio D. The best portfolio for an investor willing to accept variance equal to 0.17 is Portfolio G. Note that the investor choosing Portfolio D is more risk averse than the investor choosing Portfolio G.

LOS 64.c: Discuss diversification benefits, and explain how the correlation in a two-asset portfolio and the number of assets in a multi-asset portfolio affect the diversification benefits.

Portfolio diversification refers to the strategy of reducing risk by combining many different types of assets into a portfolio. Portfolio variance falls as more assets are added to the portfolio because not all asset prices move in the same direction at the same time. Therefore, portfolio diversification is affected by the:

- *Correlations between assets*: lower correlation means greater diversification benefits.
- *Number of assets included in the portfolio*: more assets mean greater diversification benefits.

Effect of Correlation on Portfolio Diversification

As the correlation between two assets *decreases*, the benefits of diversification *increase*. As the correlation decreases, there is less tendency for stock returns to move together. The separate movements of each stock serve to reduce the volatility of a portfolio to a level that is less than the weighted sum of its individual components (e.g., less than $w_1 \sigma_1 + w_2 \sigma_2$). No diversification is achieved if the correlation between assets equals +1. The greatest diversification is achieved if the correlation between assets equals −1.

To illustrate the effects of correlation on diversification, consider the expected return and standard deviation data derived for domestic stocks, DS, and domestic bonds, DB as shown in Figure 6.

Figure 6: Diversification Example

	Expected Return	Standard Deviation
Domestic Stocks (DS)	0.20	0.30
Domestic Bonds (DB)	0.10	0.15

The expected return, standard deviation combinations for various portfolio percentage allocations to domestic stocks and domestic bonds for each of the following correlations +1, 0, and −1 is shown in Figure 7.

Figure 7: Expected Return/Standard Deviation Combinations for Various Allocations

Correlation	DS % Allocation	DB % Allocation	$E(R_p)$	σ_P
+1	100.00	0.00	0.200	0.300
	66.67	33.33	0.167	0.250
	50.00	50.00	0.150	0.225
	33.33	66.67	0.133	0.200
	0.00	100.00	0.100	0.150
0	100.00	0.00	0.200	0.300
	66.67	33.33	0.167	0.206
	50.00	50.00	0.150	0.168
	33.33	66.67	0.133	0.141
	0.00	100.00	0.100	0.150
−1	100.00	0.00	0.200	0.300
	66.67	33.33	0.167	0.150
	50.00	50.00	0.150	0.075
	33.33	66.67	0.133	0.000
	0.00	100.00	0.100	0.150

The plot of the expected returns and standard deviations for each of the three correlations is provided in Figure 8.

Figure 8: Effects of Correlation on Portfolio Risk

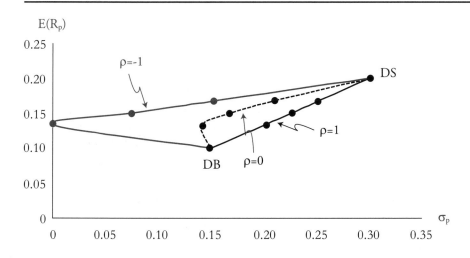

The lower and upper endpoints of the minimum-variance frontier in Figure 5 denote the risk and return of assets DB and DS, respectively. Starting at the point representing 100% invested in DB, as we increase the weight of DS and decrease the weight of DB, the frontier bulges to the left. The amount of bulge (i.e., the diversification effect) is a function of the correlation between the two assets.

As indicated in Figure 8, the lower the correlation between the returns of the stocks in the portfolio, the greater the diversification benefits. If the correlation equals +1 (the solid black line), the minimum-variance frontier is a straight line between the two points (DB and DS), and there is no benefit to diversification. If the correlation equals –1 (the dashed blue line), the minimum-variance frontier is two straight-line segments, and there exists a portfolio combination of stocks and bonds with a standard deviation of *zero* (the allocation of 66.67% to domestic bonds and 33.33% to domestic stocks).

Effect of Number of Assets on Portfolio Diversification

While the previous example shows how diversification benefits increase as correlation among assets decreases, also note that diversification benefits increase as the number of assets increases. For instance, assume we add international bonds to the asset mix. Because international bonds are not perfectly positively correlated with domestic stocks or bonds, diversification benefits will increase (portfolio risk will fall) as illustrated in Figure 9. The graph assumes that the risk on international bonds is higher than the risk of domestic bonds, the expected return on international bonds is less than the expected return on domestic stocks, and the correlation of international bonds with domestic stocks and/or bonds is less than +1.

Figure 9: Effect of Number of Assets on Diversification

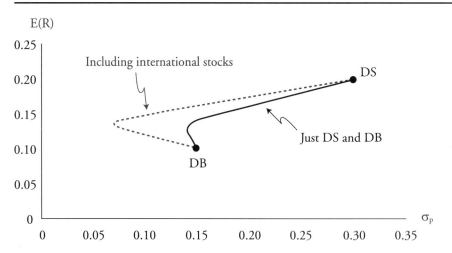

Note that portfolio risk will fall at a decreasing rate, as the number of assets included in the portfolio rises. The standard deviation of a large, well-diversified portfolio will get closer and closer to the broad market standard deviation as the number of assets in the portfolio increases.

LOS 64.d: Calculate the variance of an equally weighted portfolio of *n* stocks, explain the capital allocation and the capital market lines (CAL and CML) and the relation between them, and calculate the values of one of the variables given the values of the remaining variables.

Equally-Weighted Portfolio Risk

The formula for the variance of an *n*-asset portfolio is very complex, but the formula is simplified dramatically for equally-weighted portfolios (e.g., each w = 1/n):

$$\sigma_P^2 = \frac{1}{n}\overline{\sigma_i^2} + \frac{n-1}{n}\overline{Cov}$$

where:

$\overline{\sigma_i^2}$ = average variance of all assets in the portfolio

$\overline{Cov}$ = average covariance of all pairings of assets in the portfolio

Note that the equally-weighted portfolio variance equals the sum of two components, each of which is affected by the size of the portfolio:

- $(1/n)\times\overline{\sigma_i^2}$ gets closer to zero as *n* gets large because 1/n approaches zero.

- $[(n-1)/n]\times\overline{Cov}$ gets closer to the average covariance as *n* gets large because (n – 1)/n approaches 1.

Therefore, the following important result emerges:

The variance of an equally-weighted portfolio approaches the average covariance as *n* gets large.

Example: Calculating the variance for an equally-weighted portfolio

Consider two equally-weighted portfolios, A and B, in which the average asset variance equals 0.15 and the average covariance equals 0.09. Portfolio A comprises three assets, and Portfolio B comprises 100 assets. Calculate the variance of each portfolio.

Answer:

Variance for Portfolio A = [(1/3) × 0.15] + [(2/3) × 0.09]

= 0.05 + 0.06 = 0.11

Variance for Portfolio B = [(1/100) × 0.15] + [(99/100) × 0.09]

= 0.0015 + 0.0891 = 0.0906

Notice that for Portfolio B (the large portfolio), the first component is very close to zero and that the second component is very close to the average covariance.

With a little bit of algebraic manipulation, we can also calculate the variance of an equally-weighted portfolio as a function of the average correlation between all pairs of two stocks (ρ):

$$\sigma_P^2 = \overline{\sigma_i^2}\left(\frac{1-\rho}{n}+\rho\right)$$

The main point to take away from this equation is to notice that the maximum amount of risk reduction occurs when the number of stocks is very large, so that:

$$\text{maximum risk reduction} \Rightarrow \sigma_P^2 \approx \overline{\sigma_i^2}(\rho)$$

Thus, we have a convenient means of estimating the risk of the minimum-variance portfolio. If the average correlation is 0.3 ($\rho = 0.3$), then the maximum risk reduction possible is that the portfolio variance is 30% of individual stock variance.

Second, note how changes in the level of the average correlation affect the portfolio variance. The lower the level of correlation, the greater the potential diversification benefits, but the greater the number of securities required to realize them. For example, if the average correlation is 0.5, a portfolio of only 10 stocks gets us to within 10% of that for the minimum-variance portfolio. If the average correlation is 0.1, it takes 90 stocks to get within 10% of the minimum-variance portfolio.

Figure 10 shows the risk reduction benefits at three levels of the average correlation as the number of stocks in the portfolio changes. The numbers in the figure are the values that would be multiplied by the average stock variance to obtain the portfolio variance. For example, if the average correlation is 0.1, and a 10 stock portfolio is formed, the value 0.19 would be multiplied by the average stock variance to estimate the portfolio variance. The portfolio variance is estimated to be 19% of the average stock variance. The theoretical minimum-variance portfolio would have variance of only 10% of the average stock variance.

Figure 10: Risk Reduction Benefits of Adding Stocks to a Portfolio

	Average Correlation		
Number of stocks in portfolio (n)	*$\rho = 0.1$*	*$\rho = 0.3$*	*$\rho = 0.5$*
10	0.19	0.37	**0.55**
23	0.14	**0.33**	0.52
90	**0.11**	0.31	0.51
Maximum risk reduction benefit (minimum portfolio variance)	0.10	0.30	0.50

Professor's Note: This is a long topic review with a great deal of information. Let's not lose sight of the big picture. What we've learned so far is that (1) we can improve our risk/return prospects by increasing the number of assets in our portfolio, and (2) the minimum-variance frontier depends on the expected returns, variances and correlations of returns, and the number of assets held.

THE CAPITAL ALLOCATION LINE AND THE CAPITAL MARKET LINE

Professor's Note: Up to this point, we have discussed risky assets. Now, we add the risk-free asset to the set of asset choices and examine the effect that has on investment choices.

WARM-UP: INVESTMENT COMBINATIONS THAT INCLUDE THE RISK-FREE ASSET

Until now, our portfolios have consisted of risky assets only. But, in reality, investors usually allocate their wealth across both risky and risk-free assets. The following discussion illustrates the effects of the inclusion of the risk-free asset. A risk-free asset is the security that has a return known ahead of time, so the variance of the return is zero. Key concepts that will be discussed are the **capital allocation line** and the **capital market line**.

Consider the task of creating portfolios comprising the risk-free asset, F, and a risky portfolio, P. Assume that Portfolio P lies on the efficient frontier of risky assets. Various combinations (weightings) of Portfolio P and the risk-free asset can be created. By adding the risk-free asset to the investment mix, a very important property emerges:

The shape of the efficient frontier changes from a curve to a line after the inclusion of the risk-free asset.

Recall that the expected return for a portfolio of two assets equals the weighted average of the asset expected returns. Therefore, the expected return on Investment C that combines the risk-free asset and risky Portfolio P equals:

$$E(R_C) = w_F R_F + w_P E(R_P)$$

where:
w_F = percentage allocated to the risk-free asset
w_P = percentage allocated to Portfolio P

Also, recall that the variance of the portfolio of two assets (F and P) equals:

$$\sigma_C^2 = w_F^2 \sigma_F^2 + w_P^2 \sigma_P^2 + 2w_F w_P Cov_{FP}$$

where:

σ_C^2 = variance for Investment C

σ_F^2 = variance for the risk-free asset

σ_P^2 = variance for Portfolio P

Cov_{FP} = covariance between F and P

Observe that since we know that the variance and the standard deviation of the risk-free asset both equal zero, and that the covariance of the risk-free asset with any risky asset also equals zero, the equations for the variance and standard deviation for Investment C simplify to:

$$\sigma_C^2 = w_P^2 \sigma_P^2$$

$$\sigma_C = w_P \sigma_P$$

That is, by including the risk-free asset, we have caused the efficient frontier to become linear.

The Capital Allocation Line

The following example illustrates this important property, and leads us into our discussion of the capital allocation line. Assume that the expected return for Portfolio P equals 12% and that its standard deviation equals 24%. Also, assume that the risk-free rate equals 6%.

The expected returns and standard deviations for various combinations of the risk-free asset and portfolio are shown in the Figure 11. Notice that a weight less than zero means we've sold the asset short. For example, suppose we have $100,000 to invest in a portfolio, and we borrow an additional $25,000 at the risk-free rate. The weight on the risk-free asset is –0.25 (–$25,000/$100,000) and the weight on the risky portfolio is 1.25 ($125,000/$100,000). Notice that the weights still add up to 1, however.

Figure 11: Combining the Risk-Free Asset With a Risky Portfolio

Portfolio Possibility (C)	w_F	w_P	$E(R_C)$	σ_C
1	1	0	0.06	0
2	0.75	0.25	0.075	0.06
3	0.50	0.50	0.09	0.12
4	0.25	0.75	0.105	0.18
5	0	1	0.12	0.24
6	–0.25	1.25	0.135	0.30
7	–0.50	1.50	0.15	0.36

Notice that the relationship shown in the example between the investment combination's (C) risk and return is linear. For example, each time the expected return changes by 1.50%, the risk changes by 6%.

Figure 12 illustrates the linear relationship between expected return and risk for the investment combinations of P and F.

Figure 12: Linear Relationship Between Risk and Return When Investing in the Risk-Free Asset

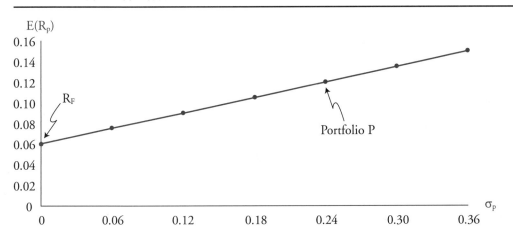

This linear relationship is a key result and is instrumental in the investor's asset allocation decisions. We will use the capital allocation line to answer several important questions. For example:

Question 1: How should the investor choose which risky portfolio among the many possible risky portfolios to combine with the risk-free asset?

Question 2: Given the investor's risk tolerance (i.e., target standard deviation), what rate of return should be expected?

Question 3: Given the investor's risk-return objectives, what percentage allocation should be given to the risk-free asset and the risky portfolio?

All of these questions are answered by employing the linear risk-return relationship that results from the opportunity to invest in the risk-free asset. The discussion will highlight the key role that the capital allocation line plays in determining optimal asset allocations for the investor.

Question 1: How should the investor choose among the many possible risky portfolios to combine with the risk-free asset? The linear risk-return relationship helps the investor make this very important decision, which can be summarized as follows: When combined with the risk-free asset, the investor should choose the risky portfolio that maximizes the reward-to-risk tradeoff.

This leads us to the *Capital Allocation Line*, which is the risk-return line that lies tangent to the efficient frontier. Figure 13 provides an example.

Figure 13: Capital Allocation Line

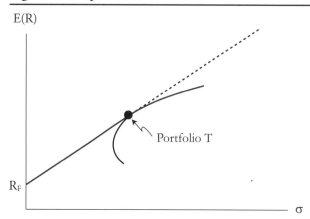

Notice that the tangency portfolio, T, is optimal in the sense that it has the highest possible reward-to-risk ratio, defined as:

$$\text{reward-to-risk ratio} = \frac{E(R_T) - R_F}{\sigma_T}$$

The reward-to-risk ratio also can be viewed as the expected risk premium, $E(R_T) - R_F$, for each unit of risk, σ_T, and is also known as the **Sharpe ratio** for Portfolio T.

Note that no other portfolio along the efficient frontier of risky assets (the curve in Figure 13) provides a higher expected reward-to-risk ratio than the tangency portfolio when combined with the risk-free asset. Stated in terms of the CAL, all risk-return lines connecting the risk-free rate and portfolios *other than* the tangency portfolio on the efficient frontier will have a flatter slope (lower reward-to-risk ratio) than the CAL. Therefore, the tangency portfolio is the *optimal risky portfolio* along the efficient frontier. The slope of the CAL represents the best possible risk-return tradeoff attainable given the investor's expectations.

Professor's Note: Under the standard CAL assumptions, investors can have different expectations about returns, variances, and covariances. Therefore, the efficient frontiers and CALs faced by investors will differ depending on the asset expectations of investors. For example, the efficient frontier derived by a highly optimistic investor might lie above the efficient frontier derived by a less optimistic investor. The CAL derived by the highly optimistic investor will have a steeper slope than the CAL derived by the less optimistic investor.

So, back to our original question—which risky portfolio should be combined with the risk-free asset? The tangency portfolio (at the point where the risk-return line touches the efficient frontier) is the optimal risky portfolio because it maximizes the investor's reward-to-risk ratio, when combined with the risk-free asset.

Question 2: Given the investor's risk tolerance, what rate of return should be expected?
To answer this question, note that investors can hold any portfolio along the CAL by changing their allocation between Treasury bills (the risk-free asset, *F*) and the

optimal risky Portfolio T. If the client invests 100% in Treasury bills, then the expected return and standard deviation on the investment equals 6% and zero, respectively. As the investor reallocates money from Treasury bills to Portfolio T, the investment combination moves up the line, increasing both expected return and risk.

All points on the line up to optimal Portfolio T represent "lending" portfolios, indicating that some money is invested in the risk-free asset (i.e., "lending" to the government treasury). All points on the line beyond optimal risky Portfolio T represent "leveraged" portfolios (i.e., borrowing money at the risk-free rate, and investing more than 100% of the original wealth in Portfolio T).

If risk-free borrowing is not available, then the CAL ends at the tangency point. Investors desiring a higher return will need to select portfolios along the original (curved) efficient frontier beyond the tangency point of the CAL. The efficient frontier without risk-free borrowing will therefore not be a straight line, but instead will consist of two segments: a straight line between the risk-free asset and Portfolio T, and the upper part of the curved portion of the original efficient frontier beyond T (shown in blue in Figure 13).

The CAL Equation

To determine the rate of return commensurate with the investor's risk tolerance, we can use the mathematical equation for the CAL.

For the CAL:

- The intercept equals the risk free rate.
- The slope equals the reward-to-risk ratio for the optimal risky portfolio.

Because the CAL is a straight line, we can express it as a linear equation:

$$Y = a + bX$$

where:
Y = dependent variable [$E(R_C)$, the expected return on the investment combination]
X = independent variable (σ_C, the standard deviation on the investment combination)
a = intercept (R_F, the risk-free rate)
b = slope (the reward-to-risk ratio for the optimal risky portfolio)

Therefore, the equation for the CAL is:

$$E(R_C) = R_F + \left(\frac{E(R_T) - R_F}{\sigma_T} \right) \sigma_C$$

The intercept and slope of the CAL in Figure 13 are:

- Intercept equals the risk-free rate of 0.06.
- Slope equals the reward-to-risk ratio for optimal risky portfolio, T, which is $(0.12 - 0.06)/0.24 = 0.25$.

Therefore, the equation for the CAL in Figure 13 is:

$$E(R_C) = 0.06 + 0.25\sigma_C$$

The slope coefficient (the reward-to-risk ratio) of the CAL indicates that the expected return on the investor's portfolio, $E(R_C)$, will change by 0.25 units for every 1-unit change in the investor's portfolio risk (σ_C).

Example: Calculating expected return from the CAL

Your firm manages a portfolio with an expected return equal to 12% and standard deviation equal to 24%. The risk-free rate equals 6%. One of your clients desires a portfolio standard deviation equal to 12%. Use the CAL to calculate the highest expected return for your client.

Answer:

Your client has a target standard deviation equal to 12% ($\sigma_C = 0.12$). Using the CAL, the expected return on an investment that combines the optimal risky portfolio, T, and the risk-free asset, F, is:

$$E(R_C) = 0.06 + 0.25(0.12) = 0.09 = 9\%$$

Therefore, the expected rate of return commensurate with your client's risk tolerance equals 9%.

Example: Calculating standard deviation from the CAL

Also, notice that the CAL can be used to calculate the standard deviation associated with a target expected return. For example, assume your client states that she has a target expected return equal to 9%. Use the CAL to calculate the standard deviation associated with her optimal investment combination.

Answer:

Start with the CAL assuming a target return of 9%, $E(R_C) = 0.09$:

$$E(R_C) = 0.09 = 0.06 + 0.25\sigma_C$$

and, then, solve the CAL for the standard deviation:

$$\sigma_C = (0.09 - 0.06)/0.25 = 0.12 = 12\%$$

Therefore, the client's investment (that combines T and F) has an expected return of 9% (as stipulated by the client) and a standard deviation of 12%.

Question 3: Given the investor's risk-return objectives, what percentage allocation should be given to the risk-free asset and the risky portfolio? The following example addresses this important question.

Example: Determining the appropriate allocation to the risk-free asset and to the optimal risky portfolio

Your client has a target standard deviation equal to 12%. Use the data above to determine the appropriate allocation to Treasury bills and to the optimal risky portfolio that will satisfy your client's risk tolerance.

Answer:

Using the equation derived in the Warm-Up, recall that the client's portfolio standard deviation (for the investment combination of Treasury bills and risky Portfolio T) equals:

$$\sigma_C = w_T \sigma_T$$

Therefore, if the client has a target standard deviation equal to 12%:

$$0.12 = w_T(0.24)$$

$$w_T = 0.12/0.24 = 0.50$$

Your client should invest 50% in Treasury bills and 50% in the optimal risky Portfolio T. And, we already know that the expected return commensurate with a 12% standard deviation equals 9%. Therefore, the investor who allocates 50/50 to Treasury bills and risky Portfolio T should expect a standard deviation equal to 12% and a rate of return equal to 9%.

Here's what you need to remember about the CAL:

- If a risk-free investment is available, investors can combine it with a risky portfolio to increase their return at all levels of risk.
- The CAL is the straight line that intersects the y-axis at the risk-free rate and lies tangent to the efficient frontier.
- The intercept of the CAL equals the risk-free rate and the slope equals the maximum portfolio reward-to-risk ratio, defined as $[E(R_T) - R_F] / \sigma_T$.
- The tangency portfolio is the optimal risky portfolio because it has the highest possible expected reward-to-risk tradeoff.
- The CAL can be used to determine the risk associated with any desired target return, or the expected return associated with any desired target standard deviation.
- The intercept and slope of the CAL depend on the asset expectations of the investor. Therefore, investors with different asset expectations will face different CALs.

The Capital Market Line

The **Capital Market Line (CML)** is the capital allocation line in a world in which all investors agree on the expected returns, standard deviations, and correlations of all assets (also known as the "homogeneous expectations" assumption). Assuming identical expectations, there will be only one capital allocation line, and it is called the capital market line.

Under the assumptions of the CML, all investors agree on the exact composition of the optimal risky portfolio. This universally agreed upon optimal risky portfolio is called the *market portfolio, M*, defined as the portfolio of all marketable assets, weighted in proportion to their relative market values. For instance, if the market value of Asset X is $1 billion, and the market value of all traded assets is $100 billion, then the weight allocated to Asset X in the market portfolio equals 1%.

The key conclusion of the CML can be summarized as follows:

> All investors will make optimal investment decisions by allocating between the risk-free asset and the market portfolio.

A graph of the CML is provided in Figure 14.

Figure 14: The Capital Market Line

The equation for the CML is:

$$E(R_C) = R_F + \left[\frac{E(R_M) - R_F}{\sigma_M} \right] \sigma_C$$

The slope of the CML is often called the *market price of risk*, and equals the reward-to-risk ratio (or Sharpe ratio) for the market portfolio. This is calculated as:

$$\frac{E(R_M) - R_F}{\sigma_M}$$

Because the CML is just a special case of the CAL, the CML also can be used to calculate the expected return commensurate with the investor's risk tolerance. All prior examples hold for the CML if we make one simple assumption—that investors have identical expectations. Under this assumption, the tangency portfolio discussed earlier for the specific investor (Portfolio T) is the market Portfolio M.

As illustrated in the previous discussion, the addition of the risk-free asset has profound implications for the efficient frontier. Most importantly, all investors can maximize their reward-to-risk ratio by investing in a combination of the risk-free asset and the market portfolio. So, with the introduction of the risk-free asset, the shape of the efficient frontier changes from a curve (the Markowitz frontier) to a line (the Capital Market Line). Stated more emphatically, the Capital Market Line dominates the Markowitz frontier.

For example, all investors would prefer Portfolio A over Portfolio B in Figure 14. Portfolio A has the same risk but higher expected return than Portfolio B. Moreover, all investors would prefer Portfolio A over Portfolio C. Portfolio A has the same expected return but lower risk than Portfolio C. Similar contrasts can be found all along the Capital Market Line and Markowitz frontier. Because optimal portfolios are now found on the Capital Market Line, the Capital Market Line becomes the new efficient frontier.

Investors with high risk aversion will invest a larger percentage in the risk-free asset and a smaller percentage in the market portfolio (for an investment combination lying on the lower end of the Capital Market Line). The reverse is true for investors with low risk aversion.

Differences Between the CAL and the CML

Although the CAL and CML are generated using exactly the same mean-variance calculations, there are a few important differences:

- There is only one CML, because it is developed assuming all investors agree on the expected return, standard deviation, and correlations for all assets.
- There is an unlimited number of CALs, because each is developed uniquely for each investor.
- The tangency portfolio for the CML is the *market* portfolio, and there is only one market portfolio. The market portfolio uses market value weights.
- The tangency portfolio for the CAL can differ across investors depending on differences in investor expectations.
- The CML is a special case of the CAL.

LOS 64.e: Explain the capital asset pricing model (CAPM), including its underlying assumptions and the resulting conclusions.

The Capital Asset Pricing Model (CAPM) is one of the most celebrated models in all of finance. The model describes the relationship we should expect to see between risk and return for individual assets. Specifically, the CAPM provides a way to calculate an asset's expected return (or "required" return) based on its level of systematic (or market-related) risk, as measured by the asset's beta.

CAPM has a number of underlying assumptions, which are very similar to those of the CML:

- Investors only need to know expected returns, variances, and covariances in order to create optimal portfolios.
- All investors have the same forecasts of risky assets' expected returns, variances, and covariances.
- All assets are marketable, and the market for assets is perfectly competitive.

- Investors are price takers whose individual buy and sell decisions have no effect on asset prices.
- Investors can borrow and lend at the risk-free rate, and unlimited short-selling is allowed.
- There are no frictions to trading, such as taxes or transaction costs.

Implications of the CAPM Assumptions

Given these assumptions, there are *four* important implications of the CAPM:

1. Because all investors have the same expectations and all use mean-variance analysis, they all identify the same risky tangency portfolio (the "market portfolio") and combine that risky portfolio with the risk-free asset when creating their portfolios.

2. Because all investors hold the same risky portfolio, the weight on each asset must be equal to the proportion of its market value to the market value of the entire portfolio. In other words, if a stock represents 1% of the total market value of all traded assets, and every investor holds the same portfolio, that stock must also represent 1% of each investor's portfolio before combination with the risk-free asset.

3. The security market line (SML), which is the graph of the CAPM, describes the relationship between the expected return and systematic risk for all assets, both individual securities and portfolios.

4. Systematic risk, measured by beta, is the only risk priced by the market.

LOS 64.f: Discuss the security market line (SML), the beta coefficient, the market risk premium, and the Sharpe ratio, and calculate the value of one of these variables given the values of the remaining variables.

The **Security Market Line** (SML) is the graph of the CAPM, representing the cross-sectional relationship between an asset's expected return and its systematic risk. Systematic risk for any asset is measured by the asset's beta, which estimates the sensitivity of the asset's rate of return to changes in the broad market's returns.

The intercept and slope for the SML are determined as follows:

- Intercept equals the risk-free rate, R_F.
- Slope equals the market risk premium, $E(R_M) - R_F$.

The **market risk premium** equals the expected difference in returns between the market portfolio and the risk-free asset. Using the CAPM, the market risk premium equals the additional return that investors require as compensation for additional units of systematic risk.

The SML equation is:

$$E(R_i) = R_F + \beta_i[E(R_M - R_F)]$$

Example: Use the CAPM to calculate the expected return on a stock

Assume you are assigned the task of evaluating the stock of Sky-Air, Inc. To evaluate the stock, you calculate its required return using the CAPM. The following information is available:

expected market risk premium 5%
risk-free rate   4%
Sky-Air beta   1.5

Calculate and interpret the CAPM expected return for Sky-Air.

Answer:

Using the CAPM, the expected return for Sky-Air is:

$$E(R_{SA}) = 0.04 + 1.5(0.05) = 0.115 = 11.5\%$$

The CAPM return can be viewed as the minimum return that investors should be willing to accept, commensurate with the risk associated with the asset. For example, if investors predict that the return will exceed 11.5%, then they should buy Sky-Air stock. However, if investors predict that the return will be less than 11.5%, then they should sell Sky-Air stock (or short sell the stock).

The graph of the SML and the location of the Sky-Air stock are illustrated in Figure 15.

Figure 15: The Security Market Line

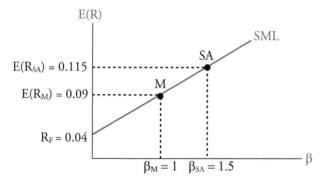

The graph illustrates the positive relationship that exists between risk (as measured by beta) and expected return. The positive relationship is a reflection of the risk aversion of investors. The SML will become steeper (i.e., the market risk premium will increase) as investors, on average, become more risk averse.

Calculating the Beta Coefficient

Systematic risk is estimated by the asset's beta, which is a standardized measure of an asset's systematic risk. The formula for the beta (systematic risk) for security i is:

$$\beta_i = \frac{Cov_{i,M}}{\sigma_M^2} = \frac{\rho_{i,M}\sigma_i\sigma_M}{\sigma_M^2} = \rho_{i,M}\left(\frac{\sigma_i}{\sigma_M}\right)$$

where:

σ_i = standard deviation of returns for stock i

σ_M = standard deviation of returns for the market portfolio

$Cov_{i,M}$ = covariance between the returns for stock i and the market portfolio

$\rho_{i,M}$ = correlation between the returns for stock i and the market portfolio

σ_M^2 = variance of the returns on the market portfolio

 Professor's Note: The equation for beta is the equation for the slope coefficient in a simple linear regression equation, specifically the market model, which is used to estimate betas.

Since beta measures the stock's reactions to movements in the market, the beta for the market as a whole must be 1.0. A stock's systematic risk can be assessed relative to the market in the following manner:

- A stock with a beta of 1 has an average level of market sensitivity. If beta is set equal to 1 in the SML, the expected return on the stock equals the expected return on the market portfolio. Stocks of large, diversified conglomerates tend to have betas close to 1.
- A stock with a beta greater than 1 has more-than-average systematic risk and will have an expected return greater than the market's expected return. Stocks of companies in industries that are more sensitive to the level of economic activity tend to have betas greater than 1 and are sometimes referred to as cyclical stocks.
- A stock with a beta less than 1 has less-than-average systematic risk and will have an expected return smaller than the market's expected return. Stocks of companies in industries not very sensitive to the economy (e.g., oil companies and grocery store chains) tend to have betas less than 1 and are referred to as defensive stocks.

Example: Calculate and interpret the beta of a stock

Assume the correlation of returns between Transport Co. and the market portfolio equals 0.80, the standard deviation of Transport Co. equals 0.60, and the standard deviation for the market portfolio equals 0.30. Calculate the beta for Transport Co.

Answer:

The beta equals the product of the correlation and the ratio of the standard deviation of the stock to the market standard deviation. Therefore, the beta for Transport Co. is:

$$\beta_{TC} = 0.80 \left(\frac{0.60}{0.30} \right) = 1.60$$

Therefore, Transport Co. is a relatively high (systematic) risk stock. The average stock beta equals 1, so TC is 60% riskier than the average stock, using systematic risk as our measure of risk.

Beta Summary

The beta for a stock is the ratio of its standard deviation to the standard deviation of the market multiplied by its correlation with the market:

$$\beta_i = \rho_{iM} \left(\frac{\sigma_i}{\sigma_M} \right)$$

It might be useful to think of beta as a measure of a stock's variability that is caused by market factors. Figure 16 summarizes the beta relationships.

Figure 16: Beta Interpretation

Beta	Risk Relative to the Market	Example Beta	Interpretation
< 1.0	Less systematic risk	0.5	Half as much systematic risk as the average stock
= 1.0	Same systematic risk	1.0	Same systematic risk as the average stock
> 1.0	More systematic risk	1.2	20% more systematic risk than the average stock

Financial Market Equilibrium

Financial market equilibrium exists when demand and supply forces cause market prices to stay at levels corresponding to expected/required returns. The CAPM is an example of an *equilibrium model*—its predictions result from market forces acting whenever prices get out of equilibrium to force them back into equilibrium.

For example, if based on its beta the required return on an asset is too low, this indicates that the market price is too high. Under these circumstances, the SML predicts that investors will sell the stock until the price falls to the point where the forecast return is again equal to its required return (i.e., equilibrium) level.

Because the CAPM assumes investors hold the market portfolio, unsystematic risk (risk that is unrelated to the market) is irrelevant. The risk related to movements in the market portfolio is all that really matters, so investors *price* only systematic risk. That's why the independent variable in the SML is beta, not standard deviation.

Professor's Note: Standard deviation measures standalone risk, which is the asset's total risk. For an individual stock, standalone risk is total systematic and unsystematic risk. For a well-diversified portfolio, however, standalone risk is only systematic risk, because unsystematic risk has been eliminated. For concentrated portfolios (i.e., partially diversified portfolios), there is systematic risk plus the unsystematic risk that has not been diversified away.

Differences Between the CML and the SML

As discussed earlier, the CML is the efficient frontier, plotting expected returns and standard deviations (total risk) for portfolios comprising a combination of the risk-free asset and the market portfolio. If markets are in equilibrium, risk and return combinations for individual securities will lie along the SML, but not along the CML. Risk and return combinations for individual securities will lie below the CML because their standard deviations include unsystematic risk that is diversified away in the market portfolio.

Figure 17: Key Differences Between the SML and the CML

	SML	*CML*
Measure of risk	Uses systematic risk (non-diversifiable risk).	Uses standard deviation (total risk).
Application	Tool used to determine the appropriate expected (benchmark) returns for securities.	Tool used to determine the appropriate asset allocation (percentages allocated to the risk-free asset and to the market portfolio) for the investor.
Definition	Graph of the capital asset pricing model.	Graph of the efficient frontier.
Slope	Market risk premium.	Market portfolio Sharpe ratio.

Professor's Note: The last part of the LOS says "calculate the values of one of these variables given the values of the remaining variables." Presumably that means using the formula for the SML, beta, the market risk premium, and the Sharpe ratio. The possibilities are almost endless here, so we'll just give you a few examples of the types of problems you might see on the exam.

Example: Using the SML

A stock has a beta of 0.75 and an expected return of 13%. The risk-free rate is 4%. Calculate the market risk premium and the expected return on the market portfolio.

Answer:

According to the SML: $0.13 = 0.04 + 0.75[E(R_M) - R_F]$.

Therefore, the market risk premium is equal to: $[E(R_M) - R_F] = 0.12 = 12\%$.

The expected return on the market is calculated as: $[E(R_M) - 0.04] = 0.12$, or $E(R_M) = 0.16 = 16\%$.

Example: Using the beta formula

A stock has a beta of 2.0. The correlation of the stock's returns with the market is 0.5 and the variance of the returns on the market portfolio is 0.04. Calculate the variance of returns on the stock.

Answer:

The variance of the market portfolio returns is 0.04, so the standard deviation of market returns is the square root of 0.04, or 0.20. Plugging that into the beta formula gives us:

$$2.0 = 0.5\left(\frac{\sigma_i}{0.2}\right) \Rightarrow \sigma_i = 0.8$$

The variance of the stock's returns is the $0.8^2 = 0.64$.

Example: Using the Sharpe ratio

Given a Sharpe ratio for the market portfolio of 0.40, calculate the expected return on a stock with a standard deviation of returns of 0.50 and a correlation with the market portfolio returns of 0.6. The risk-free rate is 5% and the standard deviation of the market portfolio returns is 0.25.

Answer:

First calculate the stock's beta:

$$\beta = 0.6 \left(\frac{0.50}{0.25} \right) = 1.2$$

Then, use the market Sharpe ratio to calculate the market risk premium:

$$\left[\frac{E(R_M) - R_F}{0.25} \right] = 0.40 \Rightarrow E(R_M) - R_F = 0.10$$

Finally, use the SML to calculate the expected return on the stock:

$$E(R) = 0.05 + 1.2(0.10) = 0.17 = 17\%$$

DERIVING INPUTS TO THE MEAN-VARIANCE MODEL

There are three methods of obtaining the inputs to the mean-variance framework:

1. Using historical means, variances, and correlations.

2. Estimating betas using the market model.

3. Calculating adjusted betas.

We will discuss each in turn.

Historical Estimates

The efficient frontier is derived by creating optimal portfolios that consider all assets in the market. However, the forecast process needed to derive the efficient frontier is daunting and arduous.

The first problem with using historical estimates is that we have to estimate a very large number of inputs. For portfolios of n assets, we will need the following number of forecasts:

n individual asset expected returns

+ n individual asset standard deviations

+ $\dfrac{n(n-1)}{2}$ covariances

For example, even if we limit ourselves to stocks in the S&P 500, the inputs required to conduct a mean-variance analysis would include 500 expected returns, 500 variances, and 124,750 covariances!

The second problem with using historical estimates is that there is typically a large amount of estimation error, particularly for estimates of expected returns and covariances.

Obviously, we need more practical methods for computing inputs to mean-variance analysis.

LOS 64.g: Explain the market model, and state and interpret the market model's predictions with respect to asset returns, variances, and covariances.

The Market Model

A more practical and useful method is the **market model**. The premise of the market model is that there are just two sources of risk:

1. Unanticipated macroeconomic events (systematic risk).

2. Firm-specific events (unsystematic risk).

In the market model, the market portfolio is the macroeconomic factor and stocks are assumed to have varying degrees of sensitivity to this one factor. In addition, each stock's returns are uniquely affected by firm-specific events uncorrelated across stocks and with the macro events.

The market model is the regression model often used to estimate betas for common stocks:

$$R_i = \alpha_i + \beta_i R_M + \varepsilon_i$$

where:
R_i = return on Asset i
R_M = return on the market Portfolio M
α_i = intercept (the value of R_i when R_M equals zero)
β_i = slope (estimate of the systematic risk for Asset i)
ε_i = regression error with expected value equal to zero (firm specific surprises)

The market model makes three assumptions:

1. The expected value of the error term is zero.

2. The errors are uncorrelated with the market return.

3. The firm-specific surprises are uncorrelated across assets.

Based on these assumptions, the market model greatly simplifies the estimation procedures needed to conduct the mean-variance analysis, as illustrated next.

Market Model Predictions of Expected Returns, Variances, and Covariances

The market model offers a simple way to derive forecasts of expected returns, variances, and covariances for individual assets. In particular, after making a few simplifying assumptions, it can be shown that:

expected return for Asset i: $\quad E(R_i) = \alpha_i + \beta_i E(R_M)$

variance of Asset i: $\quad \sigma_i^2 = \beta_i^2 \sigma_M^2 + \sigma_\varepsilon^2$

covariance between assets i and j: $\quad Cov_{ij} = \beta_i \beta_j \sigma_M^2$

In general, the *n* expected returns, *n* variances, and n(n–1)/2 covariance forecasts can be derived from just 3n + 2 parameters using the market model, which greatly simplifies the estimation procedure.

The market model makes three predictions:

1. The expected return on Asset i depends only on the expected return on the market portfolio, $E(R_M)$, the sensitivity of the returns on Asset i to movements in the market, β_i, and the average return to Asset i when the market return is zero, α_i.

2. The variance of the returns on Asset i consists of two components: a systematic component related to the asset's beta, $\beta_i^2 \sigma_M^2$, and an unsystematic component related to firm-specific events, σ_ε^2.

3. The covariance between any two stocks is calculated as the product of their betas and the variance of the market portfolio.

Example: Calculating the market model forecasts

Assume the betas for assets i and j equal 0.80 and 1.5, respectively, and that the expected return and variance for the market portfolio returns equal 0.12 and 0.04, respectively. Also assume the intercept and error variance (unsystematic risk) for Asset i equals 0.02 and 0.10, respectively. Determine the market model forecasts for expected return for Asset i, its variance, and its covariance with Asset j.

Answer:

The following forecasts can be made using the market model:

expected return for Asset i: $\quad 0.02 + 0.80(0.12) = 0.116 = 11.6\%$

variance for Asset i: $\quad 0.8^2(0.04) + 0.10 = 0.1256 = 12.56$

covariance between assets: $\quad (0.80)(1.5)(0.04) = 0.048$

To generate values for the market model (i.e., to estimate alpha, beta, and the error variance), historical returns for a stock are regressed against corresponding returns for a market index. The following example illustrates how the market model simplifies the forecasting process.

Professor's Note: The market model is simply an application of simple linear regression to portfolio management. Recall from Study Session 3 that when we ran a regression with individual stock returns as the dependent variable and market returns as the independent variable, the estimated slope coefficient was the stock's beta.

Example: The number of statistical inputs needed to derive the efficient frontier using the market model

Determine the number of statistical inputs needed to derive the efficient frontier comprising 500 assets, using the market model.

Answer:

The efficient frontier is derived after forecasting the following:

- 500 expected returns
- 500 variances
- $\dfrac{500 \times 499}{2} = 124{,}750$ covariances

This equals a total of 125,750 forecasts. However, by running 500 market model regressions, we will obtain 500 α estimates, 500 β estimates, and 500 regression error variance estimates. All we need now is one estimate of the expected market return, and one estimate of the market variance. From these 1,502 statistical inputs, we can generate forecasts for all of the 125,750 asset parameters!

LOS 64.h: Calculate an adjusted beta, and discuss the use of adjusted and historical betas as predictors of future betas.

To implement the market model estimates of expected returns, variances, and covariances, we must have regression estimates of the beta for each asset. As discussed above, one method of estimating beta is simply to use the historical regression estimate derived from the market model. There is a slight problem, however. To conduct mean-variance analysis for optimal portfolio selection, we need forecasts, not historical estimates, of expected returns, variances, and covariances.

The beta derived from the market model is a good estimate of *historical* relationships but not necessarily a good predictor of *future* relationships. This is called the *beta instability problem*. If the historical beta inaccurately predicts the future beta, then inaccurate forecasts will be used when attempting to derive the efficient frontier and to make optimal portfolio decisions. Therefore, in practice, we often apply some adjustments to the historical beta to improve its ability to forecast the future beta.

For example, if we assume that beta follows a first-order autoregressive process, then we can formulate the beta forecast as:

$$\beta_{i,t} = \alpha_0 + \alpha_1 \beta_{i,t-1} + \upsilon_{i,t}$$

where:
$\upsilon_{i,t}$ = a random error with expected value equal zero

If $\alpha_1 = 1$, then we would conclude that beta follows a random walk (the changes in beta are random over time). $\beta_{i,t}$ is the beta forecast and $\beta_{i,t-1}$ is the historical beta derived from the market model:

forecast $\beta_{i,t} = \beta_{i,t-1}$ from a market model

 Professor's Note: Remember from Study Session 3 that in a first-order autoregressive process the dependent variable is regressed against its first lagged value. In the application here, the dependent variable is beta.

More often, though, the beta instability problem is addressed by adjusting the beta to account for its tendency to gravitate to a value of 1 over time. The general form of the "adjusted beta" equation can be presented as:

forecast $\beta_{i,t} = \alpha_0 + \alpha_1 \beta_{i,t-1}$

where:
the sum $\alpha_0 + \alpha_1$ is set equal to 1

The most popular values of α_0 and α_1 are: $\alpha_0 = 1/3$ and $\alpha_1 = 2/3$.

From our understanding of first order autoregressive processes, we know that the mean reverting value for any time series variable equals the intercept divided by 1 minus the slope, $\alpha_0 / (1 - \alpha_1)$. Therefore, by assuming α_0 and α_1 sum to 1, then $\alpha_0 = 1 - \alpha_1$, and:

$$\frac{\alpha_0}{1-\alpha_1} = \frac{1-\alpha_1}{1-\alpha_1} = 1$$

The mean-reverting level of the beta is 1. If the historical beta is greater than 1, then the adjusted beta will be less than the historical beta and closer to 1. If the historical beta is less than 1, then the adjusted beta will be greater than the historical beta and closer to 1. The adjusted beta forecast will move toward 1 more quickly for larger values of α_0 (e.g., as α_0 approaches a value of 1).

Example: Calculate an adjusted beta

The historical beta for the Compware Company equals 2. Calculate the adjusted beta for Compware Company using the adjusted beta formula: $(2/3) + (1/3) \times \beta_{t-1}$.

Answer:

The adjusted beta for Compware Company equals:

$(2/3) + (1/3) \times 2 = 1.33$

Notice how the adjusted beta calculation used the historical beta estimate of 2.0 to derive a forecast beta that moved closer to a value of 1.

LOS 64.i: Discuss reasons for and problems related to instability in the minimum-variance frontier.

The risk-return characteristics of the minimum-variance frontier are determined by the expected returns, variances, and covariances among individual assets. Therefore, the shape and location of the minimum-variance frontier (in risk-return space) changes as the risk and return attributes of individual assets change over time. More optimistic expected return forecasts will cause the curve to shift up, and lowered variance and covariance forecasts will cause the curve to shift to the left (also with larger curvature or bulge to the left). Small changes in risk-return attributes of individual assets can cause large changes in the composition of the portfolios that form the minimum-variance frontier.

The instability in the minimum-variance frontier and, therefore, the efficient frontier, is a concern for a number of reasons:

- The statistical inputs (means, variances, covariances) are unknown, and must be forecast; greater uncertainty in the inputs leads to less reliability in the efficient frontier.
- Statistical input forecasts derived from historical sample estimates often change over time, causing the estimated efficient frontier to change over time (this is called time instability).
- Small changes in the statistical inputs can cause large changes in the efficient frontier (called the "overfitting" problem), resulting in unreasonably large short positions, and overly frequent rebalancing.

To address the instability problem, the analyst might consider constraining the portfolio weights (e.g., prohibiting short sales so that all portfolio weights are positive), employing forecasting models that provide better forecasts than historical estimates, and avoiding rebalancing until significant changes occur in the efficient frontier.

MULTIFACTOR MODELS

LOS 64.j: Discuss and compare macroeconomic factor models, fundamental factor models, and statistical factor models.

The market model could be described as a single factor model, because it assumes asset returns are explained by a single factor, the return on the market portfolio. A *multifactor model* assumes asset returns are driven by more than one factor. There are three general classifications of multifactor models: (1) macroeconomic factor models, (2) fundamental factor models, and (3) statistical factor models.

1. *Macroeconomic factor models* assume that asset returns are explained by surprises (or "shocks") in macroeconomic risk factors (e.g., GDP, interest rates, and inflation). Factor surprises are defined as the difference between the realized value of the factor and its consensus predicted value.

     Professor's Note: The key to macroeconomic factor models is that the variables that explain returns are not the value of the macroeconomic variable itself, but rather the unexpected part (i.e., the surprise), because we assume that the expected value has already been reflected in stock prices. For example, if the government announces that GDP grew at an annual rate of 1.5% and the consensus prediction was 2.5%, the surprise was a negative 1%. The 2.5% consensus forecast was already reflected in market prices, so the negative surprise, which was bad news to the market, should cause stock prices to fall.

2. *Fundamental factor models* assume asset returns are explained by the returns from multiple firm-specific factors (e.g., P/E ratio, market cap, leverage ratio, and earnings growth rate).

3. *Statistical factor models* use multivariate statistics (factor analysis or principal components) to identify multiple statistical factors that explain the covariation among asset returns. The major weakness is that the statistical factors do not lend themselves well to economic interpretation. Therefore, *statistical* factors are *mystery* factors.

Because most investment firms employ macroeconomic factor or fundamental factor models (or mixtures of the two), we will provide a more expanded discussion of these models.

MACROECONOMIC FACTOR MODELS

The following model is an example of a two-factor macroeconomic model in which stock returns are explained by surprises in GDP growth rates and credit quality spreads:

$$R_i = E(R_i) + b_{i1}F_{GDP} + b_{i2}F_{QS} + \varepsilon_i$$

where:
R_i = return for Asset i
$E(R_i)$ = expected return for Asset i (in the absence of any surprises)
F_{GDP} = surprise in the GDP rate
F_{QS} = surprise in the credit quality spread (BB rated bond yield – Treasury bond yield)
b_{i1} = GDP surprise sensitivity of Asset i
b_{i2} = credit quality spread surprise sensitivity of Asset i
ε_i = firm-specific surprise (unrelated to the two macro factors)

Let's take a closer look at each of the components:

- The stock's expected return comes from an asset pricing model.
- The "F's" are the factor surprises, the difference between the predicted value of the factor and the realized value.
- The "b's" are the sensitivities of the stock to the surprises. They are very similar to betas in the market model. The higher the sensitivity, the larger the change in return for a given factor surprise.
- The error term is the part of the return that can't be explained by the model. It represents unsystematic risk related to firm-specific events like a strike or a warehouse fire.

Example: Compute a stock return using a macroeconomic factor model

The following two-factor model is used to explain the returns for Media Tech (MT):

$$R_{MT} = E(R_{MT}) + b_{MT,1}F_{GDP} + b_{MT,2}F_{QS} + \varepsilon_{MT}$$

The expected return for Media Tech equals 10%. Over the past year, GDP grew at a rate that was 2 percentage points higher than originally expected, and the quality spread was 1 percentage point lower than originally expected. Media Tech's sensitivity to the GDP rate factor equaled 2 and its sensitivity to the quality spread factor equaled –0.5. Over the past year, Media Tech also experienced a 2% company-unique surprise return (i.e., unrelated to the two macrofactors). Construct the macroeconomic factor model for Media Tech, and calculate its return for the year.

Answer:

The two-factor model for Media Tech is:

$$R_{MT} = 0.10 + 2(0.02) - 0.50(-0.01) + 0.02 =$$

   0.100 (the expected return)
+ 0.040 (the return from the positive GDP surprise)
+ 0.005 (the return from the positive quality spread surprise)
+ <u>0.020 (the return from unexpected firm specific events)</u>
= 0.165, or 16.5%

The Media Tech return was higher than originally expected because MT was positively affected by higher than expected economic growth (GDP), lower than expected credit quality risk spreads (QS), and by positive company specific surprise events.

Professor's Note: Be careful to interpret the signs properly: a decrease in the quality spread (a surprise less than zero) is good news for stock MT, because it has a negative sensitivity to the factor. When credit quality spreads increase, MT's return goes down, and when credit quality spreads decrease, MT's return goes up.

The main features of the macroeconomic factor model include the systematic or "priced risk" factors and the factor sensitivities.

Priced Risk Factors

A risk that does not affect many assets (i.e., an *unsystematic risk*) can usually be diversified away in a portfolio and because of that will not be priced by the market. By "priced" we mean investors cannot expect to be rewarded for being exposed to that type of risk. The factors in our example model, GDP and credit quality spread shocks are *systematic* risk factors. That means they can affect even well-diversified portfolios. Since they cannot be avoided, systematic factors represent priced risk; risk for which investors can demand compensation.

Factor Sensitivities

In a macroeconomic multifactor model, asset returns are a function of unexpected surprises to systematic factors, and different assets have different *factor sensitivities*. For example, retail stocks are very sensitive to GDP growth and, hence, have a large sensitivity to the GDP factor. Small, unexpected changes in GDP growth cause large changes in retail stock prices, because changes in income affect retail spending. Other stocks are less sensitive to GDP and have smaller GDP factor sensitivities. Retail grocer stocks, for example, do not react as much to changes in GDP, because spending on food items is less sensitive to changes in national income. The factor sensitivities of the model can be estimated by regressing historical asset returns on the corresponding historical macroeconomic factors.

Study Session 18

FUNDAMENTAL FACTOR MODELS

Consider the following fundamental factor model:

$$R_i = a_i + b_{i1}F_{P/E} + b_{i2}F_{SIZE} + \varepsilon_i$$

where:

R_i	= return for stock i
$F_{P/E}$	= return associated with the P/E factor
F_{SIZE}	= return associated with the SIZE (market capitalization) factor
a_i	= intercept
b_{i1}	= standardized sensitivity of stock i to the P/E factor
b_{i2}	= standardized sensitivity of stock i to the SIZE factor

Let's take a closer look at each of the components of a fundamental factor model.

Standardized sensitivities (b_{i1} and b_{i2}). Sensitivities in most fundamental factor models are not regression slopes. Instead, the fundamental factor sensitivities are standardized attributes (similar to z-statistics from the standard normal distribution). For example, the standardized P/E sensitivity in a fundamental factor model is calculated as:

$$b_{i1} = \frac{(P/E)_i - \overline{P/E}}{\sigma_{P/E}}$$

where:

$(P/E)_i$	= P/E ratio for stock i
$\overline{P/E}$	= average P/E calculated across all stocks
$\sigma_{P/E}$	= standard deviation of P/E ratios across all stocks

Also note that by standardizing the factor sensitivity, we measure the number of standard deviations each sensitivity is from the average. For example, a stock with a standardized P/E sensitivity of 2.0 has a P/E that is 2 standard deviations above the mean; a stock with a sensitivity of −1.5 has a P/E that is one and a half standard deviations below the mean. This standardization process allows us to use different fundamental factors measured in different units in the same factor model. For example, P/E ratios are usually greater than 1.00 while dividend yields are in percentages (i.e., less than 1.00).

Example: Calculating a standardized sensitivity in a fundamental factor model

The P/E for Stock i is 15.20, the average P/E for all stocks is 11.90, and the standard deviation of P/E ratios is 6.30. Calculate the standardized sensitivity of Stock i to the P/E factor.

Answer:

The sensitivity of Stock i to the P/E factor is:

$$\beta_{i,\frac{P}{E}} = \frac{15.20 - 11.90}{6.30} = 0.52$$

Therefore, the P/E ratio for the stock is 0.52 standard deviations higher than the average stock P/E.

Factor returns ($F_{P/E}$ and F_{SIZE}). The fundamental factors are rates of return associated with each factor (e.g., rate of return difference between low and high P/E stocks). The return difference between low and high P/E stocks is commonly referred to as the return on a "factor mimicking portfolio." In practice, the values of the fundamental factors are estimated as slopes of cross-sectional regressions in which the dependent variable is the set of returns for all stocks and the independent variables are the standardized sensitivities.

Intercept term (a_i). Consider a stock that has fundamental factor sensitivities that equal the market-wide averages. In other words, consider the average stock in the market. All the standardized sensitivities for this representative stock will equal zero (the numerator for each standardized sensitivity will equal zero). Therefore, the expected return for the representative stock equals the intercept of the fundamental factor model (all other terms in the model equal zero).

The Macroeconomic Factor Model vs. the Fundamental Factor Model

The key differences between the macroeconomic factor model and the fundamental factor model can be summarized as follows:

- *Sensitivities.* The standardized sensitivities in the fundamental factor model (b_{i1} and b_{i2}) are calculated directly from the attribute (e.g., P/E) data—they are not estimated. This contrasts with the macroeconomic factor model, in which the sensitivities are regression slope estimates.
- *Interpretation of factors.* The macroeconomic factors (F_{GDP} and F_{QS}) are surprises in the macroeconomic variables (e.g., inflation shock and interest rate shock). In contrast, the fundamental factors ($F_{P/E}$ and F_{SIZE}) are rates of return associated with each factor and are estimated using multiple regression.
- *Number of factors.* Macroeconomic factors are intended to represent systematic risk factors, and are usually small in number (i.e., a parsimonious model). Fundamental factors often are large in number, providing a more cumbersome, yet more detailed, model of the risk-return relationship for assets.
- *Intercept term.* The intercept in the macroeconomic factor model equals the stock's expected return (based on market consensus expectations of the macro factors) from an equilibrium pricing model like the APT. In contrast, the fundamental factor model intercept equals the expected return for stocks with factor sensitivities equal to the market-wide averages.

LOS 64.k: Calculate the expected return on a portfolio of two stocks, given the estimated macroeconomic factor model for each stock.

As explained in the previous LOS, the macroeconomic model intercept equals the stock's expected return. Using the macroeconomic model, we can describe the returns for stocks i and j as follows:

$$R_i = E(R_i) + b_{i1}F_{IP} + b_{i2}F_{QS} + \varepsilon_i$$

$$R_j = E(R_j) + b_{j1}F_{IP} + b_{j2}F_{QS} + \varepsilon_j$$

The expected values of the factors and random error in a macroeconomic factor model equal zero. Therefore, using the macroeconomic factor model, the expected return for a stock equals the intercept. Using the two-factor macroeconomic factor model, the expected return on the portfolio is:

$$E(R_p) = w_i E(R_i) + w_j E(R_j)$$

Example: Calculate the expected return for a portfolio

Consider a portfolio allocated 75% to Rent Shop and 25% to Carpets Plus. Calculate the expected return for the portfolio, given the following macroeconomic model results:

$$R_{RENT} = 0.14 + 1.5F_1 + 0.8F_2 + \varepsilon_{RENT}$$

$$R_{CARPETS} = 0.08 + 1.2F_1 + 0.2F_2 + \varepsilon_{CARPETS}$$

Answer:

The portfolio expected return simply equals the weighted average of the two intercepts.

$$E(R_p) = 0.75(0.14) + 0.25(0.08) = 0.125 = 12.5\%$$

Also, note that the portfolio sensitivity to each factor equals the weighted average of the two stock sensitivities:

$$b_{p1} = 0.75(1.5) + 0.25(1.2) = 1.425$$

$$b_{p2} = 0.75(0.8) + 0.25(0.2) = 0.65$$

Professor's Note: If the macroeconomic model is used to derive the actual portfolio return (rather than the portfolio expected return), then we simply use the weighted average of the macroeconomic models for the two stocks. From the previous example, the portfolio return equals:

$$R_p = 0.125 + 1.425F_1 + 0.65F_2 + 0.75(\varepsilon_{RENT}) + 0.25(\varepsilon_{CARPETS})$$

LOS 64.l: Discuss the arbitrage pricing theory (APT), including its underlying assumptions and its relation to the multifactor models, calculate the expected return on an asset given an asset's factor sensitivities and the factor risk premiums, and determine whether an arbitrage opportunity exists, including how to exploit the opportunity.

The Arbitrage Pricing Theory (APT) refers to an asset pricing theory that assumes:

- *Returns are derived from a multifactor model.* Unfortunately, the APT provides little practical guidance for the identification of the risk factors. The lack of clarity for the risk factors is a major weakness of the APT.

- *Unsystematic risk can be completely diversified away.* This implies that unsystematic risk is not priced (has zero risk premium).
- No arbitrage opportunities exist. An arbitrage opportunity is defined as an investment opportunity that bears no risk, no cost, and yet provides a profit. This assumption implies that investors will undertake infinitely large positions (long and short) to exploit any perceived mispricing, causing asset prices to adjust immediately to their equilibrium values.

The asset pricing model developed by the arbitrage pricing theory is called the *arbitrage pricing model.*

The APT Equation

The APT describes the equilibrium relationship between expected returns for well-diversified portfolios and their multiple sources of systematic risk.

$$E(R_P) = R_F + \beta_{P,1}(\lambda_1) + \beta_{P,2}(\lambda_2) + \ldots + \beta_{P,k}(\lambda_k)$$

Each λ stands for the expected risk premium associated with each risk factor. Each λ_j equals the risk premium for a portfolio (called a *pure factor portfolio*, which is discussed later) with factor sensitivity equal to 1 to factor *j* and factor sensitivities equal to zero for the remaining factors. Remember that a risk premium is the difference between the expected return and the risk-free rate. It is the extra expected return from taking on more risk.

Each β represents the sensitivity (also called factor "loading") of Portfolio P to each risk factor. Each factor in the arbitrage pricing model is "priced," meaning that each risk premium is statistically and economically significant. Unlike the CAPM, the APT does *not* require that one of the risk factors is the market portfolio. This is a major advantage of the arbitrage pricing model.

 Professor's Note: The CAPM can be considered a special restrictive case of the APT in which there is only one risk factor, and that one factor is restricted to be the market risk factor.

Example: Calculating expected returns from the arbitrage pricing model

An investment firm employs a two-factor APT model. The risk-free rate equals 5%. Determine the expected return for the Invest Fund using the following data:

	Factor 1	Factor 2
Invest Fund factor betas	1.50	2.00
Factor risk premiums	0.0300	0.0125

Answer:

Using the two-factor APT model, the expected return for the Invest Fund (IF) equals:

$$E(R_{IF}) = 0.05 + 1.5(0.03) + 2(0.0125) = 0.12 = 12\%$$

The method for exploiting arbitrage opportunities in the APT framework is detailed in the following example.

Example: Exploiting an arbitrage opportunity

Assume your investment firm uses a single factor model to evaluate assets. Consider the following data for portfolios, A, B, and C:

Portfolio	Expected Return	Beta
A	10%	1.0
B	20%	2.0
C	13%	1.5

Calculate the arbitrage opportunity from the data provided. *Hint: Create a portfolio with 50% in A and 50% in B, and then compare the expected return and beta of that portfolio to Portfolio C.*

Answer:

By allocating 50% to portfolios A and B, we can obtain a portfolio (D) with beta equal to the Portfolio C beta (1.50):

beta for Portfolio D = 0.50(1) + 0.50(2) = 1.50

While the betas for portfolios D and C are identical, the expected returns are different:

expected return for Portfolio D = 0.50(0.10) + 0.50(0.20) = 0.15 = 15%

Therefore, we have created Portfolio D that has the same risk as Portfolio C (beta = 1.50), but has higher expected return than Portfolio C (15% versus 13%). By purchasing Portfolio D and short-selling Portfolio C, we expect to earn a 2% return (15% minus 13%).

 Professor's Note: Recall that a portfolio beta equals the weighted average of the individual asset betas, and, likewise, the portfolio expected return equals the weighted average of the individual asset expected returns.

The portfolio that is long Portfolio D and short Portfolio C is called the *arbitrage portfolio*. We have invested nothing up front because we merely use the proceeds of the short sale on Portfolio C to purchase Portfolio D. And, we have undertaken no systematic risk. The beta on our investment equals the difference in betas between our long and short positions: 1.5 – 1.5 = 0. As investors exploit the arbitrage opportunity, prices of assets in Portfolio C will drop and the (future) expected return for Portfolio C will rise to its equilibrium value.

The APT assumes there are no market imperfections preventing investors from exploiting arbitrage opportunities. As a result, extreme long and short positions are permitted and mispricing will disappear immediately. Therefore, all arbitrage opportunities such as the one described in the previous example would be exploited and eliminated immediately.

Differences Between the APT and Multifactor Models

It's important to understand the differences between the APT and the macroeconomic and fundamental multifactor models we discussed in the previous LOS.

- The APT is a cross-sectional equilibrium pricing model that explains the variation *across assets'* expected returns during a single time period. The multifactor model is a time-series regression that explains the variation *over time* in returns for one asset.
- The APT is an equilibrium-pricing model that assumes no arbitrage opportunities. The macroeconomic multifactor models are *ad hoc* (i.e., rather than being derived directly from an equilibrium theory, the factors are identified empirically by looking for macroeconomic variables that best fit the data).
- The intercept term in a macroeconomic factor model is the asset's expected return, and is derived from the APT equation. The APT intercept is the risk-free rate.

LOS 64.m: Explain the sources of active risk, define and interpret tracking error, tracking risk, and the information ratio, and explain factor portfolio and tracking portfolio.

 Professor's Note: The LOS uses the terms "tracking error" and "tracking risk," although the CFA Program Curriculum typically uses the terms "active return" and "active risk" throughout the presentation. We will use the same terminology here: active return refers to tracking error and active risk refers to tracking risk.

Active return (also known as *tracking error*) equals the differences in returns between a managed portfolio and its benchmark:

$$active\ return = R_P - R_B$$

Active risk (also known as *tracking risk*) is defined as the standard deviation of the active return:

$$active\ risk = s_{(R_P - R_B)} = \sqrt{\frac{\sum (R_{Pt} - R_{Bt})^2}{n-1}}$$

The active risk of a portfolio can be separated into two components:

1. *Active factor risk*: Risk from active factor tilts attributable to deviations of the portfolio's factor sensitivities versus the benchmark's sensitivities to the same set of factors.

©2009 Kaplan, Inc.

2. *Active specific risk*: Risk from active asset selection attributable to deviations of the portfolio's individual asset weightings versus the benchmark's individual asset weightings, after controlling for differences in factor sensitivities of the portfolio versus the benchmark.

The sum of active factor risk and active specific risk is equal to active risk squared (which is the variance of active returns):

active risk squared = active factor risk + active specific risk

Both components contribute to deviations of the portfolio's returns from the benchmark's returns. For example, consider a fundamental factor model that includes industry risk factors. In this case, active risk can be described as follows:

- *Active factor risk example*: An active portfolio manager may decide to under or over-weight particular industries relative to the portfolio's benchmark. Therefore, the portfolio's industry factor sensitivities will not coincide with those of the benchmark, and, consequently, the portfolio returns may deviate from the benchmark.
- *Active specific risk example*: The active portfolio manager may decide to overweight or underweight individual assets within specific industries. For example, a stock's market capitalization may comprise 1% of the industry, but the portfolio manager may allocate 2% of their industry allocation to the stock, causing the portfolio returns to deviate from the benchmark returns.

Example: Active risk comparisons

Consider two funds: Management Fund and Steady Fund. The benchmark for both funds is the Wilshire 5000, a well-diversified stock index. The active factor risk for Management Fund equals 20 and for Steady Fund equals 5. The active specific risk for Management Fund equals 30 and for Steady Fund equals 2. Contrast the two styles of portfolio management for the two funds.

Answer:

Management Fund is more actively managed, exhibiting both higher active factor risk and higher active specific risk. Management Fund more actively manages its factor exposures, leading to high active factor risk. Also, Management Fund is characterized by asset selection that differs substantially from the benchmark, as indicated by its high active specific risk.

In contrast, Steady Fund is much more passively managed. Note that a passively managed index fund should have zero active risk (when examining gross returns only). Also, note that a tracking fund (discussed in detail later), with active asset selection but with factor sensitivities that match those of the benchmark, will have no active factor risk, but will still have some degree of exposure to active specific risk.

The Information Ratio

Active return alone is insufficient in measuring the manager's performance over a series of measurement periods. For example, assume Manager A earned a constant 0.5% (50 bps) active return over each of the last four quarters. On the other hand, assume Manager B earned active returns of 8%, 5%, –3% and –8% over the same four quarters. The average active returns for managers A and B are both 0.5%, but Manager B experienced far more volatility (i.e., less consistency) than Manager A.

To demonstrate a manager's consistency in generating active return, we utilize the *information ratio* in which we standardize average active return by dividing it by its standard deviation. In other words, the information ratio equals the portfolio's average active return divided by the portfolio's tracking risk:

$$IR = \frac{\bar{R}_P - \bar{R}_B}{s_{(R_P - R_B)}}$$

Example: Calculating the information ratio

Assume the portfolio and benchmark returns over the past 12 months have been as shown in the following figure.

Portfolio and Benchmark Returns for Twelve Months

Month	R_p	R_B	$R_p - R_B$
1	0.0101	0.0091	0.0010
2	–0.0013	0.0062	–0.0075
3	0.0110	0.0069	0.0041
4	0.0135	0.0071	0.0064
5	0.0103	0.0067	0.0036
6	0.0093	0.0051	0.0042
7	–0.0011	0.0007	–0.0018
8	0.0085	0.0105	–0.0020
9	0.0091	0.0101	–0.0010
10	–0.0073	–0.0030	–0.0043
11	0.0186	0.0012	0.0174
12	0.0103	0.0097	0.0006
Average	**0.0076**	**0.0059**	**0.0017**
		Sample Std. Dev.	0.0063

Given the data in the figure, calculate and interpret the manager's information ratio.

Answer:

$$IR = \frac{(\bar{R}_P - \bar{R}_B)}{s_{(R_P - R_B)}} = \frac{0.0076 - 0.0059}{0.0063} \approx 0.27$$

The higher the IR, the more active return the manager earned per unit of active risk. An information ratio of 0.27 indicates the manager earned about 27 basis points of active return per unit of active risk.

Professor's Note: The information ratio is very similar to the Sharpe ratio. First, their numerators are similar in that they both compare the average portfolio return to a benchmark. The difference is that the Sharpe ratio uses the risk-free rate as the benchmark and the IR uses a portfolio benchmark return (one that best matches the investment style of the managed portfolio). In the denominator, both use standard deviation to measure dispersion, so both measure return per unit of total variability. The Sharpe ratio uses the standard deviation of portfolio returns over the measurement period and the information ratio uses the standard deviation of the active return over the measurement period.

Uses of Factor and Tracking Portfolios

A *pure factor portfolio* (or simply a *factor portfolio*) is a portfolio that has been constructed to have sensitivity equal to 1.0 to only one risk factor, and sensitivities of zero to the remaining factors. Factor portfolios are particularly useful for speculation or hedging purposes. For example, assume a portfolio manager believes GDP growth will be stronger than expected, but wishes to hedge against all other factor risks. The manager can take a long position in the GDP "factor portfolio." The factor portfolio is exposed to the GDP risk factor, but is hedged (zero sensitivity) to all other risk factors. This manager is speculating that GDP will rise above market expectations.

Alternatively, consider a manager who wishes to hedge his portfolio against GDP factor risk. Assume the portfolio's GDP factor sensitivity equals 0.80, and the portfolio's sensitivities to the remaining risk factors are different from zero. Suppose the portfolio manager wishes to hedge against GDP risk, but remain exposed to the remaining factors. The manager can hedge against GDP risk by taking an 80% short position in the GDP factor portfolio. The 0.80 GDP sensitivity of the managed portfolio will be offset by the –0.80 GDP sensitivity from the short position in the GDP factor portfolio.

The important point is that a factor portfolio is assumed to be hedged against all but one source of risk (i.e., has zero sensitivities for all but one risk factor), and has unit sensitivity to the remaining factor.

In contrast, *tracking portfolios* have a deliberately designed *set* of factor exposures. That is, a tracking portfolio is deliberately constructed to have the same set of factor exposures to match ("track") a predetermined benchmark. The strategy involved in constructing a tracking portfolio is usually an active bet on asset selection. The manager constructs the portfolio to have the same factor exposures as the benchmark, but then selects what they believe to be superior securities (subject to the factor sensitivities constraint), thus hopefully outperforming the benchmark without taking on more systematic risk than the benchmark.

For example, suppose a portfolio manager is evaluated relative to the S&P 500 benchmark, but believes she can beat the index with superior stock selection. One strategy would be to create a tracking portfolio with the same set of factor exposures as the S&P 500, but with a different set of securities. Any differences in performance between her portfolio and the S&P 500 benchmark should be the result of her stock selection ability and not from different exposures to macroeconomic risk factors.

LOS 64.n: Compare and contrast the conclusions and the underlying assumptions of the CAPM and the APT models, and explain why an investor can possibly earn a substantial premium for exposure to dimensions of risk unrelated to market movements.

Both the arbitrage pricing model and the capital asset pricing model discussed earlier are models describing equilibrium expected returns for assets, but there are some very important differences between the two models.

The CAPM suggests that all investors should hold some combination of the market portfolio and the risk-free asset. To adjust risk, less risk-averse investors simply hold more of the market portfolio, and less of the risk-free asset. More risk-averse investors hold more of the risk-free asset, and less of the market portfolio. The risk of the investor's portfolio is determined solely by the resulting portfolio beta (market risk), so the CAPM assumes there is only one source of systematic ("priced") risk.

In contrast, the APT gives no special role to the market portfolio (i.e., the APT does not require the existence of the "market portfolio"), and is, therefore, a far more flexible model than the CAPM. Also, in contrast to the CAPM, the APT states that asset returns follow a multifactor process, thereby allowing investors to manage several risk factors, rather than just one. This more targeted approach to portfolio management may help improve portfolio performance. The investor can identify and earn returns or hedge risks associated with factors such as recession risk, interest rate risk, or inflation risk. Thus, the investor's unique circumstances (different from the average investor) may drive the investor to hold portfolios tilted away from the market portfolio in order to hedge or speculate on multiple risk factors.

For example, the typical investor, who has a job and depends on a salary for income, is sensitive to recessions (which occur when GDP declines). Therefore the typical investor faces a systematic risk of recessions and will tend to avoid cyclical stocks (depressing their prices, which leads to a higher risk premium) and pursue countercyclical stocks (bidding up their prices, which leads to a lower risk premium).

The result of the behavior of the typical investor is that the business cycle actually becomes a priced risk factor (which is why GDP surprise is often used as a factor in macroeconomic models). Investors who are independently wealthy and don't depend on their salary as a source of income may be able to earn a substantial risk premium by increasing their portfolio allocation to cyclical stocks, because they are exposed to less than average systematic recession risk by virtue of not being dependent upon salary income.

KEY CONCEPTS

LOS 64.a

In mean-variance analysis, we use the expected returns, variances, and covariances of individual investment returns to analyze the risk-return tradeoff of combinations (portfolios) of individual investments.

Key assumptions made in mean-variance analysis include: investors are risk averse; statistical inputs (means, variances, covariances) are known; investors make all portfolio decisions based solely on means, variances, and covariances; and investors face no taxes or transactions costs.

The expected return on a portfolio of two assets is the weighted average of the returns on the individual assets:

$$E(R_p) = w_1 E(R_1) + w_2 E(R_2)$$

Similarly, the expected return for a three-asset portfolio equals:

$$E(R_p) = w_1 E(R_1) + w_2 E(R_2) + w_3 E(R_3)$$

The variance of a portfolio of two assets equals:

$$\sigma_P^2 = w_1^2 \sigma_1^2 + w_2^2 \sigma_2^2 + 2w_1 w_2 \rho_{12} \sigma_1 \sigma_2$$

And, the variance of a portfolio of three assets equals:

$$\sigma_P^2 = w_1^2 \sigma_1^2 + w_2^2 \sigma_2^2 + w_3^2 \sigma_3^2 + 2w_1 w_2 \rho_{12} \sigma_1 \sigma_2 + 2w_1 w_3 \rho_{13} \sigma_1 \sigma_3 + 2w_2 w_3 \rho_{23} \sigma_2 \sigma_3$$

The standard deviation equals the square root of the variance.

LOS 64.b

The minimum-variance frontier is a graph drawn in risk-return space of the set of portfolios that have the lowest variance at each level of expected return. To derive the minimum-variance frontier, we must: estimate the risk-return attributes of all assets, run an optimizer that selects portfolio weightings that minimize portfolio variance subject to expected return constraints, and calculate and graph the risk and return for the minimum-variance portfolios.

The efficient frontier is the positively sloped portion of the minimum-variance frontier. Portfolios on the efficient frontier have the highest expected return at each given level of risk.

The minimum-variance frontier and efficient frontier are unstable because expected returns, variances, and covariances change over time. This is problematic and may lead to large portfolio weighting errors.

LOS 64.c

Portfolio diversification refers to the strategy of reducing risk by combining different types of assets into a portfolio. Diversification benefits increase as the correlations among assets decrease, and as the number of assets included in the portfolio increase (but portfolio risk falls at a decreasing rate as the size of the portfolio increases).

LOS 64.d

The variance of an equally-weighted portfolio is:

$$\sigma_P^2 = \frac{1}{n}\overline{\sigma_i^2} + \frac{n-1}{n}\overline{\text{Cov}} = \overline{\sigma_i^2}\left(\frac{1-\rho}{n}+\rho\right)$$

If a risk-free investment is part of the investment opportunity set, the efficient frontier is a straight line called the CAL.

The CAL is developed using the investor's unique set of expectations.

The y-intercept of the CAL is the risk-free rate and the slope is the Sharpe ratio for the optimal risky portfolio. The CAL lies tangent to the efficient frontier of risky assets. The CAL equation is:

$$E(R_C) = R_F + \left[\frac{E(R_T)-R_F}{\sigma_T}\right]\sigma_C$$

where $E(R_C)$ = expected return on the portfolio combination of the risk-free asset and the optimal risky Portfolio T (the tangency portfolio), and σ_C is the standard deviation on the portfolio combination.

The CML is the CAL developed assuming all investors have identical expectations. All investors agree on the composition of the optimal risky portfolio, now called the market portfolio, which uses market-value weights. The equation of the CML is:

$$E(R_C) = R_F + \left[\frac{E(R_M)-R_F}{\sigma_M}\right]\sigma_C$$

LOS 64.e

The CAPM is an equilibrium asset pricing model that assumes that market risk, measured by beta, is the only risk priced by investors. The Security Market Line is the graph of the CAPM:

$$E(R_i) = R_F + \beta_i[E(R_M - R_F)]$$

The intercept of the SML is the risk-free rate, R_F, and the slope is the market risk premium, $E(R_M) - R_F$.

LOS 64.f

The market price of risk is the Sharpe ratio for the market portfolio (the slope of the CML). It equals the market risk premium per unit of market risk.

Beta is a measure of an asset's systematic risk, and equals the sensitivity to movements in the market portfolio. The formula for the beta equals:

$$\beta_i = \frac{Cov_{iM}}{\sigma_M^2} = \frac{\rho_{iM}\sigma_i\sigma_M}{\sigma_M^2} = \rho_{iM}\left(\frac{\sigma_i}{\sigma_M}\right)$$

LOS 64.g

The market model is a single-factor regression model that assumes there are just two sources of risk, unanticipated macroeconomic events (systematic risk) and firm-specific events (unsystematic risk). According to the market model, the return to Asset i is:

$$R_i = \alpha_i + \beta_i R_M + \varepsilon_i$$

The market model makes three assumptions: the expected value of the error term is zero, the errors are uncorrelated with the market return, and the firm-specific surprises are uncorrelated across assets. The market model greatly simplifies the forecast procedures needed for mean-variance analysis.

The market model makes the following predictions:
- The expected return on Asset i depends only on the expected return on the market portfolio, $E(R_M)$, the sensitivity of the returns on Asset i to movements in the market, β_i, and the average return to Asset i when the market return is zero, α_i.
- The variance of the returns on Asset i consists of two components: a systematic component related to the asset's beta, $\beta_i^2\sigma_M^2$, and an unsystematic component related to firm-specific events, σ_ε^2.
- The covariance between any two stocks is calculated as the product of their betas and the variance of the market portfolio: $Cov_{ij} = \beta_i\beta_j\sigma_M^2$.

LOS 64.h

Historical betas may be very poor predictors of future betas. Therefore, we often employ the adjusted beta formula, which adjusts the future beta toward a value of 1 over time.

LOS 64.i

The instability in the minimum-variance frontier is a concern for a number of reasons:
- The statistical inputs (means, variances, covariances) are unknown, and must be forecast; greater uncertainty in the inputs leads to less reliability in the efficient frontier.
- Statistical input forecasts derived from historical sample estimates often change over time, causing the estimated efficient frontier to change over time (this is called time instability).
- Small changes in the statistical inputs can cause large changes in the efficient frontier (called the "overfitting" problem), resulting in unreasonably large short positions, and overly frequent rebalancing.

LOS 64.j

A multifactor model is an extension of a one-factor market model in which asset returns are a function of more than one factor. There are three types of multifactor models:

- Macroeconomic factor models assume that asset returns are explained by surprises (or "shocks") in macroeconomic risk factors (e.g., GDP, interest rates, inflation). Factor surprises are defined as the difference between the realized value of the factor and its consensus expected value.
- Fundamental factor models assume asset returns are explained by the returns from multiple firm-specific factors (e.g., P/E ratio, market cap, leverage ratio, earnings growth rate).
- Statistical factor models use multivariate statistics (factor analysis or principal components) to identify statistical factors that explain the covariation among asset returns. The major weakness is that the statistical factors do not lend themselves well to economic interpretation.

LOS 64.k

Using a multifactor model, the portfolio expected return, factor sensitivities, and the error terms are calculated as the weighted average of the individual stock parameters.

LOS 64.l

The APT is an equilibrium asset-pricing k-factor model which assumes no arbitrage opportunities exist. According to the APT, the expected return on a diversified portfolio P is linearly related to its factor sensitivities:

$$E(R_p) = R_F + \beta_{P1}(\lambda_1) + \beta_{P2}(\lambda_2) + \ldots + \beta_{Pk}(\lambda_k),$$ where each λ stands for the expected risk premium associated with each risk factor

LOS 64.m

Active return is the difference between portfolio and benchmark returns ($R_P - R_B$), and active risk is the standard deviation of active return over time. Active risk is determined by the manager's active factor tilt and active asset selection decisions.

Active risk squared = active risk + active specific risk.

The information ratio is active return divided by active risk: $IR = \dfrac{\bar{R}_P - \bar{R}_B}{s_{(R_P - R_B)}}$

A factor portfolio is a portfolio with a factor sensitivity of 1 to a particular factor and zero to all other factors. It represents a pure bet on one factor, and can be used for speculation or hedging purposes.

A tracking portfolio is a portfolio with a specific set of factor sensitivities. Tracking portfolios are often designed to replicate the factor exposures of a benchmark index like the S&P 500.

LOS 64.n

The CAPM is a single-factor asset pricing model, in which only risk relative to the broad market is priced. The CAPM suggests that all investors should hold some combination of the market portfolio and the risk-free asset. In contrast, the APT captures multiple dimensions of risk besides the overall market risk, and suggests that investors make decisions relative to multiple sources of risk.

Investors who are independently wealthy and don't depend on their salary as a source of income can earn a substantial risk premium by increasing their portfolio allocation to cyclical stocks, even though they are exposed to less than average systematic recession risk.

CONCEPT CHECKERS

1. Assume the following information for stocks A and B.
    *   Expected return on Stock A = 18%.
    *   Expected return on Stock B = 23%.
    *   Correlation between returns of Stock A and Stock B = 0.10.
    *   Standard deviation of returns on Stock A = 40%.
    *   Standard deviation of returns on Stock B = 50%.

    The expected return and standard deviation of an equally weighted portfolio of stocks A and B are *closest* to:

	Expected return (%)	Standard deviation (%)
A.	20.5	33.54
B.	20.5	11.22
C.	33.5	11.22

Use the following data to answer Questions 2 through 4.

Assume the expected return on stocks is 18% (represented by *Z* in the figure), and the expected return on bonds is 8% (represented by point *Y* on the graph).

Minimum-Variance Frontier: Stocks and Bonds

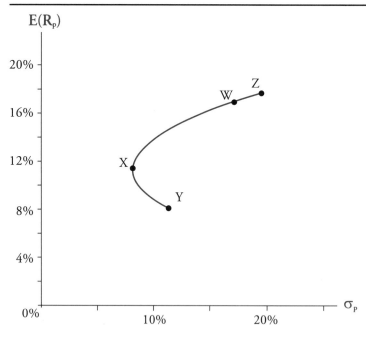

2. The graph shows the minimum-variance frontier for stocks and bonds. The point on the graph that *most likely* represents a 90% allocation in stocks and a 10% allocation in bonds is Portfolio:
    A. W.
    B. X.
    C. Z.

3.   According to the graph, the point that *most likely* represents the global
      minimum-variance portfolio is Portfolio:
      A. X.
      B. W.
      C. Z.

4.   The efficient frontier consists of the portfolios between and including:
      A. X and W.
      B. Y and Z.
      C. X and Z.

5.   The benefits of diversifying from a 1-stock to a 2-stock portfolio will be *greatest*
      when the correlation between the two stocks is:
      A. –1.0.
      B.   0.0.
      C. +1.0.

Use the following figure to answer Questions 6 and 7.

Mean-Variance Analysis

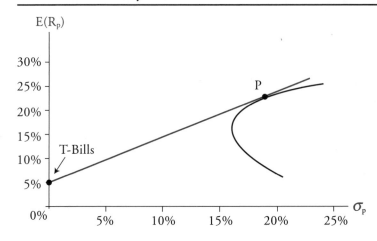

6.   Portfolio P is the point where the straight line is tangent to the curve. It is also
      the market portfolio. The market price of risk is the:
      A. expected return on the minimum-variance portfolio.
      B. slope of the line connecting T-bills and Portfolio P.
      C. point at which the straight line intersects the expected return axis.

7.   Portfolio P is the point where the straight line is tangent to the curve. It is also
      the market portfolio. The line that connects T-bills and Portfolio P is called the:
      A. capital market line.
      B. security market line.
      C. efficient market line.

Use the following data to answer Questions 8 through 12.

Samuel Perkins using the capital market line (CML) to advise his clients. Current market expectations are as follows:

- Expected return on the market portfolio   12%
- Standard deviation on the market portfolio   20%
- Risk-free rate   4%

8.   Perkins advises a client who would like to have a portfolio with a standard deviation equal to 10%. Using the CML, a portfolio meeting the client's risk tolerance will have an expected return *closest* to:
     A.   6%.
     B.   8%.
     C.   10%.

9.   Perkins advises another client who currently owns a portfolio with an expected return of 8% and a standard deviation of 15%. The amount (percentage points) by which Perkins can improve his client's expected return by using the CML while maintaining the client's 15% standard deviation is *closest* to:
     A.   2%.
     B.   4%.
     C.   6%.

10.   One of Perkins's clients has an expected return objective of 10%. Using the CML, Perkins can create a portfolio with a standard deviation as low as:
     A.   13%.
     B.   14%.
     C.   15%.

11.   What is the appropriate allocation to the optimal risky portfolio for a Perkins's client who has a 10% standard deviation objective?
     A.   30%.
     B.   40%.
     C.   50%.

12.   From the data provided, the intercept and slope of the CML are *closest* to:
     A.   4% intercept and a 8% slope.
     B.   4% intercept and a 40% slope.
     C.   8% intercept and a 40% slope.

13. At a recent analyst meeting at Invest Forum, analysts Michelle White and
     Ted Jones discussed the use of the capital asset pricing model (CAPM) and
     the arbitrage pricing theory (APT). White states that the CAPM implies that
     investors hold a risky portfolio of all assets weighted according to their relative
     market value capitalizations. Jones states that the APT implies that investors will
     make investment decisions by allocating their money between a risk-free asset
     and the market portfolio.

     Are the statements of White and Jones correct?
     A. Both statements are correct.
     B. Only one of the statements is correct.
     C. Neither statement is correct.

14. Analysts Linda Yarbrough and Pamela Burke recently discussed the application
     of the market model. Yarbrough comments that, assuming betas remain
     constant, the market model prediction of the covariance between any two
     assets rises during a period of rising market volatility. Burke states that the
     market model prediction of covariance will not be correct if the firm's unique
     components of asset returns are correlated.

     Are the statements of Yarbrough and Burke correct?
     A. Both statements are correct.
     B. Only one of the statements is correct.
     C. Neither statement is correct.

15. An equally-weighted portfolio is formed in which the average stock variance
     equals 9% and the average covariance equals 5%. As the number of assets
     included in this portfolio increases, portfolio risk will *most likely* fall at a(n):
     A. increasing rate and approach 9%.
     B. steady rate and approach 7%.
     C. decreasing rate and approach 5%.

16. Which of the following statements is *least likely* a prediction of the single-factor
     market model?
     A. The covariance between two assets is related to the betas of the two assets
         and the variance of the market portfolio.
     B. All investors hold the market portfolio, so the CML is defined as the capital
         allocation line with the market portfolio as the tangency portfolio.
     C. The expected return on Asset i depends on the market's expected return, the
         sensitivity of Asset i's returns to the market, and the average return to Asset i
         not related to the market return.

17. A multifactor model uses factors that are stock or company characteristics, such
     as price-to-book and price-to-earnings ratios, that have been shown to affect
     asset returns. This type of multifactor model would be called a:
     A. systematic factor model.
     B. fundamental factor model.
     C. macroeconomic factor model.

18.   Jones Brothers uses a 2-factor macroeconomic factor model to evaluate stocks and has derived the following results for the stock of AmGrow (AG):
- Expected return   10%
- GDP factor sensitivity   2
- Inflation factor sensitivity   −0.5

Over the past year, GDP grew at a rate that was two percentage points lower than originally expected, and inflation rose two percentage points higher than originally expected. AG also experienced a large unexpected product recall causing a firm-unique surprise of −4% to its stock price. Based on the information provided, the rate of return for AG for the year was *closest* to:

A. 1%.

B. 2%.

C. 3%.

19.   Patricia Franklin makes buy and sell stock recommendations using the capital asset pricing model. Franklin has derived the following information for the broad market and for the stock of the CostSave Company (CS):
- Expected market risk premium   8%
- Risk free rate   5%
- Historical beta for CostSave   1.50

Franklin believes that historical betas do not provide good forecasts of future beta, and, therefore, uses the adjusted beta formula:

forecast beta = 0.80 + 0.20 × historical beta

After conducting a thorough examination of market trends and the CS financial statements, Franklin predicts that the CS return will equal 10%. Franklin should derive the following required return for CS along with the following valuation decision (undervalued or overvalued):

	Valuation	CAPM required return
A.	overvalued	8.3%
B.	overvalued	13.8%
C.	undervalued	13.8%

20.   A portfolio that has the same factor sensitivities as the S&P 500, but does not hold all 500 stocks in the index, is called a:

A. factor portfolio.

B. tracking portfolio.

C. market portfolio.

21.   A portfolio with a factor sensitivity of one to the yield spread factor and a sensitivity of zero to all other macroeconomic factors is *best* described as a:

A. factor portfolio.

B. tracking portfolio.

C. market portfolio.

22.   Factor Investments manages a tracking portfolio which claims to outperform the
       S&P 500. The active factor risk and active specific risk for the tracking portfolio
       are *most likely* to be:
       A. high active factor risk and high active specific risk.
       B. high active factor risk and low active specific risk.
       C. low active factor risk and high active specific risk.

Use the following information to answer Questions 23 and 24.

The Coolum family receives a $15,000 benefit from the will of a recently deceased
uncle. Uncle Coolum, after retiring from the dry-cleaning business, became an amateur
economist and was working in the following macroeconomic factor model for two
stocks:

$$R_{Jane's\ Buttons} = 0.16 + 1.40X_1 + 0.70X_2 + \varepsilon_{Buttons}$$

$$R_{Jim's\ Shoes} = 0.08 + 2.20X_1 + 0.30X_2 + \varepsilon_{Shoes}$$

where the current factors are:

X_1	= 0.009
X_2	= 0.015
$\rho_{Buttons,Shoes}$	= 0.720
σ_{Shoes}	= 0.034
$\sigma_{Buttons}$	= 0.057

23.   The family decides to invest Uncle Coolum's money into Jane's Buttons (60%)
       and Jim's Shoes (40%). The expected return for the portfolio would be *closest* to:
       A. 12.80%.
       B. 15.30%.
       C. 13.60%.

24.   In this problem, suppose that the factor values given in the problem are forecasts
       for the upcoming year. If the family decided to invest Uncle Coolum's money
       into Jim's Shoes (60%) and Jane's Buttons (40%), the expected return for the
       portfolio would be *closest* to:
       A. 12.80%.
       B. 15.30%.
       C. 13.60%.

25.   Which of the following is the *most* important assumption underlying the market
       model?
       A. The expected value of the error term is not 1.
       B. The errors are uncorrelated to the probability distribution function.
       C. The firm-specific surprises are uncorrelated across assets.

26. The Sharpe Ratio is best formulated as:

A. $\dfrac{\bar{R}_P - \bar{R}_B}{s_{(R_P - R_B)}}$

B. $\dfrac{E(R_T) - R_F}{\sigma_T}$

C. $R_F + \left[\dfrac{E(R_M) - R_F}{\sigma_M}\right]\sigma_C$

ANSWERS – CONCEPT CHECKERS

1. **A** $E(R_P) = w_A E(R_A) + w_B E(R_B) = (0.50)(0.18) + (0.50)(0.23) = 0.205 = 20.5\%$

    $\sigma_p = \left[w_A^2 \sigma_A^2 + w_B^2 \sigma_B^2 + 2 w_A w_B \rho_{AB} \sigma_A \sigma_B \right]^{\frac{1}{2}}$

    $\sigma_p = \left[\begin{matrix} (0.5)^2 (0.4)^2 + (0.5)^2 (0.5)^2 \\ + 2(0.5)(0.5)(0.1)(0.4)(0.5) \end{matrix} \right]^{\frac{1}{2}} = 0.3354 = 33.54\%$

2. **A** Since the return to *W* is the nearest to *Z* (stocks), it is logical to assume that point *W* represents an allocation of 90% stocks/10% bonds. The return for *W* is lower than *Z*, but it also represents a reduction in risk.

3. **A** The *global minimum-variance portfolio* is the portfolio on the minimum-variance frontier that has the smallest standard deviation (or variance). This portfolio appears as the farthest left point on the efficient frontier.

4. **C** The *efficient frontier* consists of portfolios that have the maximum expected return for any given level of risk (standard deviation or variance). The efficient frontier starts at the global minimum-variance portfolio and continues above it. Any portfolio below the efficient frontier is dominated by a portfolio on the efficient frontier. This is because efficient portfolios have higher expected returns for the same level of risk.

5. **A** As the correlation between two assets decreases, the benefits of diversification increase. That's because the separate movements of the stocks serve to reduce the volatility of the combination, leaving a portfolio that is less volatile than its individual components. As we combine the two stocks, the efficient frontier *bulges* up and to the left (i.e., northwesterly if you think of the plot as a map and north as up). This bulge is what creates the diversification benefits, because we can develop portfolios above the global minimum-variance portfolio that dominate those below. The greater the bulge, the greater the benefits! The amount of bulge in the frontier is a function of the correlation between the two assets: the lower the correlation (closer to −1), the greater the bulge. The larger the correlation (closer to +1), the smaller the bulge.

6. **B** The CML is the line connecting T-bills and Portfolio P. The market price of risk is the slope of the CML, which has the same interpretation as the slope coefficient of the CAL. Had risk been measured on the graph with beta, the graph would represent the SML. The market price of risk would still be the slope of the line.

7. **A** Since risk in the graph is represented by standard deviation and P is the market portfolio, the line represents the CML. The CML is the CAL with the market portfolio as the tangency portfolio. Had risk been measured by beta, the line would be the SML.

8. **B** The equation for the CML is:

$$E(R_C) = R_F + \left[\frac{E(R_M) - R_F}{\sigma_M} \right] \sigma_C \text{, where } R_F = 0.04$$

$$\left[\frac{E(R_M) - R_F}{\sigma_M} \right] = \left[\frac{0.12 - 0.04}{0.20} \right] = 0.40$$

Therefore, the equation of the CML is:

$E(R_C) = 0.04 + 0.40\sigma_C$

Setting the standard deviation equal to 0.10:

$E(R_C) = 0.04 + 0.40(0.10) = 0.08 = 8\%$

9. **A** The equation for the CML is: $E(R_C) = 0.04 + 0.40\sigma_C$. Setting the standard deviation equal to 0.15:

$E(R_C) = 0.04 + 0.40(0.15) = 0.10 = 10\%$

Therefore, Perkins can improve the client's expected return by two percentage points:

new expected return = 10%

old expected return = 8%

10. **C** The equation for the CML is: $E(R_C) = 0.04 + 0.40\sigma_C$. Setting the expected return to 0.10:

$E(R_C) = 0.10 = 0.04 + 0.40\sigma_C$

Solving for σ_C:

$0.40\sigma_C = 0.10 - 0.04 = 0.06$

$\sigma_C = 0.06/0.40 = 0.15 = 15\%$

11. **C** The standard deviation for the investment combination (of treasury bills and the market portfolio) equals:

$\sigma_C = w_M \sigma_M$

The client wants $\sigma_C = 0.10$.

Therefore, $0.10 = w_M(0.20)$.

$w_M = 0.10/0.20 = 0.50 = 50\%$

Therefore, the portfolio should be allocated 50% to Treasury bills and 50% to the market portfolio.

12. **B**   The equation for the CML is:

$$E(R_C) = R_F + \left[\frac{E(R_M) - R_F}{\sigma_M}\right]\sigma_C,$$

where the intercept is the risk-free rate, $R_F = 0.04$, or 4%, and the slope equals the market risk premium $[E(R_M) - R_F]$ per unit of market risk, σ_M.

$$\left[\frac{E(R_M) - R_F}{\sigma_M}\right] = \left[\frac{0.12 - 0.04}{0.20}\right] = 0.40, \text{ or } 40\%$$

13. **B**   The CAPM assumes all investors have identical expectations and all use mean-variance analysis, implying that they all identify the same risky tangency portfolio (the "market portfolio") and combine that risky portfolio with the risk-free asset when creating their portfolios. Because all investors hold the same risky portfolio, the weight on each asset must be equal to the proportion of its market value to the market value of the entire portfolio. Therefore, White is correct. In contrast, the APT places no special emphasis on the market portfolio. In fact, the APT does not even require that the "market portfolio" exist. Therefore, Jones is incorrect.

14. **A**   The market model makes a number of assumptions which lead to the prediction that the covariance between two assets equals the product of the asset betas times the market variance. Therefore, Yarbrough is correct. One of the assumptions of the market model is that firm-specific events are uncorrelated across firms. If this assumption is violated, then the market model predictions of the covariances will be wrong. Burke's statement is correct.

15. **C**   The formula for the variance of an equally-weighted portfolio is:

$\sigma_P^2 = \frac{1}{n}\overline{\sigma_i^2} + \frac{n-1}{n}\overline{Cov}$, where $\overline{\sigma_i^2}$ is the average variance of all assets in the portfolio

and $\overline{Cov}$ is the average covariance of all pairings of assets in the portfolio.

As *n* increases, the first term in the formula approaches zero, and the second term approaches the average covariance. That is:

- $(1/n) \times \overline{\sigma_i^2}$ gets closer to zero as *n* gets large.
- $[(n-1)/n] \times \overline{Cov}$ gets closer to the average covariance as *n* gets large.

Therefore, as *n* increases, the variance of the equally-weighted portfolio approaches the average covariance (5%). There are limits to the benefits of diversification benefits. As more assets are added to the portfolio, the portfolio variance approaches that of the broad market variance. Therefore, as the portfolio size increases, the portfolio risk falls at a decreasing rate.

16. **B**   The single-factor market model does not predict that all investors hold the market portfolio. The market model makes three predictions:
- The expected return on Asset i depends on the market's expected return, the sensitivity of Asset i's returns to the market, and the average return to Asset i not related to the market return.
- There are two components to the variance of the returns on Asset i: a systematic component related to the asset's beta and an unsystematic component related to firm-specific surprises.
- The covariance between two assets is related to the betas of the two assets and the variance of the market portfolio.

17. **B**   *Fundamental factor models* focus on microeconomic factors. Each factor, whether a ratio or a *descriptor*, has unique factor values.

18. **A**   The 2-factor model for AG is:

$$R_{AG} = 0.10 + 2(-0.02) - 0.50(0.02) - 0.04 = 0.01 = 1\%$$

The AG return was less than originally expected because AG was hurt by lower than expected economic growth (GDP), higher than expected inflation, and by negative company specific surprise events.

19. **B**   The CAPM equation is:

$$E(R_i) = R_F + \beta_i[E(R_M - R_F)]$$

Franklin wants to use the adjusted beta formula which equals:

beta forecast = 0.80 + 0.20(historical beta)

beta forecast = 0.80 + 0.20(1.50) = 1.10

The CAPM required return for CostSave is: 0.05 + 1.1(0.08) = 13.8%. Note that the market premium, $E(R_M) - R_F$, is provided in the question (8%).

Franklin should decide that the stock is overvalued because she forecasts that the CostSave return will equal only 10%, whereas the required return (minimum acceptable return) is 13.8%.

20. **B**   A *tracking portfolio* is a portfolio with a specific set of factor sensitivities. Tracking portfolios are often designed to replicate the factor exposures of a benchmark index like the S&P 500. In fact, a factor portfolio is just a special case of a tracking portfolio. One use of tracking portfolios is to attempt to outperform the S&P 500 by using the same factor exposures as the S&P 500, but with a different set of securities than the S&P 500.

21. **A**   A *factor portfolio* is a portfolio with a factor sensitivity of 1 to a particular factor and zero to all other factors. It represents a *pure bet* on that factor. For example, a portfolio manager who believes GDP growth will be greater than expected, but has no view of future interest rates and wants to hedge away the interest rate risk in his portfolio, could create a *factor portfolio* that is only exposed to the GDP factor and not the interest rate factor.

22. **C**   A tracking portfolio is deliberately constructed to have the same set of factor exposures to match ("track") a predetermined benchmark. The strategy involved in constructing a tracking portfolio is usually an active bet on asset selection (the manager claims to beat the S&P 500). The manager constructs the portfolio to have the same factor exposures as the benchmark, but then selects superior securities (subject to the factor sensitivities constraint), thus outperforming the benchmark without taking on more systematic risk than the benchmark. Therefore, a tracking portfolio, with active asset selection but with factor sensitivities that match those of the benchmark, will have little or no active factor risk, but will have high active specific risk.

23. **A**   This problem provides too much information, inviting you to use the wrong formula, and to waste time on what is really a simple problem. The correct calculation is 0.16 × 0.60 + 0.08 × 0.40 = 0.1280. The crucial point is to distinguish "expected return" from "actual return." Since the factors are "surprises," their expected values are zero.

24. **C**   Here we are assuming that the expected values for the factors are not zero—the family has a specific forecast that can be used in the model. The correct calculation is:

$[0.16 + (1.40 \times 0.009) + (0.70 \times 0.015)] \times 0.40 + [0.08 + (2.20 \times 0.009) + (0.30 \times 0.015)] \times 0.60 = 0.1358$

Note the change in weighting.

25. **C**   The market model makes three assumptions:
    - The expected value of the error term is zero. (Choice A is tempting, but not complete enough to be correct.)
    - The errors are uncorrelated with the market return.
    - The firm-specific surprises are uncorrelated across assets.

26. **B**   The three formulas shown in the question are for: (A) the information ratio, (B) the Sharpe ratio, and (C) the CML.

The following is a review of the Portfolio Management principles designed to address the learning outcome statements set forth by CFA Institute®. This topic is also covered in:

A Note on Harry M. Markowitz's "Market Efficiency: A Theoretical Distinction and So What?"

Study Session 18

Exam Focus

Here we address a key question not covered in the previous topic review: what happens to the CAPM if one or more of its key assumptions don't hold? Make sure you know the two key assumptions: restrictions on (1) risk-free borrowing and (2) short selling.

LOS 65.a: Discuss the efficiency of the market portfolio in the CAPM and the relation between the expected return and beta of an asset when restrictions on borrowing at the risk-free rate and on short selling exist.

Key assumptions of the CAPM: Recall from the previous topic review two of the key assumptions necessary to derive the capital asset pricing model (CAPM):

1. Investors can borrow and lend at the risk-free rate.

2. Unlimited short selling is allowed with full access to short sale proceeds.

Implications of the CAPM: The two major implications of the CAPM are:

1. The market portfolio lies on the efficient frontier (i.e., the market portfolio is efficient).

2. There is a linear relationship between an asset's expected returns and its beta:

$$E(R_I) = R_F + \beta_i[E(R_M) - R_F]$$

Remember that the graph of this relationship (which we called the security market line, or SML) is a straight line with an intercept equal to the risk-free rate and a slope equal to the market risk premium $(E(R_M) - R_F)$.

If key assumptions are violated: If those two key assumptions are violated (there are restrictions on *borrowing* at the risk-free rate and/or on short selling) then the two major implications don't hold:

1. The (former) market portfolio might lie below the efficient frontier (i.e., it might be inefficient). In other words, investors who seek a level of risk greater than that inherent in the former market portfolio would be unable to use leverage and would gravitate to risky portfolios further out on the Markowitz efficient frontier of risky assets. As these investors gravitate away from the former market portfolio, this would imply a change in the asset weightings that would necessarily move the market portfolio to some point below its former place on the frontier. Thus, all investors are affected.

2. The relationship between expected return and beta might not be linear.

   Note: Even though we are talking about beta risk, and not total risk, if you think of the end of the CML becoming a curve, as illustrated in Figure 13 of the previous topic review, you can easily visualize why this might happen.

LOS 65.b: Discuss the practical consequences that follow when restrictions on borrowing at the risk-free rate and on short selling exist.

The violation of these two key assumptions has practical consequences for analysts trying to use the CAPM in their investment decision making.

- The usual explanation for why the observed relationship between expected returns and beta is not linear is that the market portfolio is difficult to observe and measure accurately. However, even if the market portfolio is measured accurately, the relationship will not be linear if there are restrictions on either (1) risk-free borrowing and/or (2) short selling. Therefore, efforts to properly measure the market portfolio may not be sufficient to make the model useful.

- The CAPM predicts that the optimal investment strategy is to hold the market portfolio and the risk-free asset. More risk-averse investors will hold a relatively larger position in the risk-free asset and a smaller position in the market portfolio, while less risk-averse investors will hold a larger position in the market portfolio. If there are restrictions on risk-free borrowing and/or short selling, the two groups of investors will hold different portfolios of risky assets, neither of which is likely to be the market portfolio:
  - More risk-averse investors will hold a diversified portfolio consisting of a large number of securities, but the portfolio will be overweighted in low-risk/low expected return securities relative to the allocation in the market portfolio.
  - Less risk-averse investors will hold a portfolio consisting of a small number of high-risk/high expected return securities.

- One common use of the CAPM is to evaluate the performance of securities on a risk-adjusted basis. For example, suppose the risk-free rate is 5% and the market risk premium is 10%. That means an average-risk security with a beta of 1.0 will have an expected return of 15%. A low-risk security with a beta of 0.8 will have an expected return of 13%, and the "risk-adjustment" relative to an average-risk security is a 2% decrease. A high-risk security with a beta of 1.3 will have an expected return of 18% and a risk-adjustment of 3%. If there are restrictions on risk-free borrowing and/or short selling, these risk adjustments might not be accurate.

KEY CONCEPTS

LOS 65.a
Two key assumptions necessary to derive the CAPM are:
- Investors can borrow and lend at the risk-free rate.
- Unlimited short selling is allowed with full access to short sale proceeds.

The two major implications of the CAPM are:
- The market portfolio lies on the efficient frontier.
- There is a linear relationship between an asset's expected returns and its beta.

If these assumptions don't hold, then:
- The market portfolio might lie below the efficient frontier.
- The relationship between expected return and beta might not be linear.

LOS 65.b
The practical consequences are:
- Even if the market portfolio is measured accurately, the expected return/beta relationship still might not be linear.
- Less risk-averse investors will hold different risky portfolios than more risk-averse investors.
- CAPM risk-adjustments may not be appropriate.

CONCEPT CHECKERS

Use the following information to answer Questions 1 and 2.

Walter Higgins has been asked by his boss to research the effects of violations of key assumptions on the predictions of the Capital Asset Pricing Model (CAPM). Higgins identifies two key violations that he believes will have major implications for the usefulness of the CAPM if they are violated:

- Less risk-averse investors hold different risky portfolios than more risk-averse investors.
- There are restrictions on investors' ability to borrow at the risk-free rate.

Higgins also draws two conclusions regarding the major implications for the CAPM if the key assumptions are violated:

- The relationship between asset expected returns and systematic risk might not be linear.
- The market portfolio might be above or below the efficient frontier.

1. Is Higgins correct in his assessment of potential violations of CAPM assumptions related to investors' holding different risky portfolios? Is he correct about borrowing at the risk-free rate?
    A. Incorrect, correct.
    B. Correct, incorrect.
    C. Both incorrect.

2. Is Higgins correct in his assessment of the implications of violations of the key CAPM assumptions regarding (1) the linear relationship between risk and return and (2) the effect on the market portfolio?
    A. Incorrect, correct.
    B. Correct, incorrect.
    C. Both correct.

ANSWERS – CONCEPT CHECKERS

1. **A**   The key assumption violations that have major implications for the CAPM are that investors face restrictions on:
    *   Borrowing at the risk-free rate.
    *   Short selling and use of short sale proceeds.

    Less risk-averse investors holding different portfolios than more risk-averse investors is not an assumption necessary to derive the model; it is a *result* of the violation of the two key assumptions.

2. **B**   If those two key assumptions are violated, then:
    *   The market portfolio might lie below *(but not above)* the efficient frontier (i.e., it might be inefficient).
    *   The relationship between expected return and beta might not be linear.

INTERNATIONAL ASSET PRICING

Study Session 18

EXAM FOCUS

This topic review covers the influence of currency risk on asset returns in the context of the international CAPM. You should be able to discuss the nature of foreign currency risk premiums as well as the currency exposure of individual companies, economies, equity markets, and bonds. This topic review has links to other concepts in the Level 2 curriculum, particularly the foreign exchange material in Study Session 4, so it's a likely source for exam questions.

INTERNATIONAL MARKET INTEGRATION

LOS 66.a: Explain international market integration and segmentation and the impediments to international capital mobility.

An efficient market is one that (almost) instantaneously impounds new information into security prices. In an international context, the notion of efficiency requires not only that individual national markets be efficient but also that the individual markets be properly priced relative to the world index. International market efficiency would preclude fund managers from using active asset allocation between countries to consistently beat the world index.

The fundamental question of international efficiency involves the issue of **international market integration** versus **segmentation**. Integrated world markets are markets where capital can flow freely across borders, allowing investors to seek the most efficient portfolios. If capital flows freely, securities with similar risk/return characteristics will be priced similarly in all markets relative to the world index.

However, if world markets are segmented, then impediments to the flow of capital prevent investors from taking advantage of relative mispricing between countries. In this case, the price of similar securities will not be equivalent in all markets, and superior performance by some investors may be possible. There are six potential **impediments to the international flow of capital**:

- **Psychological barriers.** Unfamiliarity with international markets (e.g., language and information sources) may cause investors to limit foreign investment.
- **Legal restrictions.** Institutional investors may be prohibited by domestic regulation from investing internationally. Additionally, local governments may impose restrictions on foreign investment flowing into or out of the country.
- **Transaction costs.** Transaction costs are often higher for international investing.
- **Discriminatory taxation.** Foreign investment may be taxed at a higher rate than locally generated investment.

- **Political risks.** Local government actions can cause adverse changes in the value of invested funds.
- **Foreign currency risk.** Foreign investors bear the risk of changes in the local-market value of invested funds, as well as the risk of changes in the exchange rate between the local foreign currency and investors' home currency.

These impediments are most commonly observed in emerging markets, but could be present, at least to some degree, in any foreign market.

LOS 66.b: Discuss the factors that favor international market integration.

While all of the impediments listed above potentially limit capital flows and reduce the efficiency of world markets, international market integration requires only that a *sufficient number* of investors be able to move capital between markets. Three factors have caused international capital mobility to increase dramatically over the past 20 years:

- There are many private and institutional investors who are internationally active.
- Essentially all major corporations have multinational operations.
- Corporations and governments borrow and lend on an international scale.

Given these developments, it is doubtful that markets are fully segmented today.

WARM-UP: THE STANDARD CAPM

As a starting point for a discussion of international asset pricing, consider the standard capital asset pricing model (CAPM). In a domestic framework, the CAPM (introduced at Level 1 and reviewed at Level 2 in Study Sessions 10 and 18) provides an equilibrium expected return for a security under a fairly restrictive set of assumptions that are discussed in the next LOS. The domestic CAPM leads to two basic results:

- *Separation theorem.* All investors will hold some combination of (1) the risk-free asset and (2) the market portfolio.
- A *risk-pricing relationship*. In equilibrium, the return on all assets can be calculated as:

$$E(R) = R_f + (\beta \times MRP)$$

where:
$E(R)$ = asset's expected return
R_f = risk-free rate
β = asset's beta
MRP = $\left[E(R_m) - R_f\right]$ = the market risk premium
$E(R_m)$ = expected market portfolio return

In a domestic setting, the CAPM tells us that all securities should be priced relative to the risk of the domestic market portfolio. To see this, notice that we can break down the risk of an individual asset into its *market* (or *systematic*) risk and its *firm-specific* (or *residual*) risk with the following equation:

$$\sigma^2 = \left(\beta^2 \times \sigma_m{}^2\right) + \sigma_e{}^2$$

where :

σ^2 = asset's variance

β = asset's beta

$\sigma_m{}^2$ = variance of the market

$\sigma_e{}^2$ = asset's residual risk

Since residual risk is uncorrelated with the market return, we can diversify away the residual risk in a portfolio. Hence, for a well-diversified portfolio, the risk of the portfolio is equal to:

$$\sigma^2 = \beta^2 \times \sigma_m{}^2$$

This implies that the only risk that matters (in a CAPM world) is market risk.

LOS 66.c: State the assumptions of the domestic capital asset pricing model (CAPM).

The following assumptions are necessary to derive the **domestic CAPM**:

- Investors are risk-averse: They prefer more expected return and less risk (as measured by variance), all else equal.
- Investors have homogeneous expectations: They all have the same forecast of expected returns, variances, and correlations.
- Investors are concerned with nominal returns in their home currency (e.g., Canadian investors are concerned with Canadian dollar returns).
- There is a risk-free security available, and all investors can borrow and lend unlimited amounts at the risk-free rate.
- There are no taxes or transaction costs.

LOS 66.d: Justify the extension of the domestic CAPM to an international context (the extended CAPM) and describe the assumptions needed to make the extension.

The domestic CAPM has been extended to the international environment in a model called the **extended CAPM**. The justification for the extended CAPM is to provide a common risk pricing framework that corresponds to the domestic CAPM [i.e., $E(R) = R_f + (\beta \times MRP)$]. In the extended CAPM, the risk-free rate (R_f) is the investor's domestic risk-free rate, and the market portfolio is the market capitalization-weighted portfolio of all risky assets in the world (obviously, this is difficult to proxy).

Unfortunately, the extended CAPM can only be justified with the addition of two rather unreasonable assumptions:

- Investors throughout the world have identical consumption baskets.
- Purchasing power parity holds exactly at any point in time.

In a world where these unrealistic assumptions hold, exchange rate changes would mirror inflation differences between any two countries, and real exchange rate risk would not exist.

LOS 66.e: Determine whether the real exchange rate has changed in a period, given the beginning-of-period (nominal) exchange rate, the inflation rates in the period, and the end-of-period (nominal) exchange rate.

Recall that the real exchange rate is the spot exchange rate, S, multiplied by the ratio of the consumption basket price levels:

$$\text{real } S = S \times \left(\frac{P_{FC}}{P_{DC}} \right)$$

where:
real S = the real exchange rate (domestic currency per foreign currency unit)
S = the spot rate (domestic currency per foreign currency unit)
P_{FC} and P_{DC} = the foreign and domestic price levels, respectively

Real exchange rate movements are defined as changes in the nominal exchange rate that are not explained by inflation differentials. Suppose that the 1-year inflation rate is 2% in the United States and 3% in Europe. The inflation differential is 1%. We would expect to see the euro depreciate by 1% against the dollar (remember, high inflation rate countries should expect to see their currencies depreciate). However, if the euro depreciates by 7%, there has been a *real* exchange rate depreciation of 6% (7% depreciation minus 1% inflation differential).

This can be expressed as:

$$\%\Delta \text{ in real } S = \%\Delta \text{ in nominal } S - (i_{DC} - i_{FC})$$

where:
i_{DC}, i_{FC} = inflation in domestic and foreign currency, respectively
S = spot rate as a direct quote, DC per FC unit

If the nominal spot rate doesn't change by the amount predicted by the inflation differential (i.e., $\%\Delta$ nominal $S \neq i_{DC} - i_{FC}$, then $\%\Delta$ real $S \neq 0$). The risk that this can happen is called real exchange rate risk.

Using the assumptions from the U.S./Europe example:

$$\%\Delta \text{ in real S} = -7\% - (2\% - 3\%)$$
$$= -7\% - (-1\%)$$
$$= -6\%$$

In reality, most exchange rate uncertainty is due to these real changes, because inflation is highly predictable in the short run. Let's try some examples.

Example: Changes in the real exchange rate

An investor from one country (currency = DC) invests in securities in a foreign country (currency = FC). The current exchange rate is DC2.00 per unit of FC. The ratio of the price levels of the domestic consumption basket to the foreign consumption basket is also equal to 2. Domestic inflation during the year was 7%, and foreign inflation was 3%. The end-of-year spot exchange rate is DC2.08/FC. Calculate the beginning of period real exchange rate and the new (i.e., end-of-period) real rate, and determine whether there was any change in the real exchange rate.

Answer:

Notice that the ratio of P_{DC} to P_{FC} is 2.0; that means the ratio of P_{FC} to P_{DC} is one half. The beginning-of-period real exchange rate is:

$$\text{real S} = S \times \left(\frac{P_{FC}}{P_{DC}}\right) = 2 \times \left(\frac{1}{2}\right) = 1$$

To determine whether there was any real exchange rate movement, calculate the new real exchange rate:

$$\text{real S} = 2.08 \times \left(\frac{1.03}{2.14}\right) = 1 \text{ (with slight rounding error)}$$

The end-of-period price levels are the beginning-of-period prices adjusted for inflation (foreign: 1.03 = 1 × 1.03; domestic: 2.14 = 2 × 1.07). Since the real exchange rate is the same at the beginning and end of the period, there has been no change in the real exchange rate. The constant real rate implies that the change in the nominal exchange rate (from 2.00 to 2.08) was simply a result of the inflation differential.

Another way to see this is to note that the nominal spot rate increased by 4% $\left(\frac{2.08 - 2.00}{2.00}\right)$, and the inflation differential was 4% (7% – 3%), so the percentage change in the real rate was zero.

LOS 66.f: Calculate the expected 1) exchange rate and 2) domestic-currency holding period return on a foreign bond (security), given expected, predictable inflation rates, the beginning-of-period nominal exchange rate, and the constant real exchange rate.

Example: Calculating the domestic currency holding period return

Suppose an American investor wants to add Swiss bonds to her portfolio. The current exchange rate is $2 per Sf. The expected U.S. inflation rate is 1%, and the expected Swiss inflation rate is 5%. Inflation rates are totally predictable over the next year. The ratio of the price levels of a typical U.S. consumption basket to a typical Swiss consumption basket is 2. The 1-year U.S. interest rate is 3%, and the 1-year Swiss interest rate is 7%. The real exchange rate is expected to be constant. Calculate the expected exchange rate and the expected return on the Swiss bond to the dollar investor.

Answer:

If the real rate remains constant, the change in the exchange rate will simply reflect the inflation differential. Since the differential is 4%, there should be 4% depreciation in the franc. Hence, the expected exchange rate is $1.92/Sf [= $2/Sf × (1 − 0.04)].

The expected dollar return on the bond should be approximately equal to the Swiss interest rate minus the depreciation of the franc, or 7% + (−4%) = 3%.

LOS 66.g: Calculate the end-of-period real exchange rate and the domestic-currency *ex-post* return on a foreign bond (security), given the end-of-period exchange rate, the beginning-of-period real exchange rate, and the inflation rates during the period.

Example: Calculating the domestic currency ex-post return

Use the data for the U.S. investor holding the Swiss bond. Assume that while inflation during the year was exactly as expected, the exchange rate demonstrated significant volatility, and at the end of the year the exchange rate is $1.96 per Sf versus the expected rate of 1.92. Calculate the end-of-period real exchange rate and the actual return on the bond, and describe the exchange rate risk for this investment.

©2009 Kaplan, Inc.

Answer:

The real exchange rate at the beginning of the year is:

$$\text{real } S_0 = \$2.00 / Sf \times \left(\frac{1}{2}\right) = \$1.00 / Sf$$

The *nominal* currency depreciation in the Sf is equal to:

$$\frac{1.96}{2.00} - 1 = -0.02 = -2\%$$

The ex-post return on the bond is the foreign interest rate plus the nominal currency appreciation, or:

$$7\% + (-2\%) = 5\%$$

It is also equal to the expected return plus the real appreciation:

$$3\% + 2\% = 5\%$$

This investment had a significant amount of exchange rate risk. In this case, the returns were enhanced by the real exchange rate movements. If the franc had fallen by 4% as expected, the ex-post return would equal the expected return of 3% (7% – 4%). However, if the franc had depreciated more than expected, the returns on the bond would have been less than 3%. For example, if the franc fell by 10% to $1.80, the ex-post return would equal –3% (7% – 10%).

LOS 66.h: Calculate a foreign currency risk premium and explain a foreign currency risk premium in terms of interest rate differentials and forward rates.

As the previous example demonstrates, changes in the real exchange rate can have a significant impact on realized returns. The international CAPM (ICAPM) was developed under the assumption that investors are concerned about returns in their *domestic* currency. Remember that while a U.S. Treasury bill (T-bill) is riskless to a U.S. investor, it is not riskless to a Swiss investor because of exchange rate risk.

The ICAPM requires that investors consider the real exchange rate risk associated with investing in foreign currency assets. In addition to the normal sensitivity of asset returns to changes in the market (which we will study in detail shortly), an ICAPM investor must also assess the **foreign currency risk premium** (FCRP) associated with each foreign currency. The FCRP is defined as the expected exchange rate movement minus the interest rate differential between the domestic currency and the foreign currency:

$$FCRP = \frac{E(S_1) - S_0}{S_0} - (r_{DC} - r_{FC})$$

where:
r_{DC} = domestic currency interest rate
r_{FC} = foreign currency interest rate

Interest rate parity (IRP) (which we discussed in Study Session 4) says that the forward premium or discount should be equal to the interest rate differential. Assuming IRP holds, the FCRP can also be calculated as the percentage difference in the expected exchange rate, $E(S_1)$, and the forward rate, F:

$$FCRP = \frac{E(S_1) - F}{S_0}$$

Notice that if the foreign exchange expectation relation holds $[F = E(S_1)]$, then the FCRP is equal to zero, and the hedged domestic currency expected return on an investment denominated in the foreign currency is equal to the unhedged expected return. That means there is no risk premium for remaining unhedged. If the FCRP is greater than zero, then the expected unhedged return is greater than the expected hedged return and there is a positive risk premium for remaining unhedged.

It is also possible for the FCRP to be negative. For example, if there is a 1% FCRP on the FC versus the DC, then there is a FCRP of approximately negative 1% on the DC versus the FC. The sign of the FCRP results from the net foreign investment and the relative risk aversion of the investors in the two countries.

For example, suppose U.S. investors invest more in a foreign country than the investors of the foreign country invest in the United States. That means the net foreign investment of U.S. investors is positive. Also suppose that U.S. investors are more risk averse than the foreign country investors. The United States has more hedging demand to sell the foreign currency forward than the foreign country investors have to sell the U.S. dollar forward. The result is that the forward rate (in $/FC) will drop below the expected spot rate, and the FCRP on the foreign currency relative to the U.S. dollar will be positive.

It is also important to understand that this exchange rate risk cannot be hedged in aggregate, much like global systematic risk cannot be hedged entirely. Investors can choose their own exposure to this risk, but in aggregate, someone has to hold it. Let's look at an example.

Study Session 18

Example: Calculating a foreign currency risk premium

An investor's home country has a risk-free interest rate of 7%. A foreign country has a risk-free interest rate of 3%. The current exchange rate between the two countries is 2.00 (DC/FC), and the expected spot rate in one year is 2.10. Calculate the FCRP and the unhedged and hedged expected domestic currency return on the foreign bond. Use the linear approximation.

Answer:

The expected foreign currency appreciation is:

$$\frac{2.10 - 2.00}{2.00} = 0.05 = 5\%$$

The FCRP is the expected foreign currency appreciation minus the interest rate differential:

FCRP = 5% – (7% – 3%) = 1%

The unhedged expected domestic currency return on the foreign bond should be the foreign interest rate plus the expected currency appreciation:

unhedged $E(R_{DC})$ = 3% + 5% = 8%

The unhedged expected domestic currency return on the foreign bond can also be calculated as the domestic interest rate plus the FCRP:

unhedged $E(R_{DC})$ = 7% + 1% = 8%

The hedged expected return is equal to the foreign interest rate plus the forward premium on the FC (which is equal to the interest rate differential of 4%):

hedged $E(R_{DC})$ = 3% + 4% = 7%

The investor will earn the 1% FCRP by remaining unhedged versus hedging.

LOS 66.i: State the risk pricing relation and the formula for the international capital asset pricing model (ICAPM).

As with the domestic CAPM, the ICAPM assumes that investors evaluate securities in a mean-variance framework. The two main conclusions of the ICAPM model, a separation theorem and a risk-pricing relationship, are very similar to the domestic CAPM.

The assumptions necessary to derive the ICAPM are very similar to those for the standard CAPM.

- Investors are risk-averse: they prefer more expected return and less risk (as measured by variance), all else equal. With multiple currencies, investors will also be concerned with real exchange rate risk and will want to hedge against it with forward contracts.
- Investors have homogeneous expectations: they all have the same forecast of expected returns, variances, and correlations.
- Investors are concerned with nominal returns in their home currency (e.g., Canadian investors are concerned with Canadian dollar returns).
- There is a risk-free security available in every currency, and all investors can borrow and lend unlimited amounts at the risk-free rate in any currency. However, because there is now exchange rate risk, the only completely risk-free investment for each investor (no default risk, interest rate risk, or exchange rate risk) is the risk-free asset in that investor's home currency. In other words, the Japanese default risk-free asset is not risk-free to a U.S. investor, who faces the risk of the yen-to-dollar exchange rate. In addition, because interest parity holds, investors can replicate a forward contract using a combination of borrowing and lending in two currencies.
- There are no taxes or transaction costs.

The two restrictive assumptions necessary to derive the extended version of the CAPM (all investors have the same consumption basket, and PPP always holds) are NOT necessary for the ICAPM.

The *ICAPM separation theorem* asserts that all investors will hold a combination of:

- The risk-free asset of their own country.
- The world market portfolio optimally hedged against currency risk.

The world market portfolio (market-capitalization weighted) will be the same for all investors. Unfortunately, the ICAPM does not provide operational guidelines for what constitutes an optimal currency hedge.

 Professor's Note: The model doesn't give us an easy way to construct this "optimally hedged" market portfolio. Just remember that the currency risk in the portfolio is not completely hedged away. An ad-hoc way to implement the model might be to assume the portfolio is 50% hedged against currency risk.

The **ICAPM risk-pricing relationship** (i.e., the ICAPM formula) is more complex than the domestic CAPM because the ICAPM accounts for the sensitivity of an asset to all currency changes. Hence, we must add additional risk premiums for each world currency.

The ICAPM can be written as:

$$E(R) = R_f + \left(\beta_g \times MRP_g\right) + \left(\gamma_1 \times FCRP_1\right) + \left(\gamma_2 \times FCRP_2\right) + \ldots + \left(\gamma_k \times FCRP_k\right)$$

where:

$E(R)$	= asset's expected return
R_f	= domestic currency risk-free rate
β_g	= sensitivity of the asset's domestic currency returns to changes in the global market portfolio
MRP_g	= world market risk premium $[E(R_m) - R_f]$
$E(R_m)$	= expected return on world market portfolio
γ_1 to γ_k	= sensitivities of asset's domestic currency returns to changes in the values of currencies 1 through k
$FCRP_1$ to $FCRP_k$	= foreign currency risk premiums on currencies 1 through k

 Professor's Note: Know this formula! It would form the basis of an excellent multiple regression question integrating the quantitative methods material from Study Session 3.

The ICAPM tells us that the expected return on any asset is equal to the investor's domestic risk-free rate, plus a world market risk premium (which is scaled by the asset's world market beta), plus a foreign currency risk premium for each foreign currency. Note that all returns are measured in domestic currency.

If there are only two currencies (the domestic and one foreign), the ICAPM becomes:

$$E(R) = R_f + (\beta_g \times MRP_g) + (\gamma_{FC} \times FCRP_{FC})$$

You can see from this formula that the ICAPM differs from the domestic CAPM in two ways. First, the relevant risk is world market risk. Second, additional risk premiums are added for the asset's sensitivity to changes in each foreign currency. While the risk of the world market is conceptually similar to the domestic CAPM, the sensitivities to the currency risk premiums are unique to the ICAPM.

 Professor's Note: Sometimes analysts assume the FCRPs are zero in the long run. In that case, the ICAPM reduces to $E(R) = R_f + (B_g \times MRP_g)$.

Suppose that stock in Wrinkle Company does well when the Swiss franc depreciates. This means that Wrinkle stock provides a natural hedge against franc currency risk. Hence, the stock of Wrinkle would have a low (maybe negative) sensitivity (γ_{Sf}) to changes in the franc. Let's try an example using the ICAPM.

LOS 66.j: Calculate the expected return on a stock, given its world market beta and currency exposure as well as the appropriate risk-free rates and risk premiums.

Example: Calculating expected return with the ICAPM

Suppose an investor lives in a world with only two currencies, the U.S. dollar and the Swiss franc. The investor is a U.S. citizen. The U.S. risk-free interest rate is 3%, and the Swiss risk-free interest rate is 2%. Expected appreciation of the franc is 2%. The world portfolio risk premium is 7%. You have the following statistics on two possible investments:

Betas and Currency Exposures of Stocks A and B

	Stock A	Stock B
World beta	1.0	1.2
Currency exposure (γ_{Sf})	2.0	0.5

Calculate the expected return on each security to the U.S. investor using the ICAPM.

Answer:

In this two-currency world, the ICAPM reduces to:

$$E(R) = R_f + (b_g \times MRP_g) + (\gamma_{Sf} \times FCRP_{Sf})$$

Since the dollar is the base currency (i.e., the investor lives in the United States), all sensitivities are assumed to be based on dollar returns. The franc risk premium is:

$$FCRP_{Sf} = 2\% - (3\% - 2\%) = 1\%$$

Substituting in the values of the world risk premium and the U.S. risk-free rate, the model gives an expected return for Stock A of:

$$E(R_A) = 3.0\% + (1.0 \times 7.0\%) + (2.0 \times 1.0\%) = 12.0\%$$

The expected return on Stock B is:

$$E(R_B) = 3.0\% + (1.2 \times 7.0\%) + (0.5 \times 1.0\%) = 11.9\%$$

Notice that even though Stock B has greater world market risk (it has a beta of 1.2 compared to a beta of 1.0 for Stock A), it has approximately the same expected return because of its low sensitivity to changes in the value of the foreign currency (0.5 versus 2.0).

LOS 66.k: Explain the effect of market segmentation on the ICAPM.

The ICAPM is similar to the domestic CAPM both in form and application. You should note that the ICAPM applies only in a world with integrated capital markets. If markets are segmented, risk is not priced the same in all markets, and the ICAPM does not accurately capture the relationship between risk and return across all capital markets.

WARM-UP: CURRENCY HEDGING AND EXPECTED RETURNS

The ICAPM implies that all investors should hold the world market portfolio (in combination with their domestic risk-free asset) on an optimally hedged basis. Unfortunately, the theory offers very little practical direction on how to *optimally hedge* the portfolio. Essentially, currency hedging becomes an empirical decision that depends on the investor's risk tolerance.

The hedging decision is made even more difficult because the investor is required to assess the risk premium of each currency. Unlike the risk premium on the market portfolio, which is always positive, the risk premium on any given currency can be positive or negative and is likely to be unstable over time. For short-run estimates, the investor must estimate the magnitude and sign of the currency risk premium for all relevant currencies. For long-run estimates, the usual practice is to assume that all currency risk premiums equal zero. In other words, long-run estimates of the currency risk premium assume that the best indicator of currency movements will be the interest rate differential.

LOS 66.l: Define currency exposure and explain exposures in terms of correlations.

The relationship between exchange rate movements and asset returns is central to understanding international asset valuation. We need to understand what causes a particular asset to be sensitive to movements in a particular foreign currency (i.e., we need to understand what drives γ).

Like beta in the domestic CAPM, γ in the ICAPM can be estimated with a regression; specifically, a regression of the domestic currency asset returns on exchange rate movements. It is also possible to define exchange rate sensitivity in terms of **local currency exposure**. Remember that the domestic currency return, R, is equal to the foreign currency return, R_{FC}, plus appreciation in the foreign currency, $\%\Delta S$:

$$R_{DC} = R_{FC} + \%\Delta S$$

Since the exposure of a currency to itself is 1, domestic currency exposure is equal to local currency exposure plus 1:

$$\gamma = \gamma(LC) + 1$$

where:
γ = domestic currency exposure (from the ICAPM)
$\gamma(LC)$ = local currency exposure

The biggest challenge to mastering this LOS is understanding the distinction between the domestic currency exposure, γ, and the local currency exposure, $\gamma(LC)$.

Consider a U.S. investor interested in an equity investment in a Japanese company. The U.S. investor is interested in his potential returns in dollars on his investment, but the stock is denominated in yen. If the investor buys Japanese stock, he will first convert dollars into yen, buy the stock with yen, and then, when he sells the stock, he will take the yen proceeds and convert them back into dollars. His domestic currency return is simply the percentage change from the initial dollar cost of the asset to the ending dollar proceeds.

Think of his investment as a portfolio with two components: an equity investment denominated in yen and an investment in the yen itself. His dollar return will equal the return in yen on the Japanese investment plus the percentage change in the value of the yen (the percentage change in the $/yen exchange rate). Just like any other portfolio, the risk (the "exposure") will also depend on whether the correlation between the two components is positive, zero, or negative. In this example, the U.S. dollar is the domestic currency and the yen is the local currency.

Positive Correlation

Let's take a closer look at the Japanese company. Suppose it is an importer, so its stock price (in yen) goes up when the country's local currency (the yen) appreciates. For example, let's suppose the sensitivity of the yen returns on the asset to the change in the value of the yen is 0.5. If the yen appreciates by 10%, then we would expect the stock price to go up by 5%. This is called the **local currency exposure**: the sensitivity of the *returns in the stock denominated in the local currency (yen) to changes in the value of the local currency (yen)*.

Our U.S. investor, however, is interested in how the dollar returns on his investment are affected by changes in the *value of the yen*, not how the yen-denominated returns are affected. If the yen goes up 10%, his return will be 5% on the stock plus 10% on the yen, or a total of 15%. He "wins" twice because not only did the stock go up, but so did the yen. The reason he wins twice is because the two returns are positively correlated.

Therefore, the domestic currency exposure is 1.5: the yen appreciated by 10% and his dollar return was 15%. The **domestic currency exposure** of 1.5 is the sensitivity of *the dollar returns on his investment* and the *changes in the value of the yen* itself.

Notice that domestic currency exposure is equal to the local currency exposure plus one:

$$\gamma yen = \gamma(LC) + 1 = 0.5 + 1.0 = 1.5$$

The U.S. investor would use the domestic currency exposure ($\gamma = 1.5$) in the ICAPM model as the investment's currency exposure to the yen (the gamma).

Negative Correlation

Suppose instead that the Japanese company is an exporter. Then the local currency exposure (the sensitivity of the yen returns to changes in the value of the yen) would be negative. Suppose, for example, that the local currency exposure is –0.5. If the value of the yen increases by 10%, we would expect the Japanese exporter's stock price to *decrease* by 5%. The total effect of a change in the value of the yen on the dollar return of the investment would be 5%: the 10% increase in the value of the yen offset by the 5% decrease in the stock price. The domestic currency exposure (the sensitivity of dollar returns to changes in the value of the yen) is therefore 0.5 (10% increase in value of yen leads to 5% increase in the dollar value of the investment).

$$\gamma yen = \gamma(LC) + 1 = -0.5 + 1.0 = 0.5$$

Zero Correlation

Finally, suppose that the local currency exposure is zero: changes in the value of the yen have no effect on the value of the Japanese stock. If the yen appreciates by 10%, we would expect no change in the value of the Japanese stock denominated in yen, and the combined effect on the dollar investment is 10%. Therefore, the domestic currency exposure is 1.0 (a 10% increase in the value of the yen leads to a 10% dollar return).

$$\gamma yen = \gamma(LC) + 1 = 0 + 1.0 = 1.0$$

To summarize, there are two currency exposures you need to understand:

1. γyen, the domestic currency exposure, which is the sensitivity of the U.S. dollar returns on the Japanese investment to changes in the $/yen exchange rate.

2. $\gamma(LC)$, the local currency exposure, which is the sensitivity of the yen return on the Japanese investment to changes in the $/yen exchange rate.

LOS 66.m: Discuss the likely exchange rate exposure of a company based on a description of the company's activities, and explain the impact of both real and nominal exchange rate changes on the valuation of the company.

Professor's Note: This LOS and the next two are important! They require that you apply the rather theoretical material we've covered so far to the three-step security valuation process emphasized in the CFA® Body of Knowledge: (1) analysis of alternative economies and security markets, (2) analysis of alternative industries, and (3) analysis of individual companies and stocks. Look for an exam question integrating this material with equity valuation.

The **firm's exchange rate exposure** is the way the value of an individual company changes in response to a change in the *real* value of the local currency. We can estimate the currency exposure of a particular firm by regressing the firm's stock return on local currency changes. We can further refine this process with detailed analysis of the geographic distribution of the firm's sales and the currency origin of the firm's revenues and costs.

For example, a German firm that imports products from the United States for resale in Germany has very different local currency exposure to the euro than a German firm that produces products in Germany and exports them for sale in the United States. Suppose the euro depreciates by 5% in real terms. The German importer is less competitive, and his euro profits fall because the goods purchased in the United States are more expensive (i.e., it takes more euros to buy the same goods). On the other hand, the exporter is helped by the depreciation of the euro. The exporter can effectively cut the U.S. dollar price of his goods without reducing his euro profits.

Example: Identifying a firm's currency exposure

Consider two different French firms:

- Firm 1 produces electrical components in France for sale in Great Britain. Prices are set and paid in pounds, and costs are incurred in euros.
- Firm 2 imports cars from Great Britain for sale in France.

Suppose the euro (the local currency) experiences real appreciation of 5% against the pound. Discuss how the value of each firm will be affected by appreciation of the euro against the pound. Explain how your answer changes if the change in value is completely explained by the inflation differential.

Answer:

Firm 1 will be hurt by the appreciation of the euro. The currency appreciation effectively makes Firm 1's products more expensive in the British market, so sales will fall. Cost won't change, however, so profits and stock price will also likely fall.

Firm 2 will be helped by the euro appreciation because the currency change will make the British cars less expensive in the French market. The sales, profits, and value of Firm 2 should increase.

If the currency movements are purely nominal (i.e., completely explained by the inflation differential), nominal sales and profits for both firms will change, but real sales and profits (and value) will remain the same.

 Professor's Note: Remember that importers are hurt by domestic currency depreciation, and exporters are helped by domestic currency depreciation.

LOS 66.n: Discuss the currency exposures of national economies, equity markets, and bond markets.

LOS 66.o: Contrast the traditional trade approach (j-curve) and the money demand approach to modeling the relation between real exchange rate changes and domestic economic activity.

Empirically, domestic economic activity (think GDP growth) is related to exchange rate movements. Two theories have been proposed to explain this relationship: the traditional model and the money demand model.

TRADITIONAL MODEL

The **traditional model** has both a long-run and short-run component. In the long-run, a decline in the value of a country's currency increases national competitiveness. That is, exports increase and economic activity is stimulated. However, the short-run impact is more negative. In the short run, if a country's currency depreciates in real terms, the cost of imports increases, causing a widening in the trade balance (exports minus imports) and an increase in domestic inflation. This short-run decline in the trade balance and long-run improvement is called the J-curve effect, as shown in Figure 1.

Figure 1: J-Curve Effect: Response of Trade Balance to Domestic Currency Depreciation

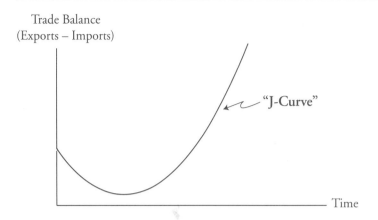

Whether the short-term or long-term effect dominates depends on the country. For developed countries, the long-run effect dominates. In the long run, the increased competitiveness of domestic industry will restore economic activity and reduce the trade gap. That is, the *traditional model predicts that depreciation in the value of the domestic currency will cause an increase in the competitiveness* of the domestic industry in a developed country and, thus, an increase in the stock value of domestic firms. (See Figure 2.)

Figure 2: Traditional Model of Equity Exposure for a Developed Country

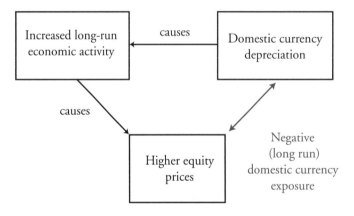

MONEY DEMAND MODEL

In the **money demand model**, an increase in real economic activity leads to an increase in the demand for the domestic currency. The increased domestic currency demand causes the value of the domestic currency to appreciate. Because stock prices are highly correlated with GDP growth, *the money demand model explains the positive correlation between changes in domestic currency and stock returns*. (See Figure 3.)

Figure 3: Money Demand Model of Equity Exposure

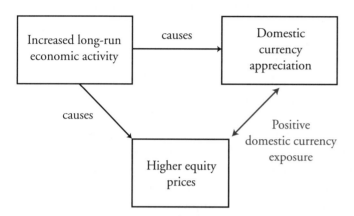

For emerging markets, currency depreciation is usually bad news because it often implies an increase in political risks or the advent of economic difficulties. Therefore, domestic currency depreciation often leads to lower equity prices in emerging markets (i.e., positive domestic currency exposure).

Bond prices are largely determined by long-term interest rates. Therefore, understanding the currency exposure of bonds requires understanding the relationship between exchange rates and interest rates. There are two conflicting theories that explain this relationship: the free markets theory and the government intervention theory.

FREE MARKETS THEORY

An increase in the domestic *real* rate of interest causes capital to flow into the domestic markets from abroad. The inflow of capital increases the demand for the domestic currency, causing an increase in its value. This creates *negative domestic currency exposure* for bond investors. That is, increases in interest rates decrease domestic currency bond values while the appreciating domestic currency increases the value of the bond in the foreign investor's domestic currency. (See Figure 4.)

Figure 4: Free Markets Theory of Bond Exposure

Professor's Note: It is important to distinguish between an increase in real interest rates and an increase in nominal interest rates caused by an increase in inflation. If rates increase because of higher anticipated inflation, the rate increase results in a decrease in the value of the currency.

GOVERNMENT INTERVENTION THEORY

Governments frequently attempt to maintain a target range for the value of their currency. If the value of the currency falls to the low end of the range, the domestic government will increase interest rates to support the currency. Likewise, a strong domestic currency will lead domestic governments to ease interest rates. This system (sometimes called the leaning-against-the-wind policy) induces positive domestic currency exposure. That is, increasing currency values (which helps foreign bond investors) leads to decreasing interest rates, increasing bond prices (which also helps foreign bond investors), and a *positive domestic currency exposure* for domestic bonds. (See Figure 5.)

Figure 5: Government Intervention Theory of Bond Exposure

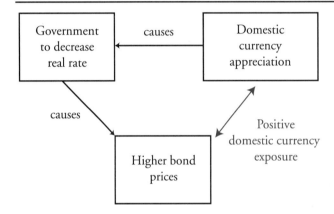

KEY CONCEPTS

LOS 66.a

Market integration requires that capital flow freely across borders. In integrated markets, assets with similar risk/return parameters will be priced similarly in all markets. Market segmentation occurs when there are sufficient impediments to cross-border capital flows. International market integration requires the elimination or reduction of impediments such as psychological barriers, legal restrictions, transaction costs, discriminatory taxation, political risk, and foreign currency risk.

LOS 66.b

Three factors have caused international capital mobility to increase dramatically over the past 20 years:
* There are many private and institutional investors who are internationally active.
* Essentially all major corporations have multinational operations.
* Corporations and governments borrow and lend on an international scale.

LOS 66.c

The following assumptions are necessary to derive the standard CAPM: (1) investors are risk-averse; (2) investors have homogeneous expectations; (3) investors are concerned with nominal returns in their home currency; (4) all investors can borrow and lend unlimited amounts at the risk-free rate; and (5) there are no taxes or transaction costs.

LOS 66.d

The justification for the extended CAPM is to provide a common risk pricing framework that corresponds to the domestic CAPM. The domestic CAPM can be extended to an international framework with the addition of two unrealistic assumptions: (1) investors throughout the world have identical consumption baskets, and (2) purchasing power parity holds at all times.

LOS 66.e

The real exchange rate is the spot exchange rate, S, multiplied by the ratio of the consumption basket price levels: $\text{real } S = S \times \left(\dfrac{P_{FC}}{P_{DC}} \right)$

Real exchange rate movements are changes in the exchange rate that are not fully explained by the inflation differential. Real exchange rate risk refers to the possibility of real exchange rate movements.

LOS 66.f

If the real rate remains constant, the change in the exchange rate will simply reflect the inflation differential. $FX_{expected} = FX_{current} * (1 - \text{inflation differential})$

The expected DC return on the bond should be approximately equal to the FC return minus the FC depreciation. $DC_{return} = FC_{return} - FC_{depreciation}$

LOS 66.g

The ex-post return on the bond is (1) the foreign interest rate plus the nominal currency appreciation, or (2) equal to the expected return plus the real appreciation.

LOS 66.h

The FCRP is defined as the expected exchange rate movement minus the interest rate differential (domestic interest rate minus foreign interest rate):

$$FCRP = \frac{E(S_1) - S_0}{S_0} - (r_{DC} - r_{FC})$$

If interest parity holds, $FCRP = \dfrac{E(S_1) - F}{S_0}$

LOS 66.i

The ICAPM risk-pricing relationship (i.e., the ICAPM formula) specifies expected return as a function of three factors: (1) the investor's domestic risk-free rate, (2) the world market risk premium, and (3) the sensitivity of the asset to changes in all foreign currencies.

$$E(R) = R_f + (\beta_g \times MRP_g) + (\gamma_1 \times FCRP_1) + (\gamma_2 \times FCRP_2) + \ldots + (\gamma_k \times FCRP_k)$$

LOS 66.j

The expected return on a stock is a function of its world market beta, currency exposure, a risk-free rate, and a foreign currency risk premium.

$$E(R) = R_f + (\beta_g \times MRP_g) + (\gamma_f \times FCRP_f)$$

LOS 66.k

ICAPM applies only in a world with integrated capital markets. If markets are segmented, risk is not priced the same in all markets, and the ICAPM does not accurately capture the relationship between risk and return across all capital markets.

LOS 66.l

For an investment in a security denominated in a foreign currency, we can identify two measures of currency exposure. The sensitivity of the foreign currency value of the security to changes in the exchange rate for the foreign currency (DC/FC, a direct quote) is termed its *foreign currency exposure*. The sensitivity of the domestic currency returns to changes in the exchange rate of the foreign currency is termed the *domestic currency exposure* of the investment and is equal to the foreign currency exposure plus one. When the correlation of the change in the foreign currency's exchange value and the foreign currency returns on a security is positive (negative) it will tend to increase (decrease) the domestic currency exposure.

LOS 66.m

The currency exposure of a particular company can be assessed by careful examination of the firm's geographical distribution of sales and the currency origin of costs and profits. If the currency movements are purely nominal (i.e., completely explained by the inflation differential), nominal sales and profits will change, but real sales and profits (and value) will remain the same.

LOS 66.n

A depreciating currency that improves domestic competitiveness will increase the stock value of domestic firms. The money demand model explains positive correlation between changes in domestic currency and stock returns—stock prices are highly correlated with GDP growth.

The free markets theory and government intervention theory model the currency exposure of bonds. The first asserts that an increase in real interest rates leads to appreciation of the domestic currency as capital flows in from abroad, so bonds have a negative exposure to currency risk. The second theory advances the idea that domestic governments frequently defend declines in their currency's value, so bonds have a positive exposure to currency risk.

LOS 66.o

The traditional model (J-Curve) predicts a negative domestic currency exposure: depreciation in the value of the domestic currency will cause an increase in the competitiveness of domestic industry. In the money demand model, an increase in real economic activity leads to an increase in the demand for the domestic currency. The increased domestic currency demand causes the value of the domestic currency to appreciate.

CONCEPT CHECKERS

1. A U.K. investor is considering the purchase of U.S. securities. The current exchange rate is £0.8 per $. If the ratio of the price of the typical consumption basket in the U.K. to the typical U.S. consumption basket is 0.8, the real exchange rate is *closest* to:
    A. £0.80/$.
    B. £1.00/$.
    C. £1.25/$.

2. A U.K. investor is considering the purchase of U.S. securities. The beginning-of-period exchange rate (in pounds per dollar) is 0.8. The ratio of the price of the typical consumption basket in the United Kingdom to the typical U.S. consumption basket is 0.8 to 1.0. After one year, inflation in the United Kingdom was 10%, and inflation in the United States was 5%. If the new exchange rate is 0.76, the end-of-period real exchange rate is *closest* to:
    A. £0.91 per $.
    B. £0.95 per $.
    C. £1.00 per $.

3. Jake Miller is a U.S. investor. Miller is considering investing either in a U.S. bond yielding 9% or a Canadian bond yielding 7%. The current exchange rate is 0.5 U.S. dollars per Canadian dollar. Miller expects the C$ to appreciate by 3%. The foreign currency risk premium (FCRP) on the C$ is *closest* to:
    A. −1%.
    B. 1%.
    C. 4%.

4. Rebecca White is a U.S. investor. White is considering investing either in a U.S. bond yielding 9% or a Canadian bond yielding 7%. The current exchange rate is 0.5 U.S. dollars per Canadian dollar. White expects the Canadian dollar to appreciate by 3%. If White's currency appreciation expectations are correct, the U.S. $ ex-post return on the C$ bond is *closest* to:
    A. 4%.
    B. 6%.
    C. 10%.

5. Shogo Suzuki is a Japanese investor. Suzuki is considering investing in the stock of a U.S. firm called Itech. The world risk premium is 6%, and the sensitivity of Itech to changes in the world index is 1.3. The only currency that Itech is sensitive to is the U.S. dollar, which has a foreign currency risk premium of 2%. The estimated sensitivity of Itech dollar-denominated returns to the U.S. dollar is 0.8. The risk-free rate is 3% in Japan and 5% in the United States. If Suzuki uses the International Capital Asset Pricing Model (ICAPM), the required return on Itech is *closest* to:
    A. 9.4%.
    B. 11.4%.
    C. 14.4%.

6.   Which of the following factors would be *least likely* to contribute to segmented international markets?
     A.   The risk of government nationalization of major industries.
     B.   Lack of consistent and accurate financial information on foreign companies.
     C.   An increase in the global U.S. dollar value of assets owned by multinational corporations.

7.   If the local currency value of a U.S. firm is uncorrelated with changes in the euro-to-U.S. dollar exchange rate, the exposure of a European investor in the U.S. firm to changes in the U.S. dollar is *closest* to:
     A.   −1.
     B.   0.
     C.   1.

8.   A U.S. firm manufactures and sells men's footwear exclusively in the United States. Which of the following situations would *most likely* cause the value of the firm to increase? Consider each situation individually. The firm's major competitors are located in:
     A.   Europe, and the value of the U.S. dollar increases relative to the euro.
     B.   Europe, and the value of the U.S. dollar decreases relative to the euro.
     C.   the United States, and the value of the U.S. dollar increases relative to the euro.

9.   A Canadian investor expects the Swiss franc to depreciate by 1.5% over the next year. The interest rates on 1-year risk-free bonds are 2.25% in Canada and 1.75% in Switzerland. The current exchange rate is C$0.75 per Sf. The foreign currency risk premium on the franc is *closest* to:
     A.   −2.0%.
     B.   −1.5%.
     C.   −0.5%.

10.   International market integration is *most likely* to improve with the reduction of:
      A.   discriminatory taxation.
      B.   environmental hazards.
      C.   barter and black-market transactions.

11.   The dramatic increase in international capital mobility is *least likely* related to:
      A.   corporations and governments borrowing and lending at the risk-free-rate.
      B.   the existence of multinational operations in almost all major corporations.
      C.   the large number of private and institutional investors who are internationally active.

12.   Which model or theory advances the idea that bonds have a positive exposure to currency risk?
      A.   Free markets theory.
      B.   Money demand model.
      C.   Government intervention theory.

13.   The ICAPM formula specifies expected return as including the:
      A. sovereign risk premium.
      B. world market risk premium.
      C. sensitivity of the asset to changes in inflation.

14.   Which of the following assumptions are necessary to derive the standard CAPM:
      A. rational investors are often risk-seekers.
      B. investors have homogeneous expectations.
      C. investors are concerned with real returns in their home currency.

15.   Extending the standard CAPM to an international framework requires the assumption that:
      A. international investors have homogeneous, unrealistic expectations.
      B. investors throughout the world have heterogeneous consumption baskets.
      C. purchasing power parity holds at all times.

CHALLENGE PROBLEMS

Use the following information to answer Questions 16 through 21.

Jetta Financial Advisors (JFA) provides services as an international fund manager. Steven Filler is a client in the United States who is interested in increasing his portfolio's exposure to Japanese and European investments. JFA gathered the following current information in preparation for a meeting with Filler. The U.S. dollar is the base currency for all of JFA's estimates.

	United States	Japan	France
One-year risk-free rate:	0.03	0.01	0.04
One-year expected inflation:	0.02	0.00	0.03

Current exchange rate:	$1 = ¥120
Ratio of U.S. to Japanese price levels:	1 to 140
World market risk premium:	0.07
Risk premium on euro	0.02
Risk premium on yen	0.015

	French Aviation	Tokyo Inc.
World beta	β_{FA} = 0.80	β_T = 1.2
Currency exposure to euro	$\gamma(LC)$ = −0.25	$\gamma_{\euro}$ = −0.5
Currency exposure to yen	$\gamma_{¥}$ = 0.40	$\gamma(LC)$ = −1.1

French Aviation's domestic currency is the euro, and Tokyo Inc.'s domestic currency is the yen.

16. Filler is considering the purchase of a Japanese government bond and asks JFA for an opinion on the expected nominal return over the next year. JFA explains that if the real exchange rate remains constant, the expected nominal return over the next year on the Japanese government bond to Filler as a U.S. investor is *closest* to:
    A. 3%.
    B. 4%.
    C. 5%.

17. JFA then proceeds to explain that the exchange rate during the next year is more likely to be volatile. JFA anticipates that the end-of-period exchange rate will be ¥130 per $. Under these assumptions, the return on the Japanese bond to Filler is *closest* to:
    A. −7.7%.
    B. −6.7%.
    C. 6.7%.

18.   Filler is interested in investing in French Aviation, which is located in France, and Tokyo Inc., which is located in Japan. The expected returns in U.S. dollars for both firms, according to the international CAPM, are *closest* to:

French Aviation	Tokyo Inc.
A. 8.70%	9.55%
B. 10.70%	10.25%
C. 11.70%	12.55%

19.   Which of the following is *least likely* to explain the differences in the expected returns between French Aviation and Tokyo Inc.? The:
        A. exposure to world risk is less for French Aviation than Tokyo Inc.
        B. currency exposures for Tokyo Inc. lower the expected return for Tokyo Inc.
        C. risk-free return lowers the expected return for Tokyo Inc.

20.   Tokyo Inc. produces computer chips for sale in France. Prices are set and paid in euros, and costs are incurred in yen. JFA anticipates that the yen will experience real appreciation of 3% against the euro. If the appreciation of the yen relative to the euro occurs, Tokyo Inc. will *most likely*:
        A. not be affected by the appreciation due to arbitrage.
        B. be hurt by the appreciation of the yen.
        C. not be affected because the change in Tokyo Inc.'s global beta will offset other effects.

21.   JFA anticipates that the yen will appreciate 3.5% in value relative to the U.S. dollar over the next year. For Filler, the foreign currency risk premium for the yen is *closest* to:
        A. 1.5%.
        B. 2.0%.
        C. 3.5%.

ANSWERS – CONCEPT CHECKERS

1. **B** Using the pound as the base (domestic) currency, we calculate the real exchange rate as follows: real S = S $(P_\$/P_£)$. Hence, the real exchange rate in this case is: real S = 0.8 (1 / 0.8) = $1/£.

2. **A** At the end of the period, the price level in the U.K. is 0.88 (= 0.8 × 1.1) and the price level in the U.S. is 1.05 (= 1 × 1.05). Using the real exchange rate formula, real S = S $(P_\$/P_£)$, we get an end-of-period exchange rate of real S = 0.76 × (1.05 / 0.88) ≈ 0.91. Based on the inflation differential, we would have expected the pound to depreciate against the dollar (the spot rate would increase from 0.8 because it would take more pounds to buy one dollar). However, the pound actually appreciated relative to the dollar on a nominal basis (from 0.8 to 0.76). That means the real value of the pound increased from 1.0 to 0.91 (again, it took fewer pounds to buy one dollar).

3. **B** The interest rate differential (U.S. minus Canada) is 2%. Hence, you would expect the U.S. dollar to depreciate by 2% over the year. Miller expects the U.S. dollar to depreciate by 3% (or conversely, for the Canadian dollar to appreciate by 3%). Therefore, the FCRP is the expected currency appreciation minus the interest rate differential:

   $FCRP_{C\$}$ = 3% − (9% − 7%) = 1%

   Remember, the foreign currency risk premium is expected foreign currency appreciation minus interest rate differential (stated as $r_{DC} - r_{FC}$). Also note that *expected foreign currency depreciation* is the same as *negative appreciation*.

4. **C** The expected U.S. $ return is 10%. You can calculate this in two ways:

   U.S. $ rate + FCRP = 9% + 1% = 10% (where FCRP = 1% is calculated in Question 3) or C$ rate + expected C$ appreciation = 7% + 3% = 10%

5. **C** The sensitivity of Itechs's returns to changes in the yen is equal to 1 + 0.8, or 1.8. Using the ICAPM, the required return is:

   $E(R_{Suzuki}) = R_f + (\beta_{Suzuki,w} \times MRP_g) + (\gamma_{Suzuki,\$} \times FCRP_\$)$

   $= 3\% + (1.3 \times 6\%) + (1.8 \times 2\%) = 14.4\%$

6. **C** Nationalization of industries and limits on repatriation of profits are political risks faced by global investors. Lack of good financial information on foreign investments increases the transactions costs of global investing. All three are barriers that might prevent the free flow of capital between countries and lead to segregated international markets. The rise of the multinational corporation in our global economy has served to break down barriers and lead to more integrated markets.

7. **C** The currency exposure on a foreign asset is equal to its local currency exposure plus one. In this case, the European investor's exposure to the U.S. investment is zero plus one, or one. For example, if the dollar depreciates by 3%, the U.S. dollar value of the U.S. firm will not change, and the euro return on the U.S. investment will also decrease by 3%. In other words, zero correlation between the investment and the dollar leaves the European investor fully exposed to changes in the value of the dollar. The size or the sign of the euro risk premium (FCRP) is irrelevant to the size of the exposure.

8. **B** If the value of the dollar relative to the euro decreases, European goods will be more expensive to U.S. consumers. Therefore, the firm should face less European competition for its product in the United States, and its stock price should increase. If the value of the dollar increases and its competitors are European, European goods will be cheaper for U.S. consumers, which is bad news for the U.S. firm. If the firm produces and sells domestically and its competitors are all domestic, then it should not be significantly affected by changes in exchange rates.

9. **A** For a Canadian investor, the interest rate differential is $(0.0225 - 0.0175) = 0.005$. Thus the Swiss franc trades at a premium of 0.5%. The foreign currency risk premium is equal to the depreciation of the Swiss franc minus the interest rate differential: $-0.015 - 0.005 = -0.02 = -2\%$.

10. **A** International market integration requires the elimination or reduction of impediments such as psychological barriers, legal restrictions, transaction costs, discriminatory taxation, political risk, and foreign currency risk.

11. **A** The three factors have caused international capital mobility to increase dramatically over the past 20 years:
    *   There are many private and institutional investors who are internationally active.
    *   Essentially all major corporations have multinational operations.
    *   Corporations and governments borrow and lend on an international scale.

12. **C** The government intervention theory advances the idea that domestic governments frequently defend declines in their currency's value, so bonds have a positive exposure to currency risk. The free markets theory asserts that rising real interest rates lead to appreciating currency and a negative exposure for bonds. The money demand model also involves appreciating currency, but not necessarily bonds.

13. **B** The ICAPM risk-pricing relationship specifies expected return as a function of three factors: (1) the investor's domestic risk-free rate, (2) the world market risk premium, and (3) the sensitivity of the asset to changes in all foreign currencies.

14. **B** The following assumptions are necessary to derive the standard CAPM: (1) investors are risk-averse; (2) investors have homogeneous expectations; (3) investors are concerned with nominal returns in their home currency; (4) all investors can borrow and lend unlimited amounts at the risk-free rate; and (5) there are no taxes or transaction costs.

15. **C** The domestic CAPM can be extended to an international framework with the addition of two unrealistic assumptions: (1) investors throughout the world have identical consumption baskets, and (2) purchasing power parity holds at all times.

ANSWERS – CHALLENGE PROBLEMS

16. **A** If the real rate remains constant, the nominal value of the yen will appreciate by the inflation differential of 2% (2% inflation in the United States minus 0% inflation in Japan). The expected return on the bond is equal to the yen interest rate of 1% plus the inflation differential of 2%, or 3%.

17. **B** The exchange rate changed from $1 = ¥120 to $1 = ¥130. Notice that the yen has depreciated (it takes more yen to buy one dollar) even though the inflation differential favored the yen. This means that the real rate has changed. The inflation differential does not fully explain the exchange rate movement. For the U.S. investor, this turns out to be bad news. Instead of appreciating by 2% as predicted by the inflation differential, the yen has depreciated by 7.69%:

$$\% \text{ change in } ¥ = \frac{\left(\$1\big/¥130\right)\ \left(\$1\big/¥120\right)}{\$1\big/¥120} = -0.077 = -7.7\%$$

Note that the price of the original quote is ¥ per $, so to compute the change in the value of the yen, we have to convert the exchange rate quotes to $ per ¥. The return to the U.S. investor is approximately equal to the yen interest rate less the yen depreciation, or 1% + (−7.7%) = −6.7%.

18. **B** The expected returns are calculated using the ICAPM as follows.

The local currency exposure of French Aviation (the sensitivity of euro returns on French Aviation to change in the $/€ exchange rate) is −0.25. Therefore, the domestic currency exposure (the sensitivity of French Aviation's dollar returns to changes in the $/€ rate) is −0.25 + 1, or 0.75.

Likewise, the domestic currency exposure of Tokyo Inc. (the sensitivity of its dollar-denominator returns to changes in the $/¥ rate) is −1.1 + 1, or −0.1.

$$E(R) = R_f + \left(\beta_g \times MRP_g\right) + \left(\gamma_€ \times FCRP_€\right) + \left(\gamma_¥ \times FCRP_¥\right)$$

$$E\left(R_{French}\right) = 0.03 + \left(0.8 \times 0.07\right) + \left(0.75 \times 0.02\right) + \left(0.40 \times 0.015\right) = 0.1070 = 10.70\%$$

$$E\left(R_{Tokyo}\right) = 0.03 + \left(1.2 \times 0.07\right) + \left(-0.5 \times 0.02\right) + \left(-0.1 \times 0.015\right) = 0.1025 = 10.25\%$$

19. **C** French Aviation has the lowest world beta and therefore the lowest exposure to world risk. The currency exposure for French Aviation is positive, which increases its expected return. The currency exposure for Tokyo Inc. is negative, which decreases its expected return. The investor's home country is the United States, so the risk-free return is based on the U.S. risk-free return for investments in both firms.

20. **B** Tokyo Inc. will be hurt by the appreciation of the yen relative to the euro. The currency appreciation will make Tokyo Inc.'s products more expensive in France, resulting in lower sales revenue. Lower sales will most likely lead to lower profits and a lower stock price for Tokyo Inc.

21. **A** Filler is a U.S. investor. Therefore, the interest rate differential (U.S. risk-free rate minus Japan risk-free rate) = 0.03 − 0.01 = 0.02 = 2%. This implies that the yen trades at a forward premium of 2%. In other words, the forward exchange rate is quoted at a premium of 2% over the spot exchange rate of ¥120 per $. The yen risk premium is the difference between the currency appreciation and the interest rate differential: 0.035 − 0.02 = 0.015 = 1.5%.

THE THEORY OF ACTIVE PORTFOLIO MANAGEMENT

Study Session 18

EXAM FOCUS

This topic review pulls together the security analysis material in Study Sessions 10 through 12 with the portfolio theory covered previously in this study session. You should be able to justify the use of active portfolio management, even when markets are assumed to be in equilibrium. Be sure to understand the logic and the steps underlying the Treynor-Black portfolio management model, which combines market inefficiency, security analysis, and modern portfolio theory.

LOS 67.a: Justify active portfolio management when security markets are nearly efficient.

Active portfolio management refers to decisions of the portfolio manager to actively manage and monitor the broad asset allocation and security selection of the portfolio. When markets are at equilibrium, asset prices equal their fair values, but we must ask what causes markets to be at equilibrium in the first place? Theoretically, markets reach equilibrium because investors constantly seek out and exploit profit opportunities arising from mispriced securities (i.e., disequilibrium). In other words, equilibrium is the desirable end result of active portfolio management.

The theory of active portfolio management can be justified based on economic and empirical arguments.

- From an economic or theoretical standpoint, active portfolio management becomes important when prices begin to deviate from fair values. For example, an efficient market draws money away from actively managed funds and toward passively managed funds. As less money is actively managed, asset prices will begin to deviate from fair values, which, in turn, will attract transfers of cash flows back into actively managed funds.
- From an empirical standpoint, active portfolio management is justified because some portfolio managers have demonstrated abnormally strong performance over extended periods. Therefore, while funds *on average* might not outperform risk-adjusted benchmarks, there may still be a few fund managers who do outperform their benchmarks. Consequently, investors seek actively managed funds that they think will be among the star performers.

Even when markets are efficient, or nearly efficient, there is still a need for a theory of active portfolio management. Recall that the mean-variance theory discussed in the Portfolio Concepts topic review leads to the following key conclusions:

- Investors should select the mean-variance efficient ("optimal") risky portfolio that maximizes the reward-to-risk ("Sharpe") ratio, and then should combine the optimal risky portfolio with the risk-free asset.
- More risk-averse investors should allocate a smaller percentage of funds to the optimal risky portfolio and a larger percentage of funds to the risk-free asset.
- Less risk-averse investors should allocate a larger percentage of funds to the optimal risky portfolio and a smaller percentage of funds to the risk-free asset.

 Professor's Note: This conclusion is often summarized as the "separation theorem," which states that the investor's optimal risky portfolio can be determined without any knowledge of the investor's risk-return preferences. Therefore, the process of identifying the optimal total investment consists of two independent decisions: (1) identifying the optimal risky portfolio that is independent of the investor's risk aversion; and (2) combining the optimal risky portfolio with the risk-free asset in a way that satisfies the investor's risk aversion.

We cannot observe the market portfolio, or its risk-return characteristics, directly. Therefore, in order to implement this passive investment strategy, an active portfolio management theory is needed to:

- Develop capital market forecasts (expected returns, variances, and covariances) for major asset classes such as stocks, bonds, real estate, international stocks, and international bonds.
- Allocate funds across the major risky asset classes to form the optimal risky portfolio that maximizes the reward-to-risk ratio.
- Allocate funds between the risk-free asset and the optimal risky portfolio in order to satisfy the investor's risk aversion.
- Rebalance the portfolio as capital market forecasts and investor's risk aversion changes (i.e., increase or decrease allocations to the optimal risky portfolio when expectations rise or fall, respectively—also known as *market timing*—and increase or decrease allocations to the optimal risky portfolio when the investor's risk aversion falls or rises, respectively).

LOS 67.b: Discuss the steps and the approach of the Treynor-Black model for security selection.

The *Treynor-Black model* is a portfolio optimization framework that combines market inefficiency and modern portfolio theory. The model is based on the premise that markets are nearly efficient—that the number of mispriced assets is limited. The objective of the model is to create an optimal risky portfolio that is allocated to both a *passively managed* (indexed) portfolio and to an *actively managed* portfolio. The active portfolio contains assets that the analyst believes are mispriced. As markets move away from equilibrium, the actively managed portfolio plays a more vital role in the overall portfolio management process.

The Treynor-Black model for security selection relies on market model forecasts of expected returns, variances, and covariances for the actively managed portfolio.

The specific steps in the Treynor-Black model are:

Step 1: Develop capital market expectations (expected return and standard deviation) for the *passively managed* market index portfolio, M.

Step 2: Identify the limited set of mispriced securities, which are securities with large (positive and negative) predicted alphas—defined as the analyst's forecast (expected) return minus the CAPM required return:

$$\text{predicted alpha for security i} = \alpha_i = \text{forecast return for security i} - \{R_F + \beta_i[E(R_M) - R_F]\}$$

Step 3: Determine weightings across the mispriced securities to form the *actively managed* portfolio, A. The weight for security *i* in the actively managed portfolio equals:

$$w_i = \frac{\alpha_i}{\sigma^2(\varepsilon_i)} \bigg/ \sum_{j=1}^{n} \frac{\alpha_j}{\sigma^2(\varepsilon_j)}$$

In this formula, *n* is the number of assets in the actively managed portfolio, and ε_i is the error term from the market model regression:

$$R_i - R_F = \alpha_i + \beta_i(R_M - R_F) + \varepsilon_i$$

Then $\sigma^2(\varepsilon_i)$ is the error variance, which measures unsystematic risk.

The Treynor-Black model places special emphasis on the predicted alpha (expected abnormal performance) and predicted error variance (unsystematic risk). Large allocations are assigned to securities with large predicted positive and negative alphas and low unsystematic risks. The Treynor-Black model penalizes securities that have high unsystematic risk because of the loss of diversification they bring to the investor's total portfolio. The following summarizes the Treynor-Black model allocations within the actively managed Portfolio A:

- Small weight for securities with small alphas and high unsystematic risk.
- Large weight for securities with large alphas and low unsystematic risk.
- Positive weight (long positions) for securities with positive alphas.
- Negative weight (short positions) for securities with negative alphas.

Step 4: Determine weightings to the actively managed Portfolio A and to the passively managed market index M to form *optimal Portfolio P*. Portfolio P is the combination of portfolios A and M that will have the highest possible Sharpe Ratio (higher than both Portfolio A or M). Recall from the previous topic review that the Sharpe ratio is:

$$\text{Sharpe ratio for portfolio P} = \frac{E(R_P) - R_F}{\sigma_P}$$

Figure 1 illustrates the optimization process leading to the selection of optimal risky Portfolio P. (Please refer to the Portfolio Concepts topic review for a discussion of the capital allocation line.)

Figure 1: The Treynor-Black Optimal Risky Portfolio

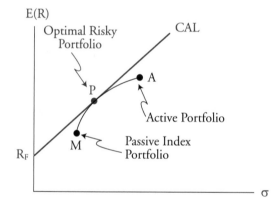

Notice how the Treynor-Black model applies the modern portfolio theory initially developed by Professor Harry Markowitz. In particular, Portfolio P is located at the tangency point of the capital allocation line and the Markowitz efficient frontier (curve M-A). Figure 1 shows that the 100% indexed portfolio, M, can be beaten by allocating funds between the risk free asset and the optimal portfolio, P. Stated mathematically, the Sharpe ratio for Portfolio P exceeds the Sharpe ratio for the passive market index M.

The active portfolio, A, is the portfolio of securities the analyst has identified as being significantly mispriced (i.e., stocks with significant alpha forecasts), and consists of long positions (positive weights) for all securities with positive alphas and short positions (negative weights) for all securities with negative alphas. The benefits of active security analysis increase as the expected return on the actively managed portfolio (Portfolio A) increase, its risk decreases, and its correlation with the market index decreases (all of which lead to an increase in the Sharpe ratio for Portfolio P, or equivalently, to a higher sloped capital allocation line) as shown in Figure 1.

Step 5: Allocate funds to Portfolio P and to the risk-free asset that satisfy the investor's risk aversion. The investor's optimal investment (combination of risk-free asset and risky Portfolio P) is represented by the tangency point of the investor's indifference curve with the capital allocation line (point C in Figure 2).

Figure 2: The Treynor-Black Optimal Risky and Risk-Free Allocation

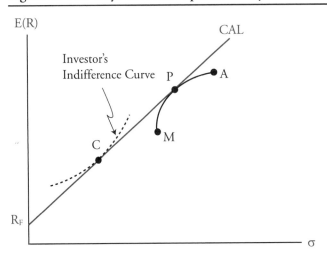

Example: Finding the optimal portfolio using the Treynor-Black model

Treyblack Inc. manages its pension using the Treynor-Black model. Assume Treyblack's optimal portfolio, P, is allocated 60% to the market index and 40% to the active portfolio. Also, assume Treyblack's asset allocation target equals 20% to cash and 80% to the optimal portfolio, P. Calculate the percentages allocated to cash, and to portfolios M and A.

Answer:

The final allocation is 20% cash, 48% indexed, and 32% actively managed. The 20% cash allocation is already provided in the question. The remaining 80% is allocated 60/40 to the index and to the active portfolio, respectively:

final allocation to the market index = 80% × 60% = 48%

final allocation to the active portfolio = 80% × 40% = 32%

Therefore, 20% is allocated to cash, 48% is indexed (Portfolio M), and 32% is actively managed (Portfolio A). Note, that as markets become more efficient, alphas will shrink, as will the allocation of funds to active management.

A key question is "if Portfolio A is so great, why don't we allocate a greater percentage of funds to it?" The answer lies in the loss of diversification associated with the actively managed portfolio. The main reason for keeping the percentage relatively low is because Portfolio A is typically highly non-diversified. The percentage allocation, then, might be relatively low because the Treynor-Black model penalizes Portfolio A for its lack of diversification. If Portfolio A is more diversified, then a larger percentage is allocated to it.

The Treynor-Black model provides a convenient way to measure the contribution of active security analysis to the portfolio performance. The improvement in performance relative to the passive market index can be measured by the difference between the squared Sharpe ratios for Portfolio P (which optimally combines the passive market index M and the actively managed Portfolio A) and the passive market index M. This difference can be shown to equal the squared alpha for the portfolio of mispriced securities (Portfolio A) divided by its unsystematic risk:

$$\frac{\alpha_A^2}{\sigma^2_{(\varepsilon_A)}} = \left(\frac{\alpha_A}{\sigma_{(\varepsilon_A)}}\right)^2$$

The ratio $\dfrac{\alpha_A}{\sigma_{(\varepsilon_A)}}$ is called the **information ratio**.

The information ratio squared measures the actively managed portfolio's squared alpha per unit of unsystematic risk.

> *Professor's Note: This ratio is the ex-ante information ratio based on expected alpha and the expected level of unsystematic risk over the upcoming time period. The information ratio,* $\dfrac{\overline{R}_P - \overline{R}_B}{s_{(R_P - R_B)}}$, *is the ex-post information ratio based on actual returns over the previous time period.*

Therefore, the Treynor-Black model provides a formal framework that exploits perceived security mispricing via active security analysis, yet still maintains a well-diversified portfolio for the investor's total investment (Portfolio P, which combines the well-diversified market index, M, and the actively managed portfolio, A).

Treynor-Black Calculations

Here is a summary of the key equations used in the Treynor-Black model for an actively managed portfolio comprising two assets:

Stock Alphas

α_i = forecast return for stock i − {R_F + β_i[$E(R_M)$ − R_F]}

Weightings within the Actively Managed Portfolio A

$$w_1 = \frac{\alpha_1}{\sigma^2_{(\varepsilon_1)}} \bigg/ \left(\frac{\alpha_1}{\sigma^2_{(\varepsilon_1)}} + \frac{\alpha_2}{\sigma^2_{(\varepsilon_2)}}\right)$$

$$w_2 = 1 - w_1$$

where: $\sigma^2(\varepsilon_i)$ is the analyst's predicted unsystematic risk for security i

Portfolio A Alpha

$$\alpha_A = \text{forecast return for Portfolio A} - \{R_F + \beta_A[E(R_M) - R_F]\}$$

or, equivalently, the weighted average of the individual security alphas:

$$\alpha_A = w_1\alpha_1 + w_2\alpha_2$$

You should also remember three additional equations from LOS 66.m in the topic review of Portfolio Concepts:

Portfolio A Expected Return

$$E(R_A) = w_1E(R_1) + w_2E(R_2)$$

or, equivalently, the CAPM required return plus expected alpha:

$$E(R_A) = \alpha_A + R_F + \beta_A[E(R_M) - R_F]$$

Portfolio A Standard Deviation Forecast (using the market model)

$$\sigma_A = [\beta_A^2\sigma_M^2 + \sigma^2(\varepsilon_A)]^{1/2}$$

Covariance of Active Portfolio A with Passive Market Index M (using market model)

$$\text{Cov}_{AM} = \beta_A\beta_M\sigma_M^2$$

The Treynor-Black Model: Efficient Market Periods vs. Inefficient Market Periods

Notice that if markets are perfectly efficient, alphas equal zero, and there is no benefit to active security analysis. According to the Treynor-Black model, during these times, the investor optimally allocates funds between the risk-free asset and the passive market index.

In contrast, when markets become inefficient, securities become mispriced, and alphas no longer equal zero. And, what's more, if a large number of securities become mispriced, then the active Portfolio A contains a large number of securities. So, not only will the active portfolio have a large predicted alpha, but it will have little unsystematic risk (unsystematic risk approaches zero as the number of securities in the portfolio increases). Therefore, during times of market irrationality or bubbles, the portfolio alpha will be high, the portfolio unsystematic risk will be small, and the potential benefits of active security selection will be large. According to the Treynor-Black model, more emphasis will be placed on security analysis—the actively managed portfolio will be heavily weighted during these times.

LOS 67.c: Describe how an analyst's accuracy in forecasting alphas can be measured and how estimates of forecasting can be incorporated into the Treynor-Black approach.

The examples provided in this topic review assume analyst forecasts are correct, but we know that analysts might be wrong from time to time. To account for the imprecision of analyst forecasts, we can impose an imprecision penalty or discount on the analyst's forecast alpha. For instance, if we know that the analyst forecast alpha is often wrong, we will shrink the forecast alpha (toward zero) accordingly. Greater weight is placed on high alpha, high quality forecasts. Since the allocation of funds to Portfolio A is determined in large part by the portfolio alpha, the allocation to the active portfolio shrinks as adjusted forecast alphas shrink.

The analyst's forecasting accuracy can be assessed by examining the analyst's forecast history. Superior analysts are usually quite accurate, in which case their forecast alphas closely track the realized alphas. To quantify the analyst's forecasting ability, we use the correlation between the analyst's forecasts alphas and realized alphas. A high correlation indicates high forecasting accuracy—indicative of a superior analyst.

The Treynor-Black weightings within the actively managed portfolio can be adjusted for the forecasting ability exhibited by the analyst. To make the proper adjustments, we rely on regression analysis. Recall from the multiple regression topic review in Study Session 3 that the R-squared (R^2) in a simple linear regression (only one independent variable) equals the square of the correlation between the dependent and independent variable.

We should also recall that the R^2 of a simple linear regression equals the proportion of the changes in the dependent variable that are explained by the changes in the independent variable. Forecast accuracy is perfect if the R^2 equals 100% and is worse the farther the R^2 drops from 100%. Therefore, we can use the R^2 to adjust the forecast alphas to account for the lack of perfect forecasting ability of the analyst.

For the Treynor-Black alpha forecasts, the R^2 equals the percentage of the changes in the realized alpha that are explained by changes in the forecast alpha. Consequently, we can use the R^2 to adjust the analyst's alpha to control for his forecasting accuracy. The specific steps are as follows:

- Collect the time-series alpha forecasts for the analyst.
- Calculate the correlation between the alpha forecasts and the realized alphas.
- Square the correlation to derive the R^2.
- Adjust (shrink) the forecast alpha by multiplying it by the analyst's R^2.

Example: Adjusting for the forecasting accuracy of the analyst

Analysts Joseph House and Elena Nukyeva derive alpha forecasts for stocks. Their firm, Active Investors, manages portfolios using the Treynor-Black model. The actively managed portfolio consists of two stocks: Software Co. (SC), which is analyzed by House, and Insure Inc. (II), which is analyzed by Nukyeva. The following forecasts were made by House and Nukyeva:

	Alpha, α	Unsystematic risk, $\sigma^2(\varepsilon)$
House	0.05	0.20
Nukyeva	0.05	0.40

The historical correlations between House's forecast and realized alphas for SC and between Nukyeva's forecast and realized alphas for II are 0.20 and 0.80, respectively.

Derive the adjusted alphas for the two stocks and analyze the effects of the adjustments on the weights of the two stocks within the active portfolio and on the weights of the active portfolio and the passive market index.

Answer:

The forecast alphas for both SC and II equal 5%. The adjusted alphas should equal:

adjusted alpha for SC = $(0.20)^2(0.05) = 0.002 = 0.20\%$

adjusted alpha for II = $(0.80)^2(0.05) = 0.032 = 3.20\%$

The original (unadjusted) weights within the active portfolio are:

$$w_{SC} = \frac{\alpha_{SC}}{\sigma^2_{(\varepsilon_{SC})}} \left/ \left(\frac{\alpha_{SC}}{\sigma^2_{(\varepsilon_{SC})}} + \frac{\alpha_{II}}{\sigma^2_{(\varepsilon_{II})}} \right) \right. = \frac{0.05}{0.20} \left/ \left(\frac{0.05}{0.20} + \frac{0.05}{0.40} \right) \right. = 0.67 = 67\%$$

or, 67% allocated to SC and 33% allocated to II (weights must sum to 100% within the active portfolio).

The adjusted weights ($ADJw_{SC}$ and $ADJw_{II}$) are:

$$ADJw_{SC} = \frac{ADJ\alpha_{SC}}{\sigma^2_{(\varepsilon_{SC})}} \left/ \left(\frac{ADJ\alpha_{SC}}{\sigma^2_{(\varepsilon_{SC})}} + \frac{ADJ\alpha_{II}}{\sigma^2_{(\varepsilon_{II})}} \right) \right.$$

$$= \frac{0.002}{0.20} \left/ \left(\frac{0.002}{0.20} + \frac{0.032}{0.40} \right) \right. = 0.111 = 11.1\%$$

or, 11.1% allocated to SC and 88.9% allocated to II.

Therefore, the weight allocated to SC decreases from 67% to 11.1% and the weight to II increases from 33% to 88.9%. The weights changed dramatically as a consequence of the large differences in forecasting accuracy for the two analysts.

Also, note that the allocation to the active Portfolio A will drop and the allocation to the market index, M, will rise as a consequence of adjusting the forecast alphas for SC and II.

KEY CONCEPTS

LOS 67.a

Active portfolio management can be justified on *economic* grounds. Theoretically, in an efficient market, investors will allocate funds to passively managed (indexed) portfolios. But, as less money is actively managed, asset prices may begin to deviate from fair values, which, in turn, will attract transfers of cash flows into actively managed funds.

Active portfolio management can also be justified on *empirical* grounds because some portfolio managers have demonstrated an abnormally strong performance over extended periods. Consequently, investors seek actively managed funds that they think will be among the star performers.

Even if markets are efficient, active portfolio management theory is needed to:
- Develop capital market forecasts for the major asset classes.
- Allocate funds across the major risky asset classes to form the optimal risky portfolio.
- Allocate funds between the risk-free asset and the optimal risky portfolio.
- Rebalance the portfolio as capital market forecasts and the investor's risk aversion changes.

LOS 67.b

The Treynor-Black model is a portfolio optimization framework that combines modern portfolio theory and market inefficiency. The model is based on the premise that markets are nearly efficient, denoting that the number of mispriced assets is limited.

The Treynor-Black model balances the need for diversification with the need for superior performance.

The specific steps in the Treynor-Black model are:
- Develop capital market expectations for the *passively managed* market index portfolio.
- Identify a limited number of mispriced securities, using security analysis.
- Determine weightings across the mispriced securities to form an *actively managed* portfolio. Weights are large for securities with high alphas and low unsystematic risk.
- Determine weightings to the actively managed portfolio and to the passively managed market index to form an optimal portfolio combination of the two.
- Determine the appropriate allocation of funds to the risk-free asset and to the optimal portfolio that satisfies the investor's risk aversion.

LOS 67.c

The Treynor-Black model can be modified to account for the imprecision of analyst forecasts. To account for poor forecast quality, alpha forecasts can be adjusted toward zero. Greater weight is placed on high alpha, high quality forecasts.

The specific steps to adjusted alphas for analyst's forecasting accuracy are as follows:
- Collect the time-series alpha forecasts for the analyst.
- Calculate the correlation between the alpha forecasts and the realized alphas.
- Square the correlation to derive the R^2.
- Adjust (shrink) the forecast alpha by multiplying it by the analyst's R^2.

CONCEPT CHECKERS

1. Thomas Jackson is the portfolio manager for Money Managers Inc., an investment advisory firm. Money Managers makes asset allocation recommendations for their clients and alternates between active portfolio and passive portfolio recommendations. The firm believes that markets are entering an extended equilibrium period. In keeping with Money Manager's predictions, are Jackson's forecasts of individual stock alpha *likely* to be high or low, and is it *likely* Jackson will recommend a high or low allocation to the actively managed portfolio?
    A. High Alpha and High Allocation.
    B. High Allocation and Low Alpha.
    C. Low Alpha and Low Allocation.

2. AP Associates is a pension advisory firm that employs the Treynor-Black framework to formulate its portfolio recommendations. Based on their framework of analysis, is it *likely* that AP Associates believes there is a large or a small number of mispriced securities, and does the firm *likely* place a large or a small weight on the importance of diversification?
    A. Large number and large weight.
    B. Small number and large weight.
    C. Small number and small weight.

3. Prudent Management Inc. (PMI) manages portfolios using the Treynor-Black model. PMI allocates funds between the passive market index and a long-only actively managed portfolio. PMI recently made adjustments for poor quality stock return forecasts by their analysts, contending that forecast errors increase with the size of the forecast alpha. By making appropriate adjustments to the alpha forecasts, will the weights allocated to low forecast alpha stocks within the PMI actively managed portfolio *likely* increase or decrease, and will the weight allocated to the actively managed portfolio *likely* increase or decrease? (Assume the changes have no effect on the unsystematic risk of the actively managed portfolio).
    A. Decrease both allocations.
    B. Increase one and decrease the other.
    C. Maintain current allocations.

Study

Cross-Reference to CFA Institute Assigned Reading #67 – The Theory of Active Portfolio Man.

CHALLENGE PROBLEMS

Use the following information to answer Questions 4 through 7.

Modern Paradigm Management, MPM, employs the Treynor-Black model to identify and weight mispriced securities. The macro unit at MPM makes the following forecasts for the passive market index:

expected market index return	10%
market index variance	0.04
risk-free rate	6%

The security analysis unit of MPM identifies two mispriced stocks: AmTech (AT) and HealthCo (HC). MPM derives the following forecasts for AT and HC:

	Forecast return	Beta, β	Unsystematic risk, $\sigma^2(\varepsilon)$
AT	15%	1.25	0.20
HC	12%	0.50	0.40

4. The weights for AT and HC within MPM's actively managed portfolio are *closest* to:
   A. 40% to AT and 60% to HC.
   B. 67% to AT and 33% to HC.
   C. 80% to AT and 20% to HC.

5. The expected return and alpha for the actively managed portfolio are *closest* to:
   A. 12% expected return and a 2% alpha.
   B. 14% expected return and a 2% alpha.
   C. 14% expected return and a 4% alpha.

6. The market model prediction for the standard deviation for the actively managed portfolio is *closest* to:
   A. 20%.
   B. 30%.
   C. 40%.

7. The correlation between the actively managed portfolio and the passive index is *closest* to:
   A. 0.40.
   B. 0.50.
   C. 0.60.

ANSWERS – CONCEPT CHECKERS

1. **C** If markets are entering an equilibrium period, then predicted returns should be very close to required returns. An asset's alpha is defined as the difference between the analyst's predicted return for an asset and its required return. Therefore, during equilibrium, alphas should equal zero. Also, if markets are expected to enter an equilibrium period, then very little weight should be allocated to active portfolio management. In equilibrium, no abnormal return opportunities exist. A high allocation should be made to passively managed portfolios (indexed portfolios).

2. **B** The *Treynor-Black model* combines modern portfolio theory and market inefficiency. The model is based on the premise that markets are nearly efficient, denoting that the number of mispriced assets is small. The model incorporates active security selection within an optimally diversified portfolio context. Therefore, the model places large value on the importance of diversification.

3. **B** The imposition of an accuracy penalty will shrink the forecast alphas for the individual securities, which will cause the entire portfolio adjusted forecast alpha to drop. Since the weights in the Treynor-Black model rise and fall with alpha, any drop in the forecast alpha will be associated with a drop in the allocation to the active portfolio (assuming no change in the unsystematic risk of the active portfolio). Also, PMI contends that the forecast errors increase with the size of the forecast alphas. Therefore, PMI will shrink the large forecast alphas significantly, but will not shrink the small forecast alphas very much. As a consequence, the weights will fall considerably for the large forecast alphas. Because the weights must sum to 100% within the active portfolio, weights will increase for the low forecast alpha stocks.

ANSWERS – CONCEPT CHECKERS

4. **B** The formula for the weights for any security i in the actively managed portfolio equals:

$$w_i = \frac{\alpha_i}{\sigma^2(\varepsilon_i)} \bigg/ \sum_{j=1}^{n} \frac{\alpha_j}{\sigma^2(\varepsilon_j)}$$

where n = 2 in this question. First, we must calculate the alphas for the two stocks, which equal the difference between the forecast return and the CAPM required return. The required returns are:

required return for AT: 0.06 + 1.25(0.10 − 0.06) = 0.11 = 11%

required return for HC: 0.06 + 0.50(0.10 − 0.06) = 0.08 = 8%

alpha for AT: 0.15 − 0.11 = 0.04

alpha for HC: 0.12 − 0.08 = 0.04

The weight for AT equals:

$$w_{AT} = \frac{\alpha_{AT}}{\sigma^2(\varepsilon_{AT})} \bigg/ \left(\frac{\alpha_{AT}}{\sigma^2(\varepsilon_{AT})} + \frac{\alpha_{HC}}{\sigma^2(\varepsilon_{HC})} \right) = \frac{0.04}{0.20} \bigg/ \left(\frac{0.04}{0.20} + \frac{0.04}{0.40} \right) = 0.67 = 67\%$$

Therefore, within Portfolio A, the weight for AT equals 67% and the weight for HC equals 0.33 (the weights within Portfolio A must sum to 100%).

5. **C** The expected alpha for the actively managed portfolio equals the weighted average of the two stock alphas:

$$\alpha_p = 0.67(0.04) + 0.33(0.04) = 0.04 = 4\%$$

The expected return for the actively managed portfolio also equals the weighted average of the two stock expected returns (the forecast returns of 15% and 12%, respectively):

$$E(R_A) = w_{AT}E(R_{AT}) + w_BE(R_{HC}) = 0.67(0.15) + 0.33(0.12) = 0.14 = 14\%$$

or, using the market model in excess return form:

$$E(R_A) - R_F = \alpha_A + \beta_A[E(R_M) - R_F]$$

$$E(R_A) = \alpha_A + R_F + \beta_A[E(R_M) - R_F] = 0.04 + 0.06 + 1[0.10 - 0.06] = 0.14 = 14\%$$

6. **C** Note that the beta for any portfolio equals the weighted average of its member betas.

Therefore, the beta for the actively managed portfolio equals:

$$\beta_A = w_{AT}\beta_{AT} + w_{HC}\beta_{HC} = 0.67(1.25) + 0.33(0.50) = 1.0$$

Using the market model, the standard deviation for the actively managed portfolio is:

$$\sigma_A = [\beta_A^2\sigma_M^2 + \sigma^2(\varepsilon_A)]^{1/2} = [(1)^2(0.04) + 0.1333]^{1/2} = 0.4163 = 41.63\%$$

To derive the unsystematic risk for the actively managed portfolio, $\sigma^2(\varepsilon_A)$, in this formula above, recall from the Portfolio Concepts topic review that the market model assumes unsystematic returns are uncorrelated across firms (i.e., the covariance of regression errors for AT and HC is assumed to equal zero). Therefore, the market model prediction of the unsystematic risk for the actively managed portfolio equals:

$$\sigma^2(\varepsilon_A) = w_{AT}^2\sigma^2(\varepsilon_{AT}) + w_{HC}^2\sigma^2(\varepsilon_{HC}) = (0.67)^2(0.20) + (0.33)^2(0.40) = 0.1333$$

Therefore, Portfolio A has an expected return of 14%, standard deviation of 41.63%, and an expected alpha of 4%. Notice that the high unsystematic risk of Portfolio A causes its standard deviation to be much higher than that of the passive market index (41.63% versus 20%) even though the betas of Portfolio A and the market index are identical. High unsystematic risk for the actively managed portfolio implies that the portfolio is poorly diversified. Treynor-Black model allocates fewer funds to the actively managed portfolio as a penalty for its lack of diversification.

7. **B** Recall from the market model discussion in the Portfolio Concepts topic review that we can forecast the covariance and correlation between Portfolio A and the passive market index, M, using the following formulas:

$$Cov_{AM} = \beta_A\beta_M\sigma_M^2 = (1)(1)(0.04) = 0.04$$

$$\rho_{AM} = \frac{Cov_{AM}}{\sigma_A\sigma_M} = \frac{0.04}{(0.4163)(0.20)} = 0.48$$

Note that the allocation of funds to Portfolio A will increase as the correlation between Portfolio A and the market index M drops. From Figure 1 in the topic review you can see that the bulge in curve A-M will increase, resulting in a more steeply sloped capital allocation line.

The following is a review of the Portfolio Management principles designed to address the learning outcome statements set forth by CFA Institute®. This topic is also covered in:

THE PORTFOLIO MANAGEMENT PROCESS AND THE INVESTMENT POLICY STATEMENT

Study Session 18

EXAM FOCUS

This qualitative material on portfolio management revisits concepts first introduced at Level 1 and provides an introduction to the extensive treatment of the topic you'll see next year at Level 3. Keep the following points in mind: (1) the investment environment is ever-changing, so investment decision making must recognize the potential for shifts in a variety of factors, and (2) every investment decision should be framed within a portfolio perspective—it is not enough to know the characteristics of a potential investment itself, you must be aware of how an investment affects the risk and return characteristics of your overall portfolio.

WARM-UP: ELEMENTS OF PORTFOLIO MANAGEMENT

Although specifying objectives and constraints and evaluating relevant economic and market conditions represent the beginning of the process, these decisions are also linked to the measurement, monitoring, and evaluation steps of the process. The integrative nature of portfolio management involves numerous feedback loops and allows managers to be as rigid or flexible (or as quantitative or qualitative) as they desire. There is no end point to the process, only evaluation of performance that may indicate a need for rebalancing. The following represents the elements of the portfolio management process.

Evaluating investor and market characteristics. The first step is to determine the objectives and constraints of the investor. Objectives are related to the risk and return expectations of the investor. Constraints are those factors that limit or restrict certain decisions or investment choices. The second step is to evaluate the economic environment. The factors relevant to an economic evaluation are mostly *macro* issues dealing with the overall state of the economy (growth prospects, inflation expectations, unemployment, and other considerations). An economic evaluation can also work down to *micro* issues, such as those related to sector-, industry-, and security-specific considerations.

Developing an investment policy statement. This next portion of the investment management process formalizes objectives and constraints into an investment policy statement (IPS), which will guide investment decisions and formalize the investment strategy (e.g., whether the portfolio will be actively managed or follow a more passive approach). Capital market expectations that take into account the economic evaluation conducted previously are also formalized in this step.

Determining an asset allocation strategy. After the formal documentation of the IPS is completed, decisions on how and where funds will be invested are completed, and a strategic asset allocation is created. Securities are evaluated as to how they might fit into a portfolio that meets the objectives and constraints of the investor. Portfolio decisions are implemented and then executed in a timely fashion so that the investor's funds can be put to use in attaining goals and objectives.

Measuring and evaluating performance. After a stated time period, which will be specified in the IPS, portfolio performance will be measured, and an evaluation as to whether the portfolio attained investor objectives and followed the IPS will be prepared. Portfolio rebalancing may be indicated by the results of the evaluation. Connecting the evaluation step to the beginning of the process must occur to ensure portfolio decisions parallel investor needs and desires.

Monitoring dynamic investor objectives and capital market conditions. Continuous monitoring of both investor and marketplace characteristics takes place throughout the entire process. Multiple feedback mechanisms throughout the entire portfolio management process indicate where significant changes in either investor factors or marketplace prospects require adjustments to the portfolio. Remember, this is a dynamic, ongoing process. There are no end points, only continuous connections between objectives and constraints to portfolio monitoring and evaluation.

LOS 68.a: Explain the importance of the portfolio perspective.

The portfolio perspective is a key underlying principle of the entire CFA curriculum, including Level 2. The equity pricing models in the Level 2 curriculum are all based on the principle that only systematic risk is priced. Furthermore, one of the basic principles of the New Prudent Investor Rule is that diversification is expected of portfolio managers as a method of reducing risk.

Investors, analysts, and portfolio managers should analyze the **risk-return tradeoff of the portfolio as a whole**, not the risk-return tradeoff of the individual investments in the portfolio, because unsystematic risk can be diversified away by combining the investments into a portfolio. The systematic risk that remains in the portfolio is the result of the economic fundamentals that have a general influence on the security returns, such as GDP growth, unexpected inflation, consumer confidence, unanticipated changes in credit spreads, and business cycle.

LOS 68.b: Describe the steps of the portfolio management process and the components of those steps.

The ongoing portfolio management process can be detailed within the integrative steps described by **planning**, **execution**, and **feedback**. Each general step contains numerous components. The planning phase consists of analyzing objectives and constraints, developing an IPS, determining the appropriate investment strategy, and selecting an appropriate asset allocation. The focus of this topic review at Level 2 is the first step: planning.

LOS 68.c: Define investment objectives and constraints and explain and distinguish among the types of investment objectives and constraints.

Investment objectives relate to what the investor wants to accomplish with the portfolio. Objectives are mainly concerned with risk and return considerations.

Risk objectives are those factors associated with an investor's willingness and ability to take risk. Combining willingness and ability to accept risk is termed *risk tolerance*. *Risk aversion* indicates an investor's inability and unwillingness to take risk.

For an individual, willingness and ability to take risk may be determined by behavioral or psychological factors, whereas for an institution, these factors are determined primarily by portfolio constraints. Some specific factors that affect ability to accept risk are as follows:

- *Required spending needs:* How much variation in portfolio value can the investor tolerate before being inconvenienced in the short term?
- *Long-term wealth target:* How much variation in portfolio value can the investor tolerate before it jeopardizes meeting long-term wealth goals?
- *Financial strength:* Can the investor increase savings (or decrease expenditures) if the portfolio is insufficient to meet spending needs?
- *Liabilities:* Is the investor legally obligated to make future payments to beneficiaries, or does the investor have certain set spending requirements in retirement (i.e., pseudo liabilities)?

If the investor's portfolio is large relative to spending and obligations, a greater ability to take risk is apparent. Appropriately connecting willingness to ability may require educating the client in risk-return principles, as shown in Figure 1.

Figure 1: Willingness vs. Ability to Take Risk

| | Ability to Take Risk | |
Willingness to Take Risk	Below Average	Above Average
Below average	Lower risk tolerance	Education/resolution required
Above average	Education/resolution required	Higher risk tolerance

 Professor's Note: When the investor's ability and willingness to assume risk are in conflict, resolution is required. If ability exceeds willingness, the investor should be counseled that the assumption of more risk is may be appropriate, with the ultimate decision up to the investor. If willingness exceeds ability, ability should define the maximum risk tolerance.

There are two risk objective measurements: absolute and relative risk objectives. Standard deviation of total return represents an example of an absolute risk objective, whereas deviations from an underlying index, or *tracking risk*, represent an example of a relative risk objective. Relative risk measures are often easier to quantify from an individual investor's perspective, but absolute risk objectives are also referred to, even if only stated in qualitative forms.

Individuals often state their willingness to assume risk in broad terms; for example, "I have a moderate level of risk tolerance." Although institutions may state specific quantitative risk measures, such as "The level of portfolio volatility should not exceed 25% in any given year," their risk objectives can also be ranked along a qualitative risk objective spectrum. It is important to incorporate whatever level of specificity is mentioned when analyzing the risk objective.

Return objectives can be classified as either a *desired* or a *required return*. A desired return is that level of return stated by the client, indicating how much the investor wishes to receive from the portfolio. A required return represents some level of return that must be achieved by the portfolio, at least on an average basis to meet the target financial obligations. As such, required returns serve as a much stricter benchmark than desired returns.

In either case, the level of return needs to be consistent with the risk objective. Desired or required returns might be unrealistic, given available market conditions or risk objectives. Educating the investor as to disconnections between return and risk may be required. Some additional considerations in calculating return levels are differentiating between *real* and *nominal* returns, and distinguishing *pretax* and *after-tax* returns.

Whatever the return level generated, one factor to remember is that the return objective should be considered from a *total return* perspective. Even if a substantial income (or spending) component is required from the portfolio, the return objective should be evaluated by the total return, the return from both income and capital gains, and the characteristics of the portfolio. The assumption is that spending needs can be met through both investment income and capital appreciation.

INVESTMENT CONSTRAINTS

Investment constraints are those factors restricting or limiting the universe of available investment choices. Constraints can be generated either internally (those determined by the investor) or externally (those determined by some outside entity, such as a governmental agency). The five main classes of constraints relate to liquidity, time horizon, legal and regulatory concerns, tax considerations, and unique circumstances.

Liquidity constraints relate to expected cash outflows that will be needed at some specified time and are in excess of available income. In addition, it is ordinarily prudent to set aside some amount (e.g., three months living expenses) to meet unexpected cash needs. Often, liquidity is required over multiple time periods. A down payment for a home, funding for children's education, and providing for special needs during retirement are all liquidity concerns. The reason liquidity constraints are important to consider is that, depending on marketability, certain assets may generate only a portion of their fair value if they must be sold quickly. Attention must be paid to an asset's ability to be turned into cash without significant impact on portfolio value or asset allocation.

Linkages between liquidity and risk objectives are also apparent. Higher liquidity requirements usually indicate a lower tolerance for risk taking. Sensitivity to liquidity is a factor potentially affecting the willingness to take risk.

Time horizon constraints are associated with the time period(s) over which a portfolio is expected to generate returns to meet specific future needs (e.g., paying for children's college education or retirement).

Tax constraints depend on how, when, and if portfolio returns of various types are taxed. Some institutional investors (e.g., pension funds and endowments) have tax-exempt status. However, income and realized gains generated by personal portfolios are taxable and attention must be paid to the taxing environment when formulating the IPS. Often, differential tax treatments are applied to investment income and capital gains, which may be taxed at a lower rate. On the other hand, returns on certain types of retirement accounts are tax deferred until withdrawals are made.

Depending on which investment vehicle is chosen for the portfolio, tax consequences may adversely impact the after-tax returns. Estate taxes can also affect portfolio decisions. As a result, investment choices must be made with careful consideration of how a portfolio's returns will be taxed.

Legal and regulatory factors are externally generated constraints that mainly affect institutional investors. These constraints are usually associated with specifying which investment classes are not allowed or dictating any limitations placed on allocations to particular investment classes. Trust portfolios for individual investors may also be subject to substantial legal and regulatory oversight, which must be considered when establishing the IPS. Otherwise, this constraint does not usually affect individual investors. An example of a legal constraint that affects the management of trust assets for an individual is the New Prudent Investor Rule.

Unique circumstances are internally generated and represent special concerns of the investor. University endowments and philanthropic organizations, for example, might not allow investments in companies selling tobacco, alcohol, or defense products. Individuals might wish to have their portfolios fund specific activities (e.g., grandchildren's education, cancer research, or support for the arts), or they might be unfamiliar or inexperienced with certain investments. These, as well as any special investor circumstance restricting investment activities, must be considered in the formulation of the IPS.

A brief summary of return objectives and risk tolerance for individual and various institutional investors is shown in Figure 2.

Figure 2: Investment Objectives of Individual and Institutional Investors

Investor	Return Requirement	Risk Tolerance
Individual investor	Depends on life-cycle stage and financial position	Depends on life-cycle stage and financial position
Defined benefit pension plan	Sufficient to fund pension liability while accounting for inflation	Depends on plan features, age of workforce, and funding status of plan
Defined contribution pension plan	Depends on life-cycle stage of beneficiaries	Depends on risk tolerance of beneficiaries
Endowments and foundations	Sufficient to cover spending needs, expenses, and inflation	Generally average or above average
Life insurance companies	Function of policy holder reserve rates	Below average because of significant regulatory constraints
Non-life insurance companies	Function of policy pricing and financial strength	Below average because of significant regulatory constraints
Banks	Function of cost of funds	Depends on business model and financial strength

LOS 68.d: Discuss the role of the investment policy statement in the portfolio management process and explain the elements of an investment policy statement.

The investment policy statement (IPS) is a formal document that governs investment decision making, taking into account objectives and constraints. The main role of the IPS is to:

- Be readily implemented by current or future investment advisers (i.e., it is easily transportable).
- Promote long-term discipline for portfolio decisions.
- Help protect against short-term shifts in strategy when either market environments or portfolio performance cause panic or overconfidence.

There are numerous elements to an IPS. Some elements that are typically included are:

- A client description that provides enough background so any competent investment adviser can gain a common understanding of the client's situation.
- The purpose of the IPS with respect to policies, objectives, goals, restrictions, and portfolio limitations.
- Identification of duties and responsibilities of parties involved.
- The formal statement of objectives and constraints.
- A calendar schedule for both portfolio performance and IPS review.
- Asset allocation ranges and statements regarding flexibility and rigidity when formulating or modifying the strategic asset allocation.
- Guidelines for portfolio adjustments and rebalancing.

LOS 68.e: Explain how capital market expectations and the investment policy statement help influence the strategic asset allocation decision, and discuss how investors' investment time horizon may influence their strategic asset allocation.

The final step in the planning stage is creation of a **strategic asset allocation**. This step combines the IPS and capital market expectations to formulate long-term target weightings for the asset classes to be included in the portfolio. The need for flexibility in the asset allocation to allow for temporary shifts (called tactical asset allocations) in response to alterations in short-term capital market expectations should also be considered.

There are three common approaches used to implement the strategic asset allocation:

- *Passive investment strategies* represent those strategies that are not responsive to changes in expectations. Indexing and buy-and-hold investment strategies are examples of passive investment strategies.
- *Active investment strategies* are much more responsive to changing expectations. These strategies attempt to capitalize on differences between a portfolio manager's beliefs concerning security valuations and those in the marketplace. Generating *alpha* and investing according to a particular investment style fall into the active investment strategy category.
- *Semi-active, risk-controlled active,* or *enhanced index strategies* are hybrids of passive and active strategies. Index tilting, where portfolio managers attempt to match the risk characteristics of a benchmark portfolio, but also deviate from the exact benchmark portfolio weights in order to earn higher returns, is one example of this approach to strategic asset allocation.

Forecasts of risk-return characteristics are required for asset classes that are included in the investor's portfolio so that the portfolio's expected risk-return profile is well-understood. The role played by this step is to connect realistic market expectations to the objectives and constraints of the investor. Should the portfolio's risk-return profile diverge significantly from the investor's objectives, the strategic asset allocation may need to be reviewed.

The length of the time horizon may also influence the investor's asset allocation. An investor with a shorter investment time horizon will often choose a strategic asset allocation that is relatively less risky, with a smaller allocation to equities, for example.

LOS 68.f: Contrast the types of investment time horizons, determine the time horizon for a particular investor, and evaluate the effects of this time horizon on portfolio choice.

The time horizon for an investment portfolio may be short, as with a couple saving to purchase a home in two years, or long, as in the case of a couple in their 30s saving for retirement. Investors may also have a combination of short and long investment time horizons, as in the case of a couple who are saving both to fund their children's educations in five years and for retirement in 30 years.

The importance of the time horizon as an investment constraint is based on the idea that the longer the investment time horizon, the more risk an investor can take on. For time horizons of ten years or more, the fact that returns will average over economic and market cycles is generally believed to justify a greater allocation to equities and perhaps to riskier equities. The uncertainty about returns and the inability to make up for poor results over a short investment horizon leads many short-term investors to select relatively low-risk (predictable) securities. For a specific investor, however, a low *willingness* to take risk may constrain portfolio risk because of sensitivity to interim results, even when the investment horizon is relatively long and the *ability* to take on risk is greater.

LOS 68.g: Justify ethical conduct as a requirement for managing investment portfolios.

The investment professional who manages client portfolios well meets standards of competence and standards of conduct. It is important to recognize that the portfolio manager, who is an expert in the field with presumably more knowledge of investment principles than the client, is in a position of trust and so must meet the highest standards of ethical conduct in order to truly serve clients. The appropriate standard of conduct is embodied by the CFA Institute Code and Standards of Practice.

KEY CONCEPTS

LOS 68.a

There are two important features about the portfolio management process to consider:
- The process is ongoing and dynamic—there are no end points, only feedback to previous steps.
- Investments should be evaluated as to how they affect portfolio risk and return characteristics.

LOS 68.b

The three phases of the portfolio management process are planning, execution, and feedback; the Level 2 curriculum focuses on the planning phase.
- The planning phase consists of analyzing objectives and constraints, developing an IPS, determining the appropriate investment strategy, and selecting an appropriate asset allocation.
- The execution process relates to portfolio construction and revision.
- The feedback process consists of monitoring, rebalancing, and performance evaluation.

LOS 68.c

The two investment objectives to consider are:
- Return objectives.
- Risk objectives.

The five common constraints are:
- Liquidity.
- Time horizon.
- Legal and regulatory concerns.
- Tax considerations.
- Unique circumstances.

Differences between an investor's willingness and ability to take risk create additional education/resolution responsibilities for the portfolio manager with regard to formulating the risk objectives.

LOS 68.d

The IPS is a written document providing guidelines for portfolio investment decision making. The IPS does the following:
- Provides guidance for current and subsequent investment adviser decisions.
- Promotes long-term discipline in investment decision making.
- Protects against short-term shifts in strategy when either market conditions or portfolio performance cause panic or overconfidence.

There are several elements to a suitable IPS: a description of the client's situation; the purpose, as well as identification, of responsibilities; formal statements of objectives and constraints; schedule for portfolio performance and IPS review; asset allocation ranges; and guidance for rebalancing and adjustment activities.

LOS 68.e

While the investment policy statement will outline the appropriate risk-return characteristics for an investment portfolio, the strategic asset allocation to provide these characteristics will depend on capital markets expectations (risk, returns, and correlations) for the various asset classes. Typically, a longer investment time horizon will lead investors to tolerate more portfolio risk and employ strategic asset allocations more heavily weighted toward asset classes with greater risk and greater expected returns, such as equities.

LOS 68.f

Investors may have short or long investment horizons, or some combination of the two when multiple investment goals are identified. Investors with longer horizons (>10 years) have the ability, but not necessarily the willingness, to employ strategic asset allocations with more risk since returns will be averaged over economic and market cycles and investors have more time to recover from periods of relatively poor returns.

LOS 68.g

The investment professional who manages client portfolios well meets standards of competence and standards of conduct. It is important to recognize that the portfolio manager, who is an expert in the field with presumably more knowledge of investment principles than the client, is in a position of trust and so must meet the highest standards of ethical conduct in order to truly serve his clients. The appropriate standard of conduct is embodied by the CFA Institute Code and Standards.

CONCEPT CHECKERS

Use the following information to answer Questions 1 through 3.

Jane Smith has an investment portfolio of $5 million. She is 68 years old, retired, and has no children. After her death, she wishes to leave her portfolio to a local art museum that has given her relatively free access to art exhibits over the past decade. Her health is better than average, and she maintains an active lifestyle consisting of frequent swimming, biking, and playing tennis with friends at her country club. Smith estimates that to maintain her standard of living, she needs approximately $250,000 per year. Expenses are expected to grow at an expected inflation rate of 2%. She states that as a retiree, her tolerance for risk is "below average." Smith has come to you for assistance in investing her assets.

1. Smith's return objective is *closest* to:
    A. 3%.
    B. 5%.
    C. 7%.

2. Smith's ability to take risk is *most appropriately* characterized as:
    A. below average.
    B. average.
    C. significantly above average.

3. In terms of Smith's time horizon and liquidity constraints, Smith *most likely* has:
    A. only a short-term time horizon.
    B. no significant liquidity constraints.
    C. two time horizon constraints.

Use the following information to answer Questions 4 and 5.

Joe Farmingham is 38 years old, married, and has two children, ages 12 and 7. He recently received an inheritance of $300,000 and is considering investing "real money" for the first time. Farmingham likes to read the financial press and indicates that if he had money to invest in the past, he could have taken advantage of some undervalued security opportunities. Farmingham believes he has an average tolerance for risk-taking in investment activities, but he also enjoys skydiving every other weekend.

4. Farmingham's ability to take risk is *most appropriately* characterized as:
    A. below average.
    B. average.
    C. above average.

5. The *most appropriate* investment strategy for Farmingham to take advantage of his stated propensity for finding undervalued investments is a(n):
    A. active investment strategy.
    B. risk-controlled active investment strategy.
    C. enhanced index strategy.

CHALLENGE PROBLEMS

6. Lanaster University's endowment fund was recently estimated to be around $200 million. The university's endowment investment committee oversees numerous asset managers and is responsible for creating the investment policy statement (IPS). Ellen Hardinger and Will Smithson have been discussing the many factors that go into an IPS and are somewhat perplexed as to how to state the fund's risk objective. Hardinger and Smithson make three statements regarding the risk objectives of the endowment fund:

    Statement 1:   The fund is relatively conservative in its investment approach.

    Statement 2:   The fund performance should not exhibit more than a 20% standard deviation in any given year.

    Statement 3:   The fund should not exhibit performance differences of more than 5% from the Wilshire 5000 over any 3-year period.

    They need assistance in understanding how to combine those risk statements into a risk objective. How many of the statements represent absolute risk?
    A. One.
    B. Two.
    C. Three.

Use the following information for Questions 7 through 9.

William and Elizabeth Elam recently inherited $500,000 from Elizabeth's father, Abraham, and have come to Alan Schneider, CFA, for assistance. Both William and Elizabeth are 30 years old. William is employed as a factory worker with a salary of $40,000. Elizabeth is a teacher's aide and has a salary of $18,000. Their four children are ages 6, 5, 4, and 3. They have no other investments and have a current credit card debt of $60,000. When interviewed by Schneider, William made the following statements:

*   I love being on top of the latest trends in investing.
*   My friend Keith told me that the really smart investor holds stocks for no more than a month. After that, if you haven't made a profit, you probably won't.
*   Technology stocks are hot! Everyone has been buying them.
*   Can you believe that my mother still has the same portfolio she had a year ago? How boring!

7. The Elams' ability and willingness to take on risk are *most appropriately* characterized as:
    A. above average willingness and ability.
    B. below average ability and average willingness.
    C. average ability and above average willingness.

8. The Elams' time horizon constraint can be *best* characterized as:
    A. long-term and single stage.
    B. long-term and multistage.
    C. variable term and single stage.

9. The Elams' liquidity and legal/regulatory constraints are *best* characterized as:
    A. significant.
    B. insignificant.
    C. liquidity significant and legal/regulatory insignificant.

ANSWERS – CONCEPT CHECKERS

1. **C** Smith states that she needs $250,000 annually to maintain her standard of living. This amount of annual expenditures represents 5% ($250,000 / $5,000,000) of the current portfolio. Accounting for an expected increase in expenses at the anticipated level of inflation indicates a return objective around 7%.

2. **B** Although her stated willingness to take risk is below average, the size of her portfolio, her good health, and relative long time horizon indicate an ability to take average risk. As a retiree, sensitivity to substantial declines in portfolio value is probably a concern.

3. **C** Barring any unexpected health-related costs, the inflation-adjusted income needed will probably not change dramatically. Smith's concern for liquidity primarily relates to unusual cash outflows (e.g., health care costs, emergency spending) that might take place during her retirement years. Smith has essentially two time horizons for her portfolio: one until the end of her life, which could be another 20 years, and one for the gift to the art museum, which is even longer-term.

4. **C** Farmingham appears to have the ability and willingness to take risk. He frequently enjoys risk-seeking activities, such as skydiving. His relatively young age indicates a somewhat long time horizon for his investment portfolio. These facts couple ability and willingness to take an above-average level of risk.

5. **A** Farmingham indicates that he follows the financial press and has spotted what he considered to be undervalued securities. This activity indicates that Farmingham pays attention to security valuation issues and that he probably will do so in the future. His portfolio, therefore, should follow an active investment strategy.

ANSWERS – CHALLENGE PROBLEMS

6. **A** The statement of "20% standard deviation in any given year" is an absolute risk measure because it quantitatively states a specified level of total risk not to be exceeded. Conversely, the statement "performance differences from the Wilshire 5000 of more than 5% over any 3-year period" is a relative risk measure. Comparing measures of portfolio risk to another investment vehicle is an indication of relative risk.

   Institutional investors tend to be more quantitative in their assessments of risk, but the statement that the fund "is relatively conservative in its investment approach" also specifies a qualitative component to the risk objective.

7. **A** Because of their long time horizon and their situational profile, the Elams have the ability to tolerate an above-average level of risk. Based on the interview with William, the Elams have stated a willingness to tolerate an above-average level of risk. Therefore, the portfolio can be constructed based on an above-average level of risk.

   Based upon their lack of investing experience and rather aggressive attitude toward portfolio risk management, however, the financial services professional should be certain that the Elam's have a clear understanding of the concepts of risk and return.

Study Session 18

Cross-Reference to CFA Institute Assigned Reading #68 – The Portfolio Management Process and the Investment Policy Statement

8. **B**   The Elams' time horizon is long term and at least two-fold: the time until retirement and their retirement years. It is possible that a third time horizon could develop should the Elams decide to support their children through post-secondary education. Should they decide to retire at age 60, their pre-retirement time horizon would be 30 years.

9. **C**   The main liquidity constraint presented in the case is immediate and significant (the $60,000 in credit card debt). Schneider should recommend that the Elams eliminate this liability with the inheritance funds immediately. No special legal or regulatory problems are apparent. Prudent investor rules apply if William is interested in creating a trust fund.

18 minutes

Use the following information to answer Questions 1 through 6.

Figure 1 represents capital markets opportunities as estimated by two analysts at Ruger Bank, Jim Henshaw, CFA, and Jill Ponder, CFA Level III Candidate. 6% is the risk-free rate. They assume that all assets are priced at their equilibrium levels consistent with the CAPM.

Figure 1: Mean Variance Analysis

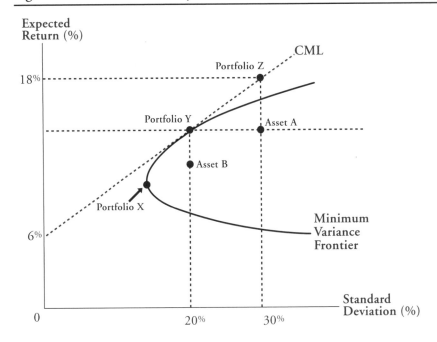

Ralph Cimins, a client of Henshaw and Ponder, is fairly risk averse and insists on keeping 40% of his portfolio in U.S. Treasury bills, which are yielding 6%. Henshaw believes Cimins' ability to tolerate risk is greater than that and would like to see Cimins invest 80% of his portfolio in risky assets. Ponder suggests that Portfolio X would be suitable for Cimins as this is the portfolio of risky assets with the least standard deviation and the least systematic risk.

Ponder is concerned about instability of the minimum variance frontier for the risky assets. Henshaw suggests that improving their historical market-model estimates of next period's risky-asset betas could reduce problems of instability, but Ponder believes the instability is just a result of changing capital markets conditions and that using only the most recent data can improve the stability of the efficient frontier.

They also consider a multi-factor model of securities returns and the use of factor portfolios. Henshaw states that they might be able to improve the Sharpe ratio of the portfolio they are constructing for Cimins by using a tracking portfolio to match a benchmark portfolio's risk along several dimensions. Ponder suggests that they use their firm's research to construct a tracking portfolio that has a Sharpe ratio greater than that of Portfolio Y in Figure 1.

1. Assuming the CAPM holds and that Portfolio Y in Figure 1 is a proxy for the market portfolio, it's Sharpe ratio is *closest* to:
    A. 0.30.
    B. 0.40.
    C. 0.50.

2. Ponder claims that Asset A is too risky with a standard deviation of 30%, and none of Asset A should be included in Cimins's portfolio. Henshaw claims that Asset A will plot on the Security Market Line and that including some of Asset A in Portfolio Y will not increase its risk. With respect to these claims:
    A. Ponder is correct and Henshaw is not.
    B. Ponder is incorrect and Henshaw is correct about Asset A plotting on the SML but not about the effect of adding it to Portfolio Y.
    C. Ponder is incorrect and Henshaw is correct in both his claims.

3. If Ponder and Henshaw construct Cimins' portfolio with his desired allocation of 40% to T-Bills and the remainder invested in Portfolio Y, the beta and expected return on Cimins' portfolio will be *closest* to:

	Beta	Expected return
A.	0.40	9.6%
B.	0.60	9.6%
C.	0.60	10.8%

4. With respect to their claims about the instability of the efficient frontier:
    A. both Henshaw and Ponder are incorrect since the instability of the efficient frontier cannot be improved by either method.
    B. Henshaw is correct but Ponder is not.
    C. Ponder is correct but Henshaw is not.

5. Assume that Portfolio Y is the market portfolio, that the research department at Ruger Bank can identify a number of stocks that are priced either above or below their equilibrium levels, and that a multi-factor model rather than the CAPM describes returns on risky assets. Ponder and Henshaw could increase the expected return of Crimins' portfolio without altering its risk by:
    A. using a factor portfolio that is overweight the underpriced stocks combined with an allocation to T-bills.
    B. constructing a tracking portfolio for Portfolio Y that has none of the stocks identified as overpriced.
    C. constructing a portfolio that is long the overpriced stocks and short the underpriced stocks and hedging its additional risk with a factor portfolio.

6. Ponder and Henshaw are estimating the beta of Asset B in Figure 1 and feel that adjusting their estimate of historical market-model beta is appropriate. This adjustment to their calculated beta, assuming that Asset B is priced at its equilibrium value according to the CAPM, would *most likely* be to:
    A. increase the historical market-model beta.
    B. decrease the historical market-model beta.
    C. not change the historical market-model beta for this asset.

SELF-TEST ANSWERS: PORTFOLIO MANAGEMENT

1. **B**   The Sharpe ratio is the slope of a line (the CML) from the risk-free rate to Portfolio Y, which can be calculated from the values for Portfolio Z. (18-6)/30 =0.40.

2. **C**   According to the CAPM, at least some of all tradable risky assets are in the tangency (market) Portfolio Y. Since all assets are assumed to be priced at their equilibrium values, they will all plot on the SML. Since Asset A has the same expected return as Portfolio Y, it must have the same beta as the market portfolio, which is one.

3. **C**   The portfolio beta will be a weighted average of the beta of T-bills (= 0) and the beta of Portfolio Y (= 1), (0.4)(0) + (0.60)(1) = 0.60. Given that the slope of the CML in Figure 1 is 0.40, the market risk premium is 0.40 × 20% = 8% and the expected return according to the CAPM is 6% + (0.60)(8%) = 10.8%.

4. **B**   The instability of the efficient frontier is due to estimation (sampling) error in historical betas (or asset returns parameters) as well as the fact that historical estimates are not forecasts; that is, they are not forward looking. Better historical estimates will reduce sampling error, while use of a forecasting model can yield forward looking estimates. Either of these can reduce instability of the estimated efficient frontier. Using less data, as Ponder suggests, will aggravate the instability problem as it will lead to greater estimation error and not address the problem of changing betas over time.

5. **B**   A tracking portfolio is constructed to match the factor risks of a benchmark portfolio such as the market portfolio, Portfolio Y. By going either overweight the underpriced stocks or underweight the overpriced stocks within a tracking portfolio (relative to their benchmark weights), the portfolio manager can increase the expected returns of the portfolio of risky assets, while still matching the risk characteristics of the benchmark portfolio. Since Portfolio Y is the market portfolio and contains all stocks in some positive amounts, omitting the overpriced stocks will increase the expected portfolio return. The long-short portfolio may have quite different risk characteristics from those of Portfolio Y and unsystematic risk as well. A single factor portfolio cannot be expected to hedge away these risk differences.

6. **A**   Assuming assets are priced according to the CAPM, Asset B must have a beta less than one since it has a lower expected return than Portfolio Y, the market portfolio. Because betas are mean reverting toward one, the adjustment to the historical market-model beta for Asset B is to increase it toward one.

FORMULAS

STUDY SESSIONS 16 & 17: DERIVATIVE INVESTMENTS

definition of the basis:

$$\text{basis} = S - F$$

definition of the futures price:

$$\text{futures price} = \text{spot price} \times (1+r)^{(T-t)}$$

forward contract price: $FP = S_0 \times (1+R_f)^T$

forward contract value of long position:

at initiation: zero, because priced to prevent arbitrage

during life of contract: $S_t - \left[\dfrac{FP}{(1+R_f)^{T-t}} \right]$

at expiration: $S_t - FP$

equity forward contract price:

$$FP(\text{on an equity security}) = (S_0 - PVD) \times (1+R_f)^T$$

$$FP(\text{on an equity security}) = \left[S_0 \times (1+R_f)^T \right] - FVD$$

equity forward contract value: $V_t(\text{long position}) = \left[S_t - PVD_t \right] - \left[\dfrac{FP}{(1+R_f)^{(T-t)}} \right]$

equity index forward contract price:

$$FP(\text{on an equity index}) = S_0 \times e^{\left(R_f^c - \delta^c \right) \times T} = \left(S_0 \times e^{-\delta^c \times T} \right) \times e^{R_f^c \times T}$$

equity index forward contract value:

$$V_t\left(\text{of the long position}\right)=\left(\frac{S_t}{e^{\delta^c\times(T-t)}}\right)-\left(\frac{FP}{e^{R_f^c\times(T-t)}}\right)$$

fixed income forward contract price:

$$FP\left(\text{on a fixed income security}\right)=\left(S_0-PVC\right)\times\left(1+R_f\right)^T$$
$$=\left[S_0\times\left(1+R_f\right)^T\right]-FVC$$

fixed income forward contract value: $V_t\left(\text{long position}\right)=\left[S_t-PVC_t\right]-\left[\dfrac{FP}{\left(1+R_f\right)^{(T-t)}}\right]$

currency forward contract price: $F_T\left(\text{currency forward contract}\right)=S_0\times\dfrac{\left(1+R_{DC}\right)^T}{\left(1+R_{FC}\right)^T}$

currency forward contract value:

$$V_t\left(\text{currency forward contract}\right)=\left[\frac{S_t}{\left(1+R_{FC}\right)^{(T-t)}}\right]-\left[\frac{F_T}{\left(1+R_{DC}\right)^{(T-t)}}\right]$$

continuous time price and value formulas for currency forward contracts:

$$F_T\left(\text{currency forward contract}\right)=S_0\times e^{\left(R_{DC}^c-R_{FC}^c\right)\times T}$$

$$V_t\left(\text{currency forward contract}\right)=\left[\frac{S_t}{e^{R_{FC}^c\times(T-t)}}\right]-\left[\frac{F_T}{e^{R_{DC}^c\times(T-t)}}\right]$$

generalized no-arbitrage futures price:

$$FP=S_0\times\left(1+R_f\right)^T+FV\left(NC\right)$$

$$FP=S_0\times\left(1+R_f\right)^T-FV\left(NB\right)$$

Treasury bond futures contract price: $FP=\left[\text{bond price}\times\left(1+R_f\right)^T-FVC\right]\times\dfrac{1}{CF}$

put-call parity for European options: $C_0 + \left[\dfrac{X}{\left(1 + R_f\right)^T} \right] = P_0 + S_0$

put-call parity for European options with cash flows:

$$C_0 + \frac{X}{\left(1 + R_F\right)^T} = P_0 + \left(S_0 - PVCF\right)$$

binomial model:

$$D = \frac{1}{U}$$

$$\pi_U = \frac{1 + R_f - D}{U - D}$$

$$\pi_D = 1 - \pi_U$$

expiration value of caplet $= \dfrac{\max\ \{0,\ [(\text{one-year rate} - \text{cap rate}) \times \text{notional principal}]\}}{1 + \text{one-year rate}}$

expiration value of floorlet $= \dfrac{\max\ \{0,\ [(\text{floor rate} - \text{one-year rate}) \times \text{notional principal}]\}}{1 + \text{one-year rate}}$

delta and dynamic hedging:

$$\text{delta}_{call} = \frac{C_1 - C_0}{S_1 - S_0} = \frac{\Delta C}{\Delta S}$$

$$\Delta C \approx N\left(d_1\right) \times \Delta S$$
$$\Delta P \approx \left[N\left(d_1\right) - 1\right] \times \Delta S$$

forward put-call parity: $C_0 + \dfrac{X - F_T}{\left(1 + R_f\right)^T} - P_0 = 0$

fixed swap rate (with four payments): $C = \dfrac{1 - Z_4}{Z_1 + Z_2 + Z_3 + Z_4}$

payoff to cap buyer:

periodic payment $= \max\left[0,\ (\text{notional principal}) \times (\text{index rate} - \text{cap strike}) \times \left(\dfrac{\text{actual days}}{360}\right)\right]$

payoff to floor buyer:

$$\text{periodic payment} = \max\left[0, (\text{notional principal}) \times (\text{floor strike} - \text{index rate}) \times \left(\frac{\text{actual days}}{360}\right)\right]$$

STUDY SESSION 18: PORTFOLIO MANAGEMENT

expected portfolio return (two assets): $E(R_p) = w_1 E(R_1) + w_2 E(R_2)$

portfolio variance (two assets): $\sigma_P^2 = w_1^2 \sigma_1^2 + w_2^2 \sigma_2^2 + 2w_1 w_2 \text{Cov}_{1,2}$

correlation: $\rho_{1,2} = \dfrac{\text{Cov}_{1,2}}{\sigma_1 \sigma_2}$

variance of equally-weighted portfolio: $\sigma_P^2 = \dfrac{1}{n}\overline{\sigma_i^2} + \dfrac{n-1}{n}\overline{\text{Cov}} = \overline{\sigma_i^2}\left(\dfrac{1-\rho}{n} + \rho\right)$

reward-to-risk ratio = $\dfrac{E(R_T) - R_F}{\sigma_T}$

CAL: $E(R_C) = R_F + \left(\dfrac{E(R_T) - R_F}{\sigma_T}\right)\sigma_C$

CML: $E(R_C) = R_F + \left[\dfrac{E(R_M) - R_F}{\sigma_M}\right]\sigma_C$

SML: $E(R_i) = R_F + \beta_i\left[E(R_m) - R_F\right]$

Beta: $\beta_i = \dfrac{\text{Cov}_{i,M}}{\sigma_M^2} = \dfrac{\rho_{i,M}\sigma_i\sigma_M}{\sigma_M^2} = \rho_{i,M}\left(\dfrac{\sigma_i}{\sigma_M}\right)$

market model: $R_i = \alpha_i + \beta_i R_M + \varepsilon_i$

$$\sigma_i^2 = \beta_i^2 \sigma_M^2 + \sigma_\varepsilon^2$$

$$\text{Cov}_{ij} = \beta_i \beta_j \sigma_M^2$$

adjusted beta: $\beta_t = \alpha_0 + (1 - \alpha_0)\beta_{t-1}$

Arbitrage Pricing Theory (APT): $E(R_P) = R_F + \beta_{P,1}(\lambda_1) + \beta_{P,2}(\lambda_2) + \ldots + \beta_{P,k}(\lambda_k)$

active return $= R_P - R_B$

active risk $= s(R_P - R_B)$

information ratio: $IR = \dfrac{\bar{R}_P - \bar{R}_B}{s_{(R_P - R_B)}}$

expected domestic currency return:

$$\text{unhedged } E(R_{DC}) = E(R_{FC}) + E(\%\Delta S) = E(R_{FC}) + \frac{E(S_1) - S_0}{S_0}$$

$$\text{hedged } E(R_{DC}) = E(R_{FC}) + \frac{F - S_0}{S_0}$$

real exchange rate: $\text{real } S = S \times \left(\dfrac{P_{FC}}{P_{DC}}\right)$

$$\%\Delta \text{ in real } S = \%\Delta \text{ in nominal } S - (i_{DC} - i_{FC})$$

foreign currency risk premium: $FCRP = \dfrac{E(S_1) - S_0}{S_0} - (r_{DC} - r_{FC})$

$$FCRP = \frac{E(S_1) - F}{S_0}, \text{ assuming IRP holds}$$

ICAPM: $E(R) = R_f + (\beta_g \times MRP_g) + (\gamma_1 \times FCRP_1) + (\gamma_2 \times FCRP_2) + \ldots + (\gamma_k \times FCRP_k)$

domestic currency sensitivity: $\gamma = \gamma(LC) + 1$

predicted alpha: $\alpha_i = \text{forecast return} - \{R_F + \beta_i[E(R_M - R_F)]\}$

weights in actively managed portfolio, A: $w_i = \dfrac{\alpha_i}{\sigma^2(\varepsilon_i)} \Big/ \displaystyle\sum_{j=1}^{n} \dfrac{\alpha_j}{\sigma^2(\varepsilon_j)}$

INDEX